Advance Praise for
East Winds

[A] soulful debut memoir . . . Rueckert's reminiscences present readers with an evocative travelogue and a remarkably sensitive and insightful portrait of the difficulties of modern marriage and the compromises that one makes to feel both autonomy and connection . . . Rueckert's grappling with uncertainty yields courage and a luminous sense of hope. An engrossing exploration of a hard but ultimately exhilarating trek toward love and commitment.

—*Kirkus Reviews*, starred review

Is it an ethnography, a travelogue, a memoir, a love story, or a true confession? Whatever its genre, it is funny, inciteful, poetic, and engaging. A delightful read!

—Laurel Thatcher Ulrich, PhD
Pulitzer Prize winner
author of *Well-Behaved Women Seldom Make History*

Trouble abounds in this brave, stirring, engaging memoir, but the protagonist proves equal to every bit of it, thanks to her self-awareness and pluck. A travel account that takes us deep into the author's inner life and spiritual struggles while delivering vividly detailed accounts of the lands she explores, this satisfying record of the growth of a self should please readers of every type. It certainly pleased me.

—Phillip Lopate, PhD
American essayist & editor of *The Art of the Personal Essay*

Thoroughly smart and clear-eyed. *East Winds* invites the reader to question their assumptions. Rueckert asks unique questions that resonate on a universal level.

—Gary Shteyngart
author of *Little Failure*

Rachel Rueckert's *East Winds* is outstanding. A captivating reflection on love and faith found in unexpected places, it's a chronicle of the early days of marriage. Rueckert is a writer to watch. In lovely, candid prose, she shares intimate insights about partnership and the connections that exist because of it. I could not put it down.

—Wendy S. Walters, PhD
Nonfiction Concentration Director at Columbia University
author of *Multiply/Divide*

The engine that drives this delightful memoir is the rash condition the author puts on her fiancé: immediately after marrying, they must embark on a low-budget, one-year-long honeymoon around the world. This would strain any relationship to the breaking point, but Rueckert and her husband triumph in surprising and moving ways. Both are socially progressive Mormons; they rebel against their faith without rejecting it. By turns comical and serious, this passionate, searchful book will speak especially to readers who grapple with the cultural pressure to marry and the taboo of divorce. In strange, far-off cities and miserable hotels, Rueckert investigates this conundrum with a restless and insightful mind. The writing is filled with funny, shivery, illuminated moments. *East Winds* brims with intelligence.

—Michael Greenberg
author of *Hurry Down Sunshine*

In *East Winds*, Rachel Rueckert journeys around the world and into the heart of a marriage, asking how we can truly know our partner, ourselves, and the truth of our bond. Exploring communities in Asia, South America and Europe as well as excavating her own Mormon roots, Rueckert's warm, frank voice takes the reader across oceans and generations, examining how love, family, connection and commitment are reflected in and through culture. A fascinating travelogue and a charmingly bumpy love story, *East Winds* is an ultimately joyous struggle for identity as and with a partner that many women will recog-nize within themselves.

—Allison K Williams
author of *Seven Drafts*

EAST WINDS

BCC PRESS

BY COMMON CONSENT PRESS is a non-profit publisher dedicated to producing affordable, high-quality books. BCC Press's mission includes finding manuscripts, mentoring authors, nurturing projects to completion, and distributing important books to an audience at the lowest possible cost.

RACHEL RUECKERT

EAST WINDS

A GLOBAL QUEST TO RECKON WITH MARRIAGE

East Winds: A Global Quest to Reckon with Marriage

For information contact
By Common Consent Press
4900 Penrose Dr.
Newburgh, IN 47630

Cover design: D Christian Harrison
Book design: Andrew Heiss

www.bccpress.org
ISBN-13 (paperback): 978-1-948218-68-9
ISBN-13 (hardcover): 978-1-948218-63-4

10 9 8 7 6 5 4 3 2 1

For Austin

Also for:

The sixteen-year-old who felt concerned about where to attend college, only to be told by her boyfriend, "It doesn't matter where you go. You'll only need your degree if your husband dies."

The girl who received dishes, pans, and towels for holidays (while her brother received stereos and skis), then received a hope chest filled with linens and quilts for her high school graduation.

The twenty-three-year-old who was cornered by a bishop's wife after church and asked, "Do you feel like an old maid, wishing you were already married?"

The young woman who was encouraged to wear makeup because "the frosted cookies are always the first to go."

The twenty-something, struggling with eating disorders and depression, who was often told by people at church, "You're so beautiful. I don't understand why you aren't married yet," to which she'd reply, "It must be my horrible personality."

The woman who was told that if she wore her Army Class A uniform to church, she would never "attract" a husband because he would feel like he wasn't the boss in the relationship.

The woman who showed up to her new congregation's meet and greet and was asked by the same person, multiple times, who her husband was, then had to keep stating that she was unmarried—it was just her.

The twenty-year-old who felt like running on her wedding day when she heard that she was promising to hearken to and obey her husband, but he didn't have to do the same for her in return.

The thirty-something who gets placed at the kids' table during family reunions while her nineteen-year-old, married cousins sit with the adults.

The senior who showed her BYU undergrad advisor her grad school acceptance letter from Stanford and was met with: "How lovely. Maybe you'll marry a nice linguist!"

The woman who stayed in an abusive marriage
because leaders told her that once you choose your
love, you love your choice—no matter what.

The biomedical PhD specializing in cancer
immunology who was constantly told that having
a family was a holier pursuit, that her
priorities weren't in order.

The twenty-something whose honored grandparents
warned her that if she didn't stop traveling and
exploring so much, no man would be able to catch
her. So she reined herself in so she could be caught.

The third-generation missionary who *was* taught
that she could balance career and family, with a wise
grandmother stating that she had "better things to do
than climb into bed with some damn man."

For all these Mormon women, and hundreds of others,
who shared with me these and other experiences—
some similar, some opposite, all different.
We are never a monolith. Here, I add my
singular truth to the mosaic.

Marriage brings one into fatal connection with custom and tradition, and traditions and customs are like the wind and weather, altogether incalculable.

—Søren Kierkegaard
The Laughter Is on My Side

It is only necessary to know that love is a direction and not a state of the soul. If one is unaware of this, one falls into despair at the first onslaught of affliction.

—Simone Weil
Waiting for God

Contents

PART 1

SOUTH AMERICA

CLEAVE | klēv |

verb

1. to split or sever (something), especially along a natural line or grain
2. to adhere strongly to (a particular pursuit or belief)
3. to become very strongly involved with or emotionally attached to (someone)

CHAPTER 1

Casa de Ari

I FACED THE BOLTED GATE of Hostel de Chocolate at 1:00 a.m. in Bogotá. The weight of my traveler's backpack, haphazardly stuffed with the possessions meant to last me a year, felt both reassuring and heavy as I stood in the darkness.

Austin, my husband of two weeks, searched for a notice or phone number through the curling barbed wire. I clutched the confirmation receipt from the reservation we'd made sometime between the dash to mail our wedding thank-you cards at the nearest post office and boarding the plane for Colombia.

"Now what?" I asked, ready to blame Austin for having clicked the "book" button on a reservation we'd both agreed to.

"We find something else," he said, unfazed.

I'd never done well with permanent. *Husband* represented a commitment toward the stereotypical package I'd spent most of my millennial life resisting: Mormon, Married, Mother. The End. Yet here I was, at step 2. I stared at Austin in his J.Crew collared shirt, a buttoned-up look that hid his wildness that I loved. We often debated who was The More Experienced Traveler: Austin had served a two-year Mormon mission to Ukraine and had a long history of outdoorsmanship; I had done anthropology fieldwork as an undergrad and held a more decorated passport. But all traces of my travel confidence had dissolved into anxiety.

Our taxi driver called us back. "Peligroso." Dangerous. "I know another place," he said in strained English.

We thanked him and piled into the car again. I gripped my backpack in my lap. Though I had fallen in love fair and square—had agreed to marry Austin of my own free will and had all the agency in the world—sometimes I still felt as if some external wave of happenstance had carried me here.

Austin and I met two years earlier at an interfaith discussion group between Latter-day Saints and Quakers. I'd just moved from Utah to Boston for grad school and a job with Teach For America. He sat across from me in a small circle of folding chairs. He reminded me of a Ken doll—boyishly handsome, brown-blond hair, a square jaw, blue eyes. A Quaker woman asked about women's roles in Mormonism. "I heard women can't get to heaven unless they have a husband," she said, leaning forward, barely hiding her contempt. "Can people get divorced?"

"Divorce happens," I weighed in. "I don't think it's any more stigmatized than in other religions in the US. My parents are divorced." I wasn't ready to face, let alone answer, the first part of her question.

"It's not encouraged," Austin said, before explaining the orthodox stance: A temple marriage represents the pinnacle of choices to be made and, whether it happens here or in the afterlife, stands as a prerequisite to reach the highest degree of heaven. A temple marriage, also known as a sealing, binds people to their families forever. This is part of the plan of salvation, a name sometimes interchanged with the plan of happiness.

In other words, divorce may be commonplace for modern Mormons (a mere 5 to 10 percent lower than the national average of 50 percent), but theologically, it's complicated.

I avoided Austin after that comment.

Months later, at a mutual friend's party, we brushed shoulders on the threshold of a doorway. He paused. "You and I should have a long, philosophical conversation," he said with a smile, seemingly pleased with his line.

Before long, we were shrieking and leaping into half-frozen lakes in New England under a canopy of stars. He was biking with ice-frosted lashes through blizzards to surprise me at my doorstep, standing there in the spring with a fistful of flowers plucked from the neighbor's garden, and blowing off homework to take me on picnics at Walden Pond. I was salivating over his book collection and in love with laughing again and keeping a stash of ice cream at his apartment. He "knew" within weeks. His flattering, swift confidence in our relationship exuded an intoxicating persuasion, softening the edges of my concerns.

Austin and I waved off our first impressions from the interfaith discussion and all it said about the different ways we inhabited Mormonism—all it said about how we each viewed marriage.

The taxi headlights and a lone streetlamp revealed a graffiti-lined street. A crowd of men surrounded a radio at a humming pizza stand.

"We'll be fine," Austin said, reading my emotions as he looked out the window. "We won't blow our budget by finding a safe place to stay tonight."

I frowned. "We may not have enough for the trip to start with." I'd spent the past two arduous years scrimping, saving twenty thousand dollars from a high school teaching salary to fund a solo trip so I could circumnavigate the globe.

Then, one of two things happened: my relationship with Austin became serious and we decided to make a honeymoon of it; or, as he tells it, I told Austin I would only marry him if he agreed to come. I no longer remember the truer story, just that my original vision morphed into something else. I'd always believed that any trip longer than a few weeks required some sort of inquiry focus, a reason to get up in the morning. Though many subjects interested me (post-colonial literature, dream interpretations, international folktales, etc.), I planned to learn more about marriage and wedding symbolism around the world. I hoped other cultures might reveal some wisdom as I wrestled with the idea of marriage for myself, not realizing that living it—that intensely personal experience—was perhaps the only way to find out. Austin, disillusioned with his MBA program and inspired by my project, wanted to do something similar and study health-care innovations in emerging markets.

Since my savings had not meant to cover two people, Austin had agreed to chip in by working odd jobs virtually whenever he could during our travels. *Work hard, play hard.* But for every good thing I'd given up to save money—movie tickets, a coat worthy of Boston winters, meals that didn't feature peanut butter—I felt Austin had indulged himself. He believed in what he called "the good life," this radical notion that life was to be enjoyed and not just endured. He had a pile of student debt and no savings to his name. Sharing money didn't sit well with me.

A few minutes later, the taxi rolled to a stop in front of a pale building with Colombian and Israeli flags. A sign read "Casa de Ari."

The driver pushed a buzzer three times. I held my breath until the door cracked open. A squat woman with puffy gray hair appeared in a nightgown.

The woman unlocked a thick chain, then ushered us in as I offered apologies and gratitude in textbook Spanish. She and the driver stepped outside, speaking in hushed voices.

Austin and I placed our backpacks on the checkered linoleum peeling at the corners of the lobby. There was a faint smell of rotten produce. Framed collages with pictures of tourists covered the walls. We stared at the open door and waited for direction. Dust coated the sun-bleached couches and cobwebs clung to the ceiling. Austin scanned the dim room with curiosity. His lack of distress annoyed me.

The hostel manager pulled a set of faded floral sheets and a mop from a closet, muttered, then walked away.

"I'm going to get some pizza from that place we saw down the road," Austin said. "I'm hungry."

"Uh, this is Bogotá. You can't wander around at night. You don't even know Spanish." On the plane, I'd been reading Juan Gabriel Vásquez's novel, *The Sound of Things Falling*, set in Bogotá—the gunshot scenes fresh in my mind.

"It's only a few blocks away," Austin said. "And I didn't know you were such an expert on Bogotá."

He was right. Despite my belief in the importance of studying a culture before visiting a new place, we'd done little research before booking our one-way tickets to Colombia days earlier. Our time and energy had been spent on wrapping up our jobs and wedding planning. We'd settled on Bogotá because it was the cheapest flight to enter South America from the States.

Austin paused at the doorway, his hair a mess. "Want to come?"

"No. I'll check us in."

"I don't think she's coming back anytime soon. What did she say to you?"

I had no idea. "Hurry back."

Standing in the lobby, I heard a crash on the floor above. Then, a large white dog bounded down the stairs. She sat at my feet, panting. A lacy, zebra-striped thong hung from her mouth.

"Hello there." I crouched to pet the fluffy dog, careful to avoid touching the underwear. I looked up, hoping to see the hostel manager. The dog then fetched a bottle of opened mascara. She cracked the plastic tube with her back teeth. Black goop smeared through her fur as she played.

I tried to get the mascara away from the dog when Austin returned. He held out a parcel of tinfoil. "They called it 'American pizza,'" he said. "I got the cheapest one. I knew that's what you'd want." He paused for my reaction. "Where'd the dog come from?"

The hostel manager, hearing the front door open, reappeared. She led us through a maze of concrete steps to a room on the top floor. The dog trailed us, its bushy tail thwacking the door as we entered. Twin beds flanked each wall. It wasn't much, but considering our unexpected arrival, we were lucky she could offer us anything. The hostel manager smiled and said something in Spanish, then disappeared again with the dog prancing after her. Austin perched on the edge of one of the mattresses and opened the tinfoil package to examine our dinner.

The room reeked of mildew. Austin watched as I wrinkled my nose while investigating the sheets, finding brown stains on the pillows.

"What?" I asked, my voice strained.

"This pizza has corn on it. That's what makes it 'American.'"

I managed a genuine grin, letting go of my backpack with a loud thud.

"I'm not sleeping in these sheets," I said, pressing my hands to my hair. "I doubt I can sleep at all."

"It's going to be okay." He stood and hugged me with one arm as he cradled a slice in his other hand. I leaned into him.

"Some first night of our honeymoon," I said.

He offered me a square piece of pizza. A hunk of pineapple slid off in a cascade of rubbery cheese as I took a bite. The crust was crunchy and perfect, but I wasn't sure I wanted to show too much gratitude after his recklessness.

"At least we have each other," he said, raising an eyebrow.

I rolled my eyes. "I am not having sex with you here." Austin huffed, then laughed, and I couldn't help but laugh too, relieved we'd had a few nights together before leaving home.

After devouring the pizza, we pushed the twin beds together and pulled out one of the few wedding gifts we'd brought on the trip: sheets sewed into thin sleeping bags. I held the clean linen up to my nose, the smell of fresh detergent lingering in my nostrils. I knew it would be a long time before I'd smell that powdery scent again.

I flipped off the lights, kicked off my Chaco sandals, and crawled into my linen sleeping bag with my clothes still on. The bedsprings squeaked. Austin cozied up to me in an awkward sleeping-bag cuddle. "I'm glad to be here with you," he whispered. I nuzzled into him, thankful we could cope with Casa de Ari together despite my perennial fantasies of solo travel. Soon Austin's breathing slowed. I felt his warm chest rise and fall against my back. I lay awake.

I'd spent nights with sheets far worse than these in other countries without a second thought. But here I was, caught between the ideal, liberating trip I'd built up for years and the unknown world of commitment I'd entered into. Past travels had offered me some freedom from expectations back home, a chance to revel in the sweet sensation of losing and getting lost, to strip away excess, untether, and immerse myself in the marvelous present—the instant calm of incense, the texture of a moss-eaten wall, the hushed conversation between old women on neighboring balconies. In other words, to continually remember and witness the infinite ways people can live.

But I worried this trip might feel more like an ending, a last hurrah, a fun way to delay the impending death blow to my sense of self. Unlike my other travels, now there seemed something to lose and expectations I could no longer outrun. I felt happy to be with Austin—that wasn't the problem. I didn't know if I believed in marriage, let alone *eternal* marriage.

The night before my wedding, I'd stayed up late trimming baby's breath bouquets while listening to my dad and stepmom yell at each other behind their closed bedroom door—something about her being late to the rehearsal dinner, regrets about moving back in together. I tightened the aqua ribbons and snipped off the stems. My hands shook. The cheap bouquets smelled like body odor. I spent the night in the twin-size bed from my teenage days, which did not feel that long ago, the bedroom walls bare because I always thought of my dad's house as temporary.

I arrived late to the Salt Lake Temple, the iconic Mormon venue: a white granite fortress with six Gothic spires. The steeples flashed with August sunlight. My ancestors, who'd endured the exodus across the plains of the United States to escape religious persecution in the East, helped build this dazzling temple in the middle of a desert. They determined its location a mere four days after their arrival on July 24, 1847. The temple represented a cornerstone of the faith, an urgent project to undertake despite fleeing one temple in Ohio and watching another in Illinois be swallowed up in flames. The Salt Lake Temple required forty years of construction and unimaginable sacrifice. This is where my family members had married for generations, sealed together for eternity. My bagged wedding dress bounced on my shoulder as I ran. I did not like the dress but had not told anyone. As I sprinted for the door, I had time to think:

I'm only twenty-five.

It's not too late to call it off.

I wonder if my mom will come.

CHAPTER 2

East Winds

DAVIS COUNTY, UTAH, sits near the mouth of a canyon. The county mostly receives calm wind from the west. Other times, a high-pressure pocket of Wyoming air races a hundred miles down from the east. The pressure generates a surging wind that pushes in waves over the Rocky Mountains, slamming into the valley below with the force and speed of a hurricane.

Eastern winds topple power lines, demolish roofs, and uproot thousands of trees. Some argue these winds that tear through the Wasatch Front of the Rockies deserve a name, like the mistral and foehn winds from the Alps or the Santa Anas from Southern California. For now, the locals settle on "east winds."

Mormons have documented these storms and their wreckage since the pioneers' arrival. People lost their homes, their church buildings, crops, livestock, even family members. An east wind storm in 1864 pinned a woman and her infant son against a fence, battering them until they froze to death. While traveling during that same 1864 storm, Brigham Young rebuked the winds in the name of the Lord. His travel companion, Wilford Woodruff, wrote that the east winds subsided until the late 1890s. But years later, while serving as the fourth president of the church, Woodruff reported that "in late years, these winds have occurred in some of their old-time severity." Perhaps he was familiar with the biblical accounts, that east winds often embodied God's vengeance. They announced seven years of famine in Genesis, ripped open the sea for Moses, carried people off in Job, scattered others in Jeremiah, broke the ships of Tarshish in Psalms, dried springs in Hosea, and beat Jonah until he said, "it is better for me to die than to live."

In one of my first memories, I clutched my pigtails and cowered by the mailbox during a massive east wind storm. I sobbed as I stared at the bending trees, debris flying down the road. My mom and dad chased down our uprooted mailbox. I rushed to the garage to monitor my toys and bike, the wind pounding on the metal door like a fist. I was scared for the birds, worried my plastic playground in the backyard would blow off like the peeling shingles.

Mom took me inside. We stood at the bay window. She put a hand on my shoulder. I still gripped my hair, fearing I would blow away too. She asked me what I was so afraid of while trying to suppress a laugh. It must have seemed like a ridiculous fear. But the three of us—my father, then me, then my mother—in our own turn, in our own way, would blow away from that home.

Dad was twenty-two when he met my mother. Mom was four years his senior and only getting older. He'd recently returned from his Mormon mission when they met at a church dance, hosted at the Snowbird ski resort. As a college student living off mac and cheese, he felt drawn to her beauty, independence, and intrepid spirit: she had a successful career as an elementary school teacher, money she used to dote on him, an apartment, and travels to boast about. Her name, Ava, meant "life." She also drove a sporty white Isuzu

Impulse. Everyone agreed the car fit her: *Impulsive. Fun. Playful. Different.*

They went to Los Angeles on a weekend road trip a few months later, though my mom now claims with regret that her preferred date for the getaway, a Johns Hopkins–trained doctor, had cancelled.

Soon after California, they found themselves cuddling on the couch in her parents' basement to watch a movie. Still high off the fumes of the spontaneous trip, my mom asked, "Could you see us getting married?"

A pause. The thought hadn't yet crossed his mind. "Yeah, sure."

She ran upstairs to announce their engagement to her parents as a knot formed in his stomach. He sensed he should have called it off but cited the pressures, his aversion to conflict, the fear of hurting her feelings. Not even falling asleep at the wheel—crashing his car into a concrete barrier days before their wedding and escaping with his life—made him reconsider.

Mom told a different version. "He had the worst proposal. On a drive one day, he told me the ring was in the glove box."

I never could reconcile their polarizing accounts. My family lacked an origin story, splintering us from the start. The narratives never added up, never clarified how I arrived here as the creation of these two people.

But they both liked each other once. This I gather from extended family who still remember them dating. It's hard for me to imagine.

While my parents were married, they seemed like strangers—a classic "stay together for the kids" couple. They hated each other as fiercely as they loved my three younger siblings and me. My dad worked at an insurance company and spent most of his evenings in the basement, hunched behind his desk or watching his big-screen TV. My mom stayed home to raise the kids, which my dad never understood given her independent streak and thriving career before they married. Dishes piled in the sink, dust covered the forest-green carpet, closets bulged with trinkets and dollar store finds for birthday parties. He hardly recognized her anymore. She endured him.

In the single memory I have of my parents showing affection, they were standing in the kitchen. My dad faced the sink, distracted by something on his mind, when my mom gave him a tight hug from behind. She held on for a moment, rested her head on his shoulder and closed her eyes. My dad patted her arm, exhaled.

In the same way that I clutched my pigtails and feared blowing away, I wonder if my mom held my dad at that moment because she sensed his eventual abandonment. She had thrown all of herself into motherhood—giving and giving without reservation, never concerning herself with what happens when children grow up, losing sight of herself and whatever affection she may have once felt toward my father. As much as she resented him, he provided stability.

After fourteen years, my dad decided he deserved a chance at happiness. He took my mother to Chili's, her favorite restaurant (a thoughtless gesture he would later regret), to tell her he wanted a divorce. They then tried marriage therapy, a short-lived experiment that ended in colossal failure. My dad felt the relationship had been dead far too long to revive the flames. My mom suspected another woman.

One day when I was thirteen, my mom shipped me off to Colorado with my grandparents and favorite cousin. I spent a week riding horses and climbing red rock formations in national parks. I later learned my mom had also sent my younger siblings to other homes so we wouldn't see our dad haul his belongings into the front yard. At the time, I didn't remember any families in the neighborhood who'd been through a divorce.

When I returned from Colorado, I went to my parents' bedroom and slowly pushed open the door. The hinge squeaked—the noise I would hear before jumping into my parents' bed to watch Saturday morning cartoons, snuggle between them after a nightmare, or urge them awake on Christmas mornings.

The air smelled stale. There was something tired about the sage-green walls, the purple floral comforter on the bed. I shuffled to the walk-in closet. My dad's side was empty, except for a few ties. I crouched with my back against the wall, his abandoned ties dangling above my head—they belonged to the same man who'd hummed The Eagles to himself in the kitchen before anyone in the house woke up, who'd noticed my creativity from the hundreds of 3D animals I'd fold out of paper or build out of beads, who'd taken me on the roof (despite Mom's protests) on a day when the space shuttle flew overhead. He'd placed me on his shoulders, wanting me to be as close as possible to the sky. By leaving his marriage, he would create the escape velocity he needed to feel alive again. He would become a more attentive father.

I held my bony knees to my chest. Under the ties, I understood that I was no longer a carefree child. The real possibility that a person—any person—could leave, hit me for the first time. One day, sooner than I could have imagined, it would be my turn to go. Not like a gentle beach breeze, but like an east wind storm.

After a night of sleep at Casa de Ari, I woke up with a cramp in my neck. Austin had left the room, his unzipped bag spilling travel-size shampoo bottles and a razor. Chilled, I pulled on the only sweater I'd packed.

Austin returned. Water droplets clung to his hair. "Good morning," he said, shirtless with his muscular torso. "Warning: the shower is cold. And don't mind the mold."

Each year in church, as a teenager, I had been instructed to list the qualities I wanted in my future husband. I wrote out things like

"I want a husband who can play the guitar" or "I want a hot husband who has long hair." Never had I written, "I want a husband who is a morning person," no matter however beautiful he might be.

"Let's get out of here," I said, a cold shower far from my mind.

We explored La Candelaria all morning, the old city and historic neighborhood of Bogotá. It was Sunday, and few places were open. Vibrant walls tattooed with brilliant graffiti art featured backdrops of yellow, red, and key-lime green. Almost all the buildings had arched Spanish doors. My spirit lifted.

What were you so worried about? I thought as I admired the vivid architecture. Daylight illuminated the city's beauty in a way I couldn't have imagined the night before.

See?

Nothing to fear.

After breakfast, Austin and I hiked up a hill in the rain, triple-checking the address for our next accommodation where we'd stay a week or two in Bogotá. The street numbers followed a sequential pattern unfamiliar to us. After an hour, we found it and buzzed the doorbell. A face appeared in a barred window above our heads. "Austin?"

"That's us," Austin said with visible relief as he wiped rain from his forehead.

Lili was a plump, middle-aged woman who was born and raised in Bogotá. She ran this Airbnb for university students, Peace Corps volunteers, and visitors like us. She unlocked the door. Austin rattled off his thanks to her in English, but she held up her hand.

"Solo español," she said. "I teach you. Maestra de español." Austin's mouth fell open in confusion, perhaps wondering if this was the person he'd been corresponding with in English over email. "Google Translate," she said with a coy smile before bounding up the stairs.

Lili led us through a sparsely decorated common area to a small room. A full-size bed with a Disney princess comforter took up most of the space. She squeezed through the narrow aisle between the mattress and the empty TV stand as she held a tray with mugs of coca tea. We each grabbed a cup and felt the warmth transfer to our palms. As we studied the clear liquid with olive-colored leaves on top, Lili sat on the bed's edge and asked us about our plans. I sipped at the bitter tea. Austin looked at me to translate.

My rusty Spanish creaked with uncertainty. Lili nodded and corrected when necessary, ensuring I took notes in my notebook. "Museo del Oro," she said, waiting for me to write it down along with a few other tourist must-sees and foods to be had. Austin repeated her words with a perfect accent, to which Lili laughed, rubbing his head and ruffling his curly hair. She emphasized the importance of *ajiaco* soup four times and taught us a few ways to say "cool" like a local. "Qué chido," she enunciated, "Qué chevere."

Lili showed us pictures of Colombian beach-town destinations like Cartagena, but she insisted that visiting the Amazon should be a priority. We hadn't listed it on our still-evolving itinerary due to the rebel FARC group ruling over these parts of the rainforest, but Lili assured us some areas were safe now. Austin had a life-long dream to see the Amazon. His eyes gleamed. As a third grader in his school's Rainforest Club, he'd donated all his meager allowance to rainforest conservation. Austin became obsessed. Every Sunday during church, he would draw pictures of jungle scenes: monkeys holding onto balloons, snakes dangling from trees, toucans perched on branches.

"It would mean skipping Ecuador," Austin said as we replotted a potential path through Colombia to Peru, where we were planning to spend a few months in Cusco before spending the rest of the year in Asia and Europe. I didn't mind skipping Ecuador, imagining I could go another time despite my improbable concern that this was my last globe-trot, that marriage would render me homebound in an apron as I chased after twelve children. Relaxing on a beach or salsa dancing in Cartagena sounded divine, but it couldn't compete with Austin's emotional investment in the Amazon. Besides, Cusco had been my idea, and we would get there soon enough.

I saw how much this meant to Austin, far more than my stake in the next leg of the journey. I could play nice, do this compromise-in-marriage thing. Right? There would be plenty of future opportunities for Austin to do the same for me when it came to something I felt passionately about.

We were Amazon bound.

I took an overdue shower. The warm water slid down my face, my hair a wet mat resting heavy on my back.

I have my mother's hair—thick and dark, limp with an inconsistent wave. I call this look "Jesus hair," the opposite of stylish in the '90s.

Everyone says I resemble my mother. Of her four children, I am the only one to inherit her chestnut-brown eyes rather than my dad's Scandinavian hazel. When I look at her childhood pictures, I can't deny the similarities between us.

"You were late," my mom used to tell me. "You had a headful of hair, thick eyelashes, and long fingernails." She enjoyed repeating my birth story.

"You almost killed me," she would then say. Mom reiterated a series of issues posed as facts—facts I cannot verify given her now-diagnosed delusional disorder, though I believe many of them were true. She told me about the tearing. Toxemia. The unbearable agony of labor. She cannot remember what time I finally made my way into the world, the exact moment I cried with my own lungs, whether it was morning or night.

My mother loved me. She took me home from the McKay Dee Hospital swaddled in one of dozens of girlish outfits as my dad drove us to their Salt Lake City apartment. We moved two weeks later. My dad had landed an accounting job in Mission Viejo, California. They found a deal on a brand-new apartment complex opening three blocks from a beach in Laguna Niguel.

My first moments of consciousness bloomed on that Californian shore. The memories are just out of reach. I rely on stories and pictures. Often I am there, with her, every single day: my bonnet with pink bows, the stroller's wheels caked with beach, the waves tumbling and rolling onto the shore. I wore a blue swimsuit over my diaper. I ate sand by the fistful. When I got older, I ran, ran as fast as I could under the bright sun to that big, open ocean. My mother loved me. She would chase me, stop me before the edge, before my toes met the cold. In my imagination, her laugh sounds like bells as she sweeps me off my toddler feet.

But can that be right? Perhaps there were some days we didn't go to the beach, days where she lay in bed with a headache following a fight with my father or begged for rest after my brother was born a year and a half after me. Was motherhood, not marriage, what cracked open her bottomless fear? I suspect these domestic transitions stirred up the unaddressed abuse of her childhood, an unspoken pain she wanted to protect us kids from at all costs. My mother loved me. Perhaps her heart thumped in her chest as she imagined me tumbling into the dark water without her notice. Perhaps she scolded me, shaping my forming mind with the notion that the world was dangerous, as she would so many times afterward. But I don't think so, not yet. I look at my three younger siblings now, all functioning adults. This is the gift, the foundation of secure love she gave us at the onset, despite the storm to come.

But this life, this "fantasy" as my dad would later call it, could not last forever. Rent skyrocketed. His salary couldn't compete. It was time to return to Utah.

Her fears became more pronounced in Utah, bordering on paranoia. As I grew, the world was not safe enough for me.

"You can't sit on the back of that truck!" she once scolded me when I tried to join my cousins on the ledge of Old Blue, Grandpa's beloved 1981 Ford F-250. She ushered me away. My cousins swung their dangling legs over the lip of the parked truck. My aunts exchanged glances.

"Children can *die* from falls like that."

"But it isn't moving!" I protested.

"It could roll. Grandpa could start driving without noticing you. You're too small to see in the mirrors."

"Never sit in the front seat of a car. Airbags kill children."

"Don't go outside if it's raining. You could get electrocuted."

"Your brother could have *died*!" she blustered at me once as I watched my little brother play on the recently fertilized grass in the front yard. "He could become handicapped now, brain damaged! Do you understand?" I waited years, watching my brother grow, wondering if my moment of neglect would manifest.

"Don't sit on your dad's lap anymore. You're too old."

"Lock your door at night. You don't know what your dad is capable of."

When I was eleven, a few years before my dad moved out, Mom called me into her dark bedroom after school.

"I have something to tell you," she said, upright in bed, her voice heavy, her liquid eyes wide with fear. She spoke as if it pained her to speak.

"I had a dream about you," she said. "And your dad."

My chest tightened. The walls seemed to fall away. She believed in dreams, and I believed in her.

"In my dream, your dad was holding an enormous snake. Soon, the snake became so powerful that it crushed him. He couldn't get away. It was too late for him." I gulped. "You were standing next to him, playing with a smaller snake. Your father has been overcome by sin, but there is still time for you to escape." A pause. "Is there anything you want to tell me?"

I only had questions. "What does that mean? What am I doing wrong?"

She shook her head and rose to leave. She never lingered in difficult conversations. She said what she had to say, then drifted away, always on the move, always shifting, deflecting, then defensive.

I followed her out of the room, down the staircase, into the messy kitchen, begging her to tell me the meaning, to tell me what was wrong with me, desperate to make myself right again in her eyes. There was nothing left to say. My mother loved me. She wanted to keep me safe, innocent, good.

After Dad left, her approach sharpened. Her fear of losing me to my increasing independence masqueraded under a guise of rigid contempt. I began missing curfew. Hanging out with boys. Her prophetic warnings became more pointed.

Once, after my dad dropped us kids off after our Tuesday night outing dictated by the custody order, Mom sat on the white living room couch, waiting, her face shadowed with rage.

"What are you doing?" I asked. My brothers and sister scattered to their rooms, sensing a squall to avoid.

Her jaw tightened. She eyed me carefully. I stood my ground in the tiled entryway.

"You have a darkness about you," she said, already rising for her exit. "You're different after spending time with your dad."

"What do you mean?" I asked with thin skepticism veiling my own insecurity, my utter exhaustion of being pulled apart and pitted against both parents.

"You have a bad spirit about you," she said, her voice trailing her as she bolted upstairs to her bedroom. "I can't explain it. There's a darkness around you." The east winds were coming.

A few months later, I blew away.

It was an average June afternoon. Dad's Dodge Durango idled in the driveway. Hoping to start saving for a car, I'd taken a summer job near his house, forty minutes away from Mom's, at a fast-food restaurant that hired fifteen-year-olds.

It'll only be for a few weeks, I thought. *Until I turn sixteen. Until I'm old enough to get a job at the movie theater.*

I shut the front door of the house, my red carry-on at my side. I couldn't see my mother's face in the side window. I didn't hug any of my siblings goodbye. I didn't have any idea this *was* goodbye—didn't know my action of going to live with my dad would be seen as an unforgivable betrayal to my mother, that she didn't have the tools to navigate conflicts, that she would stop speaking to me for years, or that our relationship would never be the same.

I walked down the concrete steps, the ones I'd run up and down since before I could remember—where I'd gotten that tear-shaped scar on my knee, where I'd placed my carved pumpkins each fall. My roller bag, up close, had a fabric printed with dozens of mini suitcases—vibrant, dizzying details, a riot of patterns, the bags yet to be opened, the journeys to be taken. I did not know that way leads on to way, and I felt certain I would come back. The wheels hit every step.

Smack.

Step.

Smack.

Dad popped the trunk and gently lifted the little bag inside. The suitcase was so light. I slipped into the passenger seat. We pulled away.

Did I look back? Did I feel, on some intuitive level, that this was the before and after? The last glimpse of home when my key still worked in the lock?

No.

I drove off, headstrong, away into the after.

Silent weeks turned into silent months. Thanksgiving went by without a call from my mom. People told me what she'd been saying to anyone and everyone but me: *Disobedient. Sleeping around. Drugs. Smoking. Disappearing in the night. Paid off by her dad.* Though my mom wouldn't speak with me, she made my "bad spirit" widely known to my extended family, people at church, my friends and their parents. She didn't have evidence, though people seemed inclined to believe her more than the absent teenager. I ached to return to my old existence but began to accept that impossibility. My reputation had combusted. I changed schools and began to face my new reality: that like my father before me, I'd become my mother's greatest enemy.

In English class at my new high school, we read the play *Inherit the Wind*, published during the 1950s about the Scopes "Monkey" Trial in the 1920s, debating whether or not evolution should be taught in schools. I recall little about the plot of the play, retained nothing about the themes of creationism vs. evolution, ignorance vs. science, harmony vs. the search for truth. All I recall is the haunting title taken from Proverbs 11:29: "He that troubleth his own house shall inherit the wind: and the fool shall be servant to the wise of heart."

My dad's house never felt like my home in the same way, but we bonded over our shared misfortune. He understood my pain and advocated for me and my siblings. I could depend on him. Settling into his place, I remember pestering him at his desk: "Can I change my middle name to Adventure?" My middle name was a family name, one given to me by my mother. And adventure was such a fun, new word in my vocabulary, a way of manufacturing entertaining stories out of more complicated ones harboring trauma. Perhaps I wasn't a person in exile; I was an *adventurer*.

"Sure," he said as he continued to type, a neutral response I didn't anticipate.

I never followed through with the change. A part of me knew that, for better or worse, my mother and I were intertwined. From this, time would teach me, there would be little escape. Maybe this is where I began internalizing my windy nature as fate—not just external forces outside of me, blowing against me, but *me*. My restless nature. My "badness." My potential for leaving and terrible destruction. I would carry the name my mother gave me, along with this inheritance of fear, and the moral lesson of her tragedy that seemed to have begun with—or was at least exacerbated by—marriage.

CHAPTER 3

The Amazon

THE AMAZON RIVER COULD BE MISTAKEN for a lake given its shocking width. The cloudy brown water resembled chocolate milk. Trees thick like a carpet of broccoli rolled in every direction. We teetered on the rickety Tabatinga dock, a small port on the Brazilian side of the Amazonian Trapezoid—a region where the points of Colombia, Brazil, and Peru meet. People moved between the three countries freely in this area, as if borders didn't exist in the jungle. Fishermen shuffled past and hauled their loads up the rotted-out wooden walkway. A group of men sat shirtless on benches made of planks and watched a football match on a cracked TV screen. They shook their fists and erupted with outrage every few minutes. Long, thin canoes with motors on the back floated in and out of the dock, tethered by makeshift buoys. The air smelled of fish and gasoline.

The day before, as Austin and I had trudged from the remote Leticia, Colombia airport down the shoulder of the road to get to town, a man had pulled up on a sputtering motorcycle and introduced himself as "George of the Jungle." He pitched us an "authentic" two-day excursion in Brazil led by a local expert named Miguel. The tour promised a full-day hike through the rainforest, an overnight stay in a bungalow, a lesson in how to catch piranha for lunch, an evening of caiman spotting, and a chance to swim with pink river dolphins. George of the Jungle gave us a business card with a link to a website we later discovered was discontinued. He required all the money up front, in cash. When we declined, he showed us a convincing book of handwritten, raving reviews dated over the past ten years. Austin and I considered the risks (Austin's proposed alternative, a "self-directed" Amazon tour, made me more nervous than the George of the Jungle option). Despite our skepticism, we couldn't say no to the chance. Just in case it was real.

Lina and Ivan, our Colombian companions for the expedition, were both medical students in Cali—a city west of Bogotá. Lina had a thin ponytail and defined collarbones. Ivan's thick, dark eyebrows contrasted with his light complexion. They too had been dubious about this venture and, like us, relieved when Miguel, our native guide, had shown up that morning.

Fishermen shouted at each other as they tossed ropes and brought in crates of the morning's catch. Miguel, who'd left us on the dock as he'd finalized our travel arrangements, returned in a narrow boat to pick us up.

"This is Juan," Miguel said, nodding toward a skinny boatman with a shy smile. "He will be with us for the journey."

We greeted Juan as he bailed out a thin layer of water with a magenta plastic bucket.

Miguel leaped onto the dock with rubber boots spilling from his short arms. "Take your size."

"Where's George of the Jungle?" asked Austin.

"He's just the business guy. It will only be us and Juan."

The boat quivered as the four of us stepped inside the boat after Miguel. The engine coughed to life. Juan steered using a long pole hanging out the back with a prop at the end. A blue tarp canopy, which blocked the scorching sun, flapped in the wind. We spent an hour riding to the part of the jungle where our hike would start.

Miguel offered us finger-sized bananas still attached to the vine and yelled some geographic information above the motor: "You have to ride sixty days on the river to get to the headwaters," Miguel said, matter-of-factly, waving ahead, "thirty to get to the middle of the river." Miguel pointed behind us. "And if you go that way for five days, you need a very expensive permit. Thousands of US dollars. Only well-funded institutions like National Geographic can afford it. If you make it ten days after that, you risk being killed by people who have never had contact with outside civilization. If you go fifteen days more, you can be eaten by people who practice cannibalism."

I studied Miguel's face for any sign of embellishment. Reflected light rested on his button nose and bronze cheekbones. He lacked the typical tour-guide sensationalism—it didn't seem necessary in the Amazon. His affect reminded me of a local friend sharing stories over drinks and less like a packaged brochure speech. Though he hailed from the Peruvian highlands, he'd spent fifteen years in this area after marrying his Colombian wife.

Much to Austin's delight, some fishing spears and machetes rested below our wooden bench.

"I need a machete," Austin had said on our final descent into Leticia, his face pressed against the plane's window at the unknown below.

My stomach had lurched. Though we'd both been oldest children, both bookworms, both raised with traditional Latter-day Saint values, both eaten our fair share of Mormon funeral potatoes and Jell-O salad mixed with cottage cheese, and both shared a craving for adventure—something that had attracted us to each other—that desire manifested differently and had been viewed differently within our respective contexts. I carried much of the fear, a lifetime of lessons from my mother and culture to exercise caution as a girl. Austin never seemed conflicted about who *he* was or what he should or should not want. A machete, to me, screamed "weapon" louder than "tool."

I shook Austin's knee to break his trance. "You're not Indiana Jones."

"I definitely need one," he'd said, only half-teasing. "We've come this far. Let's see what's out there."

I had a sense of where his explorer's thrill came from. Austin grew up at the end of a long dirt road in a small town in Wyoming where his father owned a vet clinic specializing in large animals. When he wasn't building fences, pouring concrete, or shoveling out the animal stalls, Austin roamed the Big Horn Mountains directly behind his house with his yellow Labrador, Nellie. Eventually, he'd make his way home again before dark and assume his place as the oldest of five boys at an oak dining table in a loving family with supportive parents. One of his first words was "actually." His tendency toward mischievousness and pushing limits were interpreted as endearing and clever by those around him, rarely entitled or sinful. The stories have become legendary.

There was the time he flooded the house by placing the garden hose in the dryer vent. Just to see what would happen.

When he continued to brush off his younger brother's attempts to claim a video game controller by saying, "It's not my fault it's always my turn."

Or when he wrote cuss words on little notes to pass to kids on the bus. After he got caught, the principal called his mother but started with the good news: "Everything was spelled correctly."

When he snuck out of church each Sunday during the children's hour—whose services he found boring beyond measure—to draw on the sidewalks with rocks. This enraged a fellow Mormon kid named Bobby, who'd chase Austin around the church premises with fists raised to inflict righteous punishment. (Bobby went on to become county attorney.)

In third grade, a lunch lady caught Austin stuffing food into his coat pockets—napkins full of dry Spanish rice and mixed vegetables—so he could have seconds of "the good stuff," like tapioca pudding. The lunch lady dragged him to the principal's office by the ear. On the way, they passed a lost-and-found bin. Austin blindly reached for a coverless book on top. Left alone, facing a wall in an administration office for the rest of recess, Austin read with increasing interest. The book happened to be *The Hobbit*.

For years, he reread that story and *The Lord of the Rings*, completely enchanted by Bilbo's and Frodo's journeys. The book unearthed a universe along with excitement about life's possibilities. As a kid, he'd already lived with his grandparents stationed in Belgium for a summer, which formed some of his first magical memories of mouth-watering *frites*, gold-trimmed architecture, and a curious fountain featuring a little boy peeing into the basin. In Wyoming, he camped and hiked at every opportunity. He would go on to see other countries: hopping moving trains on his mission in Ukraine (he knew all his life he'd serve a mission for the church, as is expected of young men); researching the media in Russia for his international relations college thesis; kayaking through the Bahamas to spear fish for firepit dinners outside the tent he pitched on tiny islands.

But things didn't always work out for Austin. Sometimes he experienced the harsh costs of his thoughtlessness and undiagnosed ADHD, like the time he owned a beloved canary named Sunny. As a kid, Austin sang songs to his pet, let Sunny perch on his finger or shoulder, let him flap his pretty yellow wings between branches of a tree in the living room. But his mom had to remind him to feed the bird. Over and over. Or he'd forget.

One day, Austin returned from a camping weekend with his Scout troop. He found Sunny stiff in the bottom of his cage. Sunflower seed shells scarred by peck marks littered the metal floor, evidence of Sunny's desperate attempts to fight starvation. Austin cringes to tell this story—the searing consequence of his negligence, his inability to care for this creature he was responsible for, a creature he adored.

Juan cut the engine and nudged the boat forward to a muddy shore as Miguel instructed us to gather our things. Juan would meet us at a distant tributary after our six-hour hike.

I took a deep breath and wiped my sweaty hands on my T-shirt. My knees felt hot after an hour of sitting in black jeans. Nerves and *what-ifs* buzzed in my mind when all I wanted was to focus on the unrivaled landscape before me, ahead of me. *What if we go missing? What if someone gets hurt?* Austin wore a white-and-navy-checkered button-up. His tall boots over khakis made me think he did look a little like Indiana Jones.

The group formed a single-file line up the river bank. Miguel took the lead at the front, chopping down growth taller than me to find the start of the trail. Palms marked with fresh slashes would prevent us from getting lost. I felt caught between a desire for safety and the lure of the unknown. But I didn't want fear to define me, or this trip. Turning around, I watched Juan and the motorized canoe disappear from view.

"This way," Miguel shouted after an uncomfortable pause. He waved his machete above the brush. We followed him into the shadows as the trees swallowed up the blue above.

"The sky is bigger in Wyoming," Austin liked to say when we dated. And, listening to him narrate his life, I believed that for him, it was.

I grew up in a Utah suburb sandwiched between Gentile Street and Gelding Road, curious names given I knew few "Gentile" non-Mormons and the farms (along with whatever horses may have inhabited them) had long been replaced by subdivisions. As a kid, I considered the borders of my neighborhood—my world—to be the same as the boundaries of my church congregation. My family rarely visited the nearby mountains, content with our small corner of the planet. My wildest space was the wetlands, an off-limits patch of nature reserve fenced behind rows of houses where, as a child, I would sneak in to snap cattails and unleash a blizzard of feathery seeds to run through.

Our sidewalks connected like circuits. I could count the number of non-Mormon households: the home on the corner where five lanky boys with white-blond hair kept to themselves, my friends who lived across the street with their mother who wore tank tops, the unseen man who we suspected was allergic to the sun on account of his neglected lawn, a swath of crabgrass. How terrible—the worst thing—I remember thinking, to be allergic to the sun. The gray-rock Latter-day Saint chapel served as the nucleus. Our homes, standard A-frames with rectangle windows like cartoonish eyes over a double-garage mouth, were no more than a 0.3-mile radius away from the church, though most people drove there on Sundays. Mom once told me when we built our home in this new development in 1992 the congregation had three different nurseries to accommodate seventy-one toddlers during Sunday School.

On the whole, women stayed home to raise the children. Men went off to jobs as truck drivers, mechanics, and teachers. The system worked well for me when I believed I fit in. For years, before my family's unraveling and my eventual exile—I was happy there. I could sprint barefoot for no reason at all, tie a jump rope around the handles of my bike and pretend it was a stallion, imagine shooting a bow and arrow like my brothers did at Scout camp while I attended Achievement Days and the Young Women program—church initiatives for girls eight to eighteen—where I learned to bake cookies, tole paint, pose for fashion photo shoots, and play the occasional game of backyard croquet. I didn't question why my activities differed from my brothers'—it's just how it was.

My well-meaning mother used to pray with my siblings and me each day before we left for school. "Please bless that the boys will go on missions and the girls will get married in the temple." She once wrote these as family goals next to our individual names on a pink Post-it note and stuck it to the refrigerator. I couldn't have been older than ten, but at that moment I sensed my brothers had the better deal. Young men could go on missions to far-flung places around the globe, *then* get married. Never mind that they often went to places like Idaho or that I would later decide proselytizing wasn't for me. They had more options. At that time, there was a fading-but-enduring stereotype that women only went on missions if they had failed to snag a husband by the time they turned twenty-one. Now, almost a quarter of missionaries are women, and they can serve as young as nineteen. But in 2007, the year I graduated from high school, women represented only 17 percent of full-time missionaries. This wasn't surprising given the 1985 statement from the fifteenth president of the church, Gordon B. Hinckley, that "while we recognize the vast good that sister missionaries do, and while we greatly appreciate their tremendous service, we are reluctant to have in the field the same or a larger number of sister missionaries" than brothers since "we regard a happy marriage as the greatest mission any young woman can enjoy."

No one expected or encouraged me to serve a mission, though I often stared at my dad's Japanese doll collecting dust in a glass case in the basement. The doll was a souvenir from the Tokyo mission he rarely talked about. The object resembled nothing else in the house. I'd place my chin in my hands and stare at the doll—her pale, expressionless face; her heart-shaped lips; her black hair divided into three buns; her dress a mix of fire-engine red and bold oranges with swirls of silver embroidered on the fabric that seemed permanently frozen in motion, floating around her like a spirit. I understood this artifact as a portal to another realm I didn't understand. The doll was nothing like the Barbies I played with. I stole glimpses whenever I could. Once, without the glass case on, I extended a finger to touch the doll's hair, startled at its plastic crunch.

In time, the doll disappeared without warning, thrown away by my mother.

As I grew, I realized education would be my ticket to options, the safest gateway toward a vague form of freedom I sensed outside the walls of my world. My mom, a former elementary school teacher, encouraged us to take school seriously. We had a closet library filled with worn children's books and outdated encyclopedias. College was never a question for me as it was for other girls my age. Of the fifteen neighbor girls I spent most of my time with as a teen, only four went to college (unusual for Latter-day Saints, who generally value education). A few married soon after high school graduation. They all had their own valid, complicated life paths, but I wanted to know what else was out there.

"Get your degree," Mom said to me, but often with the refrain: "Your husband could die. You never know what could happen. It's a good backup plan."

I threw myself into studying, stockpiling As as if my entire future depended on them. Though it didn't occur to me that I could apply to college outside of Utah, I felt elated to get accepted into the most selective school in the state: Brigham Young University. However, I also remember how my stomach dropped when I took a BYU entrance survey with a question about my primary motive for attending school. Among the multiple-choice selections was "to find an eternal companion." By then, I imagined I was "different." I desired something less traditional for myself, though the contours remained blurry. Career wasn't a thing I'd been encouraged to consider with specificity, but I wanted one. I knew I was ambitious. I knew I liked to write. I knew I loved to read and critically engage with books. I knew I craved authentic, meaningful conversations and connections, had a knack for listening, and a capacity for empathy. I knew I wanted to contribute to the world, help others, and maybe even go to that elusive thing called grad school. All of this, at the time, seemed impossible to negotiate with a husband. I didn't want to get married before graduating from college, maybe not ever, though the second thought frightened me and seemed preposterous. No one had taught or presented the choice to remain single as a possible—let alone favorable—life model. I'd internalized that *good* people married, wanted to marry.

I pushed this red flag on the questionnaire aside: BYU offered, on the whole, a quality education with a tuition rate I could afford if I worked two jobs.

At BYU, a campus tucked against a gorgeous-but-harsh Rocky Mountain face in Provo, I allowed some of my internal resistance to peek through.

I speed walked through campus with my heavy school bag, nursing resentment toward my seemingly homogeneous peers—mostly white students, men with missionary-short haircuts and cargo shorts, young women wearing DownEast Basics T-shirts layered under tank tops with straight, long hair who happened to look a whole hell of a lot like me. Despite BYU's vibrant campus, I sulked and judged the world as I wanted to see it, feared to see it—a world inundated with messages about how I needed to settle down. I felt stunned when my freshman roommate accepted a proposal, and I struggled to understand my many classmates who squeezed their weddings into weekends during the semester. The typical engagement period spanned a few months, but a few weeks wasn't unheard of. Long engagements were not encouraged in order to minimize sexual "mess ups," since the church teaches abstinence until marriage.

Though I was sick of the rules and itching to escape, I didn't want to be perceived as "bad," as anything like the way my mother and childhood neighborhood, I feared, had come to see me. Though three years had passed since leaving home, Mom and I didn't talk. Though we reached a point of polite civility, we never healed. I saw her a few times a year—on Christmas and Mother's Day—always with my siblings present, always stiff, always pretending that she hadn't spread delusional lies about me to anyone who would listen.

I still had so much to prove. I wanted to make her proud, or maybe sorry—just in case she ever called. I felt I could only risk so much, yet the pressure found other paths of escape. My "rebellion" intensified.

I cut off my long hair and dyed it hot pink,
then black, then purple, then a dull blue—like a bruise.

"Isn't this a nice color?" my grandma said,
slipping me a magazine featuring a brunette.

For no apparent reason, I stopped wearing shoes,
even when it meant getting kicked out of grocery stores.

"That's inconsiderate," my stepmom would say.
"Beneath you."

I illegally drove my red moped at top speeds
on campus sidewalks past midnight to feel the wind on my face.

"Motorcycles will kill you," my boyfriend warned.

In the winter, I would take off my coat and lie on the frozen grass outside the dorms, longing to feel something—anything.

"Try looking at the glass half-full," Dad suggested.

I often drove my car into the mountains at night and parked at a secluded spot with a full view of the blue and yellow city lights. I would sit on the hood of my car for hours and watch the valley. Sometimes I spent the night there on the mountain. Once, late on a Friday night, I got an hour or two toward California before coming to my senses and turning around. I had class on Monday.

During my freshman year, I enrolled in an astronomy course. The class met in the planetarium, where I sat in the back, tucking my longboard in the aisle. My longboard made for a cool, *unconventional* form of transportation I'd adopted from the skater boys I worked with. I used to ride down Provo Canyon before quickly realizing how much I hated speed wobble and asphalt's finite mercy. Most days during college, I walked home without once taking it out of my backpack straps, its shadow casting wings.

The plush planetarium chairs reclined so everyone could tilt their gaze up at the fishbowl as if seeing the night sky. For a few weeks, I thought it *was* the night sky, broadcast onto the dome via a powerful telescope. Students often fell asleep in those chairs. But not me. I watched as the nervous professor moved through slide after slide.

"Does anyone know where the word *planet* comes from?" the professor asked one day.

Silence. "Anyone?"

Click.

"Planet comes from the word *planete*, meaning 'wanderer,'" she explained. "Each time the ancient Greeks tried to plot the stars in the sky, a few pesky dots would retrograde. Of course, those dots were planets. They never remained in place."

A deep part of me awoke when I saw those Greek letters on the screen.

That's me, I thought.

That's me, that's me. Just when a determined, happy road seemed clear, at the moment I saw the next step I should take, I felt hesitation. I paused. I retreated and slipped. I baffled and confused and questioned. I could not be plotted. I never fathomed this was human nature, bigger than me and my projections.

Planete.

Wanderer. I let the word ring in my mind, as if hearing it for the first time.

Soon after, I went to Denny's with some friends for midnight pancakes (a ritual for sober BYU kids). There, I met Zach, a cute hitchhiker who'd recently graduated from the University of Michigan. He carried a school backpack with a few sets of clothes and a Moleskine. "The key to successful hitchhiking is to not look homeless," he said, tossing his curly dark hair. He needed a place to stay. My roommates weren't in town. Feeling bold and eager to hear more, I offered up my couch.

Zach and I stayed up late talking in my living room. He told me about his journey so far, how to survive without money, the hospitality everyone had shown him, the freedom and liberation he now enjoyed. He asked me questions about The Church of Jesus Christ of Latter-day Saints, bewildered by my restricted choices, which I was naïvely surprised to read about later on his blog. His goal was to make it to the East Coast and find a way to Europe, maybe work on a boat for free passage. I absorbed every word with an attention that had little to do with Zach or a sense of attraction but everything to do with an awakening power, an unconscious tingling of momentum, the kind of evocative energy described in one of my favorite poems from high school, "The Name" by Don Marquis:

> My heart has followed all of my days
> —Something I cannot name!

"Come with me," Zach said with gusto after a few hours. "I can tell you are made for the road, like me."

Was that true? Was *this* the nagging buried within me, clawing its way up? My heart quickened. Time puttered to a stop. "You have a hitchhiker's thumb," Mom had told me. In third grade, I'd once made a lifecast model of my thumb featuring a grotesque, ninety-degree arch. Mom displayed the cement model in the living room, on the cedar hope chest she'd been given as a girl, the cedar chest that held her wedding dress with hand-sewn beads and plastic pearls.

I considered what I would leave behind: a low-paying restaurant job, an apartment lease, my family, an upcoming semester with a full-ride scholarship. But my overwhelming feeling was not a sense of loss or fear of irresponsibility but a sense of transgression. I was a woman. I felt I wasn't allowed. *Dangerous. Taboo for a single woman to travel alone with a man.*

"I can't," I said to Zach, followed by a heavy, disappointing silence.

We heard a knock at the door. Two of my guy friends from the Denny's group dropped by to make sure I was safe.

I rolled my eyes. Zach didn't seem too miffed. I said goodnight to my friends, then Zach, and retreated to my bedroom alone. The next morning, I went into the living room. Bright bars of light sifted through the blinds. Zach was gone, but he'd left behind a dream I could almost articulate.

Austin could not contain his grin as he paused to stare at the rainforest canopy. We spotted a few monkeys, which some locals eat, though Miguel argued that eating monkeys was immoral. He showed us rubber trees and giant *cashaponas* with thick roots shooting from the ground with arched legs. We watched a proud toucan fight off a sizable dog using its razor-sharp beak edged with sea-foam green and aqua. Soldier ants crawled everywhere my boots stepped.

We halted every so often so Miguel could scan for the pale slashes he'd made as markers with his machete over the years to keep us on his homemade trail. "There is no telling what would happen if we lost them," he said as he cut through branches creeping up to block the path. I tensed every time he stopped and spun around with a quizzical expression. I sensed the potential for excitement, but more the devastating consequences, of going missing in the uncharted Amazon. My mind was used to considering consequences. Austin relished the risk, seemed almost at home in it, a little giddy when we were running low on water. Mosquitoes hung around us like a fog.

"Look here!" Miguel pointed at a fist-sized tarantula. The spider crouched with brown-striped legs in the nook of a tree.

I screamed a little and the furry tarantula curled inside. While remarkable, this kind of expedition was not my ideal kind of travel. I liked to settle into one place, buy a paper map, find the good food, and chip away at a project. Maybe that was brave too.

Austin laughed. Ivan peered into the trunk to glimpse the spider. No luck. I felt bad for spoiling the moment for the others. Miguel shook his head with disappointment.

My ever-logical dad didn't understand my perplexing discontent at BYU when everything seemed to be going well for me according to outward measures. He and my stepmom, Lisa, doting and concerned by the changes in me, recommended I try something else. "What about a semester at BYU's Hawaii campus?" my dad said. Perhaps a change in scene could help me outgrow this phase.

So I went.

Compared to BYU's main campus of thirty thousand students, BYU–Hawaii had 2,500 representing seventy-six different countries. These church members looked different from me, expressed different thoughts than me, held side conversations and sang hymns in languages I had never heard before. Despite the wide range of backgrounds, they still identified as Mormon. People wore sarongs and flip-flops and never began meetings on time; they didn't care that I didn't wear shoes. Hitchhiking, which was commonplace, became my form of transportation around the island. I tacked anthropology onto my English major, a plan I would finish out at BYU–Provo which had more international research opportunities—ones I would take full advantage of upon my looming return.

Hawaii gave me a glimpse of how big the sky could be. One evening, after a long day of surfing, I sprawled out in the back seat of my friend's car on the coastline drive home. I closed my eyes and felt the rush of humid breeze from the open windows, drying my suntanned skin and sandy beach hair that I hadn't bothered to comb or wash in days. I felt a stinging sensation on my hand. When I opened my eyes, I noted a new coral wound in the shape of a goofy smile on my palm. I admired the red cut and erupted into giggles. I hoped it would scar, stamp me forever.

"What's so funny?" my friends asked.

I laughed. I laughed until I cried. Had I ever felt so alive?

"Nothing," I said.

In Hawaii, I also had the safe space to confront, head-on, the most urgent, dangerous question of my heart: *Should I settle down and become the wife and mother I'm supposed to be, or should I listen to my growing impulse to travel?*

Now, I ache a little for this nineteen-year-old, wrestling with such a misguided question at the onset of her adulthood. Yet this was the first time I'd tackle, with total sincerity, this dichotomy. I thought travel was the name for my restlessness. For a while, I fancied I could define myself by being somewhere else.

Being the earnest Mormon that I was, I took my honest question, along with my leather-bound Bible + Book of Mormon scripture set, to a meditative setting called The Point, a half-mile lithified cliff jutting out into a sea thirty feet below. I considered it my spiritual responsibility to know and reconcile—even if that meant coming to terms with a path I might find unpalatable—what God wanted for me. I'd also packed a paper copy of what is known as a patriarchal blessing, a special blessing given to Latter-day Saints once in their lives at a time when they are seeking guidance. The blessing serves as a kind of guide map, a promise of things to come if you live your life well.

The ocean roared as I stepped cautiously to the very edge of The Point and looked out at the vast horizon—massive sky meeting massive water. I felt hope and terror as I settled into an uncomfortable position on a black lava rock. I cracked open my scriptures to find my patriarchal blessing tucked between the thin Bible pages.

I'd received my patriarchal blessing soon after being banished from my mom's home. I needed guidance, comfort, certainty, something. Alone, I went to the patriarch's house, an elderly man I'd never met, the person in our region specifically ordained to administer this kind of blessing. Due to their importance in Latter-day Saint culture, patriarchal blessings are recorded, then transcribed for later reference.

The patriarch's name was Storer. He had white hair and translucent fingers that twitched as he shook my hand. He asked my name and made a few points of small talk before directing me to sit in a wooden kitchen chair. He retrieved a tape recorder from the closet. Then, the patriarch placed his shaky palms on my head. I closed my eyes, eager for God's mysterious, elusive plan for my life to reveal itself, like a cosmic fortune cookie, despite everyone's warnings that this wasn't how it worked.

The blessing said I was promised a mind that would comprehend many things, a strong marriage, the chance to study abroad and travel the globe, to be free from fear. Just as I began to rejoice that I could indeed have it all, Patriarch Storer closed the prayer.

"One moment," he said, biting his lower lip. "I think we have a problem."

"What?"

"It seems the blessing did not record. We'll have to do it again."

He offered me another blessing. To my dismay, it wasn't the same. It wasn't bad, just different: all the bits about marriage and children, nothing about travel or studying abroad.

The textured rocks on The Point reminded me of Patriarch Storer's wrinkled hands. A large wave crashed, sending mist in all directions. I tasted salt on my lips as I read over my two patriarchal blessings—one official document creased into thirds, the other a scrawling bulleted list I'd jotted down on a piece of paper from memory after visiting Patriarch Storer. They were *both* mine, I realized. Many others were also mine. I didn't have to pick. There was not one correct path. A stillness swelled in me, a sense of being seen, or perhaps seeing more clearly. I squeezed my eyes shut and let the sensation overtake me, a rare feeling I was beginning to know by name: peace. A peace I took as a spiritual confirmation that God wanted *me* to decide my future.

Though it would be easy to view these two blessings as disillusioning, I found the experience faith-inspiring. This stake anchored me (if loosely) to Mormonism. If God did exist, and if that God knew me at all, that God would give me options—not a map. That God would give me space and courage big enough to bravely choose the life I wanted to live. Not even God was going to dictate what I should do, and perhaps this was God's way of telling me my question was not the right question to begin with. But kudos for trying.

"Amen," I said aloud after a few minutes of silently pondering this insight. I stood, warm with a newfound permission within me. The friendly wind whipped at my hair as I bounded home on lighter feet.

The glimpse faded. The experience got boxed away in a back closet of memory. I was still learning when and how to trust myself.

Miguel and our band of hikers made it out of the Brazilian jungle near sunset. On seeing the Amazon River again, we cheered. My shoulders relaxed with relief. Everyone skirted down a steep slope, our boots caked with layers of mud and bugs. Juan waited in the boat at the bottom of the bank. He poked at the water with a spear, jabbing absently without looking. He pulled up a fish every few stabs. Austin's Wyoming mind burst; even for him, this represented an abundance he couldn't believe existed.

We saw no other boat or sign of other humans as we sliced through the calm water to get to our bungalow. Palms framed the glassy river. With enthusiasm, Miguel identified birds in English (for Austin and me) and Spanish (for Lina and Ivan) by their unique warbles. The sun sank lower, the purplish-blue clouds gathering in trails.

Austin sat at the nose of the boat. Without making a scene, he pulled Miguel's gray machete out from under the bench and examined it with both hands.

I couldn't help but feel happy for him, for his intrepid spirit that had guided us here, to the Amazon. *His machete moment*, I thought.

But what about mine? What would be the equivalent?

Though skewed and too self-deprecating, I used to see Austin as my alluring contrast. He grew up in a wilderness; I grew up in a suburb. He was uncommonly happy; I was discontent without knowing why. He welcomed risk; I still couldn't silence the fear of crossing boundaries. He came from a good home; I wasn't sure what home meant. He trusted himself; I second-guessed everything. He thought he knew what he wanted; I still didn't know how to disentangle what I wanted from what I should want.

I watched Austin's eyes study the sharp blade then gaze at the reflection of clouds shining back along the water's surface, gliding along with us.

CHAPTER 4

Waking Up

"I DON'T KNOW IF I SHOULD DO THIS," I said, squirming as a nail technician clipped back my cuticles for a bridal pedicure. The salon smelled of acetone. A harsh light pummeled through the window with a view of the strip mall parking lot.

"I like the classic look you picked," Jane said from the chair on my left. "The shellac gel will last longer."

I shook my head. "I don't know if I should get married." My throat tightened. My eyes began to burn.

Jane winced slightly, like everyone did lately when I expressed doubts about my engagement. She reached over and took my hand. Her blonde ringlets bounced.

"But you love Austin." Jane searched my face, her head cocked, eager to resolve the awkwardness. Jane and I had spent three months doing anthropology fieldwork in a remote village in Ghana. She'd seen me in stressful situations—learning how to research and interview people at the local secondary school, visiting the clinic for malaria symptoms, shopping in the ever-bustling Kejetia, the largest open-air market in continental Africa. She'd also seen me through relationships and gutting breakups since. But she'd never seen me like this.

I shrugged. By now, full-on tears were streaming. And they weren't letting up soon.

"You've dated for two years. He's supportive of you." Jane paused. I didn't respond. "But you know I will support you no matter what."

I *did* love Austin. And yet, I couldn't shake the feeling of resistance, couldn't articulate what, precisely, I was resisting—like trying to describe air. My windy disposition meant I was no stranger to cyclones of cold anxiety mixing with my hot, brazen courage. Yet I could not fully see or identify this particular haze—not the reason for why I was getting married, but why I felt I *had* to get married. This was always my choice, but one with a perceived right answer in the thick, powerful atmosphere all around me.

The clarity could only come years later, in examining the cumulation of moments.

When I was in children's Sunday school, singing at the top of my lungs bordering on a scream,

> I LOVE TO SEE THE TEMPLE.
> I'M GOING THERE SOMEDAY!

The woman conducting the children's hymn held up a poster of the Salt Lake Temple against a backdrop of pastel clouds.

"This is the Lord's house," she said. "It's where people get married. A temple sealing is different from getting married outside of the temple, where people have to say 'till death do us part.' The sealing makes it so families can be together forever."

She did not say that a temple sealing is required to enter the highest level of heaven—the celestial kingdom—where God lives.

She did not say that the dominance of the nuclear family narrative didn't emerge in full force until post–World War II, simultaneous with America's embrace of 1950s gender roles. She did not offer any non-heteronormative models of marriage or mention the people excluded from participation. She did not say that my family, in time, would look nothing like the ideal talked about at church.

"Do you want your family to be together forever?" the conductor asked.

A roar of yeses.

I sang the children's hymn again, yell-singing in my foofy Easter dress, barely able to remain seated in my tiny plastic chair. This was during the days when I flung open my bedroom window and serenaded the neighborhood, the era before I became embarrassed of my voice.

> I'LL PREPARE MYSELF WHILE I AM YOUNG;
> THIS IS MY SACRED DUTYYYYYYYYYY!

When I was fourteen, I sat with my friend in the middle school cafeteria as she told me about her birthday. She'd received some teen-appropriate gifts from her family, along with a vacuum cleaner and some queen-size furniture. She said her parents wanted her to have a few items to help ease the transition into marriage. At the time, I thought this sounded like a great idea and wondered if I should ask my parents to do the same.

Fast-forward to the Young Women organization, the gender-segregated church program where I spent my Sundays between the ages of twelve and eighteen. The image of the Salt Lake Temple appeared on all my pink Personal Progress church workbooks. It featured on the embossed Young Womanhood Recognition medallion, a reward for those who completed the program. The temple image reinforced the ultimate goal—to be taken by the hand, presented before a sacred altar, and married "for time and all eternity" so mine could be a happy, forever, covenant family. Almost annually, I participated in an activity where everyone listed desirable qualities in a future husband. My local leaders encouraged me to pray for my future husband to have a good day, do well in school, etc. Because even though I hadn't met him, he was out there somewhere. I followed their directives until the excitement morphed into unease.

In high school, my boyfriend gave me a synthetic ruby promise ring before serving his mission in Canada. "Will you wait for me?" he asked, eyes misty as he opened a white ring box on his parents' driveway. The gray letterman's jacket he got from the swim team smelled of chlorine, and it hung heavy on my shoulders.

I accepted, shivering in the dry December air—not fully understanding what it meant—and wore it on my wedding finger with the commitment that I'd "wait for him." No adult in my life pulled me aside to warn me of the dangers of picking a life partner at the age of seventeen.

When he returned two years later, the relationship didn't last a week. I still remember his barrage of questions:

"How often do you swear now?"

"Why are you going to Ghana?"

"Do you even want to be a mom?"

After breaking up with him, I burned with resentment, fearing that I'd disappointed everyone for not wanting what I was supposed to want: marriage to a *good* returned missionary. Instead of returning the ring, I pawned it to help pay for a plane ticket to India. My travels, from the beginning, seemed to be in direct conflict with prioritizing marriage.

During college, I became aware of "Super Cute Sunday," the first

Sunday of a new academic year at BYU, where thousands of anxious women across campus wake up early to curl their hair, apply their best makeup, and pull on their favorite dress. First impressions matter. Student "singles ward" congregations, beginning at eighteen and continuing until someone marries or "ages out" at thirty-one, were created to encourage meeting and marrying. I participated like anyone else. Having dates most weekends gave me a sense of security, a false sense of confidence and worth. I didn't want to get married yet, maybe ever, but that didn't mean I couldn't get married if I *had* to. I went on good dates, awkward dates, terrible dates—like the one where a guy picked me up in his two-seater car to go rock climbing, met a friend at the indoor gym, then let the friend ride shotgun while I rode in the trunk all the way home. I designed an ice cream litmus test, where I'd suggest going out for milkshakes, order the same size as my date, then pepper him with questions along the lines of, "Do you pee in the shower?" and "What species would you be in *The Lord of the Rings?*" and "Are you a fire person or an ice person?" If I finished my shake and he was only halfway done, I could judge him for talking too much, showing more interest in himself than in me. I didn't really know how to turn men down. As a result, I probably hurt a lot of people.

Swapping dating stories with friends used to be one of my favorite pastimes: stories about being taken to Temple Square in Salt Lake City on a first date and receiving a proposal, stories about enduring hide-and-go-seek games at Walmart, stories about guys showing up on women's doorsteps with original song compositions to ask them out (and then the women feeling like they couldn't say no after such an effort). The specifics of the tales changed, but I was never surprised or shocked. My friends and I howled with laughter to prevent examining the more troubling truths behind them.

I audited a marriage preparation class at BYU three times—never telling a soul, never officially enrolling, sure I'd die if it was on my transcript. But my distrust for marriage began to make me feel a little insane, and I wanted to understand what I might be missing. I snuck into the back row and purchased the binder of readings, which contained talks from high-ranking church leaders:

From "To the Single Adult Sisters of the Church" (1988) by Ezra Taft Benson:

> I would also caution you single sisters not to become so independent and self-reliant that you decide marriage isn't worth it and you can do just as well on your own. . . . Our priorities are right when we realize there is no higher calling than to be an honorable wife and mother.

From "Receive the Temple Blessings" (1999) by Richard G. Scott:

> An essential priority of a prospective wife is the desire to be a wife and mother. She should be developing the sacred qualities that God has given His daughters to excel as a wife and mother: patience, kindliness, a love of children, and a desire to care for them rather than seeking professional pursuits.

From the *Eternal Marriage Student Manual* (2003):

> Honorable, happy, and successful marriage is surely the principal goal of every normal person. Marriage is perhaps the most vital of all the decisions and has the most far-reaching effects, for it has to do not only with immediate happiness, but also with eternal joys.

Some of these sources may seem dated, but that stale air continued to circulate. For me (and for my mother who raised me), the old air was never contradicted. No one threw open a window. The importance of marriage remained the same, regardless of the decade. As recently as 2019, the president of the church asserted that "in God's eternal plan, salvation is an individual matter; exaltation is a family matter."

I never did finish that marriage prep course. Each time, I stopped going after the class that featured the stats for children of divorce. The School of Family Life professor never changed his slides. Sometimes I wasn't sure which I feared more: repeating my parents' incompatible marriage or the hellfire end of it.

"If this is you, don't worry," the professor said. "There is a bimodal distribution in the curve. The likelihood of future divorce is less about your parents and more about *your own commitment* to the idea of marriage."

For that lack of commitment, for all my doubts and brave concerns I harbored then and in that nail salon, I'd blamed myself.

Blue mosquito netting veiled the bright morning sun. Tangled in my hammock, I rubbed my eyes. I wore a gag gift from my cousin, a tank top with the word *BRIDE* embossed with glitter across the chest, the white fabric now reddish from swimming and relaxing on the Amazon's petal-soft muddy banks. Austin's hammock was empty, as were Ivan's, Lina's, Miguel's, and Juan's. As I stumbled into consciousness, I caught a glimpse of my pedicured toenails lined with dirt. A tiny ant corpse clung to the corner of my big toe, but the pearly French tip design appeared unscathed. I laughed to myself, smelling my sweat and the layers of DEET and eucalyptus bug spray. This hammock was another curious honeymoon bed.

I wiggled my toes. Jane had been right about at least one thing at the salon a world away: the shellac gel lasted longer.

A moment later, Austin came back into the room in his swimsuit. He flashed a radiant grin. "I bailed water out of a canoe from the bay so we can go for a ride."

Later that night, Miguel gathered the group back to the boat. I held a flashlight in the pitch black.

Miguel shined his spotlight on each of us. "Did everyone wash their hands? Bug repellant hurts the caiman's skin. We want to do this responsibly." I nodded. Juan started the motor, and the boat puttered away from shore as Miguel illuminated a path. Every few minutes, a fish lured by the light jumped into the boat, flopping and flailing at our feet. I shrieked as each one landed with a thud. Austin threw them back into the river with the bail bucket.

"We're looking for baby caimans, a species of alligator," Miguel said above the rumbling engine. "They appear at the edges of the water at this time of night. Siblings stick together. You can find them because their eyes glow red in the lamplight. Our task is to sneak up on them, gently lift them by the firm part of their necks, and put them back in the river safely."

Everyone's faces appeared nervous in the harsh lighting. I wondered why we were disturbing perfectly nice baby caimans.

"How big are they?" I asked. Miguel held up his fingers to measure about eight inches.

"Where are the bigger ones?" said Austin.

"They come out around three or four in the morning." I gulped. Miguel sensed my concern. "Don't worry," he said. "We aren't looking for those ones."

It didn't take long to spot a pair of red dots looming in the distance. Juan cut the motor. Miguel leaned out the front, his hand raised and ready. I closed my eyes and held my breath.

There was a splash. Miguel pulled back his hand and revealed a tiny caiman.

"Come here!" he said. No one needed to be beckoned. Lina snapped pictures. Ivan stroked the caiman first.

"Closer, Rachel. They don't bite! Don't be afraid."

I inched forward and brushed the spine of the reptile, its skin hard but slimy. Miguel returned it to the water, then found a few more.

He fished out a small one for me. "It's a girl," he said, examining the sex before pushing her in my direction. "Take it."

Something about the word *girl* caused me to slowly reach out my hand.

I pinched the caiman near the back of her neck, careful to support her head as Miguel had coached, then lowered her body onto my arm. I beamed. I couldn't believe this prehistoric creature perched on my bare skin. She was an evolutionary wonder—perfect as is, millions and millions of years older than Homo sapiens and the many cultures humans came to construct. Her young neck was so strong, her textured skin a bumpy armor. Her yellow eyes glowed with the otherworldly, like a galaxy, limitless.

I exchanged a smile with Austin, lingering there. Maybe, just maybe, I wouldn't cease to exist as I feared. Imagine if I could stay true to myself, that Austin wanted me that way. What if I could make marriage my own, something new, something unlike anything else I had ever seen before, much like a place I had never been before—a place as untamed and dynamic and alive as the Amazon?

When I felt ready, I carefully placed the caiman back into the dark water, the way Miguel had shown. The fresh night air embraced me as I released her into the wild, where she would always belong.

CHAPTER 5

You Knew What I Was

NO ROADS CONNECT TO IQUITOS, PERU—the capitol of the Peruvian Amazon, a city of almost five hundred thousand people that is known for little government control, child sex tourism, rainforest excursions, and the chance to get high on ayahuasca in the jungle in pursuit of a spiritual experience. Austin and I only went to Iquitos to catch the cheapest flight out of the rainforest bound for Cusco, Peru, where we were planning to stay for a few months. To get to Iquitos, we could take either a three-day slow boat or a fifteen-hour "fast" boat up the Amazon, departing from Santa Rosa (the Peruvian port in the Amazonian Trapezoid). Both boats were rumored to be miserable, stopping every few hours to pick up and deliver livestock. We chose the fast one.

Austin and I arrived in Iquitos, exhausted, at the Flying Dog Hostel in the pouring rain. A shaggy-haired receptionist greeted us. We placed our damp passports on the counter and looked around at the tomato-red walls. The center of the hostel was outdoors, the rain dancing off the concrete floor. Twenty-somethings walked in and out of the communal kitchen in the back.

"I need to see your immigration card too," the young man said as he thumbed through our documents.

Austin and I looked at each other. After our tour with Miguel, we'd raced to the airport in Leticia to stamp out of Colombia, the official way out of the Amazonian Trapezoid, minutes before the customs office closed. We'd arrived breathless and panting. The immigration officer glanced at me, then at the clock on the wall. He said something in Spanish about us not having enough time to collect a stamp into Peru.

Not enough time, I repeated in my mind. Did he mean we were cutting it close if we wanted to catch a ride across the Amazon River to get to Santa Rosa, Peru, before nightfall? We had boat tickets from Santa Rosa to Iquitos the next morning.

Or was it something else?

Rather than taking precious time to clarify what the immigration officer meant, we dashed back to the port. I didn't trust my Spanish, but I wondered if I should this time—if I should trust myself. I expressed my doubts to Austin. "The boat company will give us a stamp," he assured. Someone had misinformed us that a Peruvian immigration officer would give us a stamp as we boarded for Iquitos.

No one did.

"We're going to the Oficina de Inmigración as soon as they open tomorrow," Austin said to the receptionist. I watched the man's face shift from annoyance to pity. But pity wouldn't fix our problem.

"I don't think you can stay here," he winced. "It's illegal to host anyone without an immigration card." He examined our passports, sighed. "What a mess. Let me talk to my boss."

Austin and I waited in the lobby. He returned with the manager.

"You can stay here for the night," the manager said. "But I have to warn you. You'll probably be sent back."

Austin and I gawked. The very thought of enduring the fifteen-hour boat ride back to the Amazonian Trapezoid made my skin crawl. Our flight to Cusco left in two days. We couldn't go back; there wasn't time.

We explained our circumstances. The manager agreed it was unfair and the boatmen should have noticed the problem, but he doubted anything could be done. "I had a friend who had this happen a few months ago," the manager said. "They didn't do anything for him, even with a bribe."

We thanked them for their generosity in letting us stay, then dragged our bags to a room with three bunks. The six beds had red covers tucked around crisp, white sheets. I sat on one and immediately regretted it. I was still covered in the accumulation of days-old Amazon dirt and body odor. My throat constricted as I prepared to strike out at the closest target. Austin rummaged through his backpack for soap.

"I told you earlier what I thought the immigration officer in Leticia said. I *told* you we might need to be in Peru earlier for a stamp. You always assume things will work out, and then they don't."

Austin grabbed the shampoo and frowned. "You're actually suggesting this is my fault?"

"We wouldn't be in this mess if you would've listened to me."

We bickered until tears rolled down my face and Austin slammed the door on his way to the shower. I pulled off my sweater and looked at my tank top underneath, tie-dyed with iron-rich stains. I ripped it off, not caring if a stranger walked in. I held my knees to my chest until Austin returned. He didn't look at me. I snatched the shampoo from his hand and stormed past. In the shower, I scrubbed away DEET repellent and clumps of mud from my hair, ankles, ears. Auburn water swirled around the drain. Suds burned my eyes. *Things don't work out. Of course we're getting sent back. Of course this is all a mistake.* I scoured my skin raw and stood under the spigot until the heat waned.

When I returned, Austin was talking with a young German who'd checked into one of the bunks. She was complaining, saying how closed-minded she found her ayahuasca group. She felt ripped off and afraid. Austin listened with sympathy. I wanted to throw a shoe at him but climbed into a top bunk and cowered under the sheets instead. They smelled like Tide detergent. I listened to rain pelt the window. The weak daylight faded, and the room grew darker.

The German left. Austin climbed up the ladder. He found my hand under the blanket. "Going to sleep?"

I pulled my hand away.

"We need dinner. You haven't eaten all day."

"I don't care."

"You've got to eat."

"I don't have to do anything."

He peeled back the sheets to look me in the eyes. "Can I bring you back anything?"

"No."

"Are you going to sleep in your jeans?"

"Just go."

The door shut. I sniffled until a group of three American Peace Corps volunteers claimed the other beds, throwing their bags on their bunks and venting about how impossible their tasks were in their various host villages. I held the red blanket over my head, pretending to be asleep, and tried to listen to the methodical rain.

You and I should have a long, philosophical conversation. Austin's pickup line when he brushed shoulders with me for an electric moment in the doorway of a mutual friend's party in 2012. I was twenty-three, he was twenty-eight. He lifted his chin slightly as he grinned—such a beguiling grin—and I felt a gravity behind the honey sound of his voice.

That weekend, I decided to message him. Why not? I was casually dating a few great guys at the time—Mormon and non-Mormon—but no one exclusively. Dating provided a needed distraction during my first year of Teach For America:

"Would you rather have everything or know everything?" I texted. So philosophical.

He wanted, like me, to know everything. Then he asked me out.

A few weeks later, I stood in front of the mirror in my bedroom, undertaking the herculean effort of curling my thick hair. The room reeked of White Rain hairspray.

"What are you doing this weekend?" my colleagues had asked.

"I'm going on a date," I said. They probed. "To some MBA schmoozy dance party called 'Holidazzle,'" I laughed, playing it off like an anthropologist—"an interesting cultural experience." I'd spent another week working from dawn until dusk on my feet, prepping lessons, grading, performing unwavering enthusiasm, and fighting the copy machine. When I got home each night, I'd slip into baggy sweatpants and go straight to sleep at 7:00 p.m. Anything called Holidazzle sounded dizzying, an almost-comic charade compared to the reality of my job and the challenges my underserved students faced. I wondered if saying yes to Austin's invite had more to do with getting a free meal, a nice change from my usual granola bars.

Yet here I was, crunchy curls, my fingers sticky with hairspray residue. I slipped on a crimson, tea-length dress I'd worn in high school, the fanciest thing I owned, then dug out the heels I'd received from my stepmom, Lisa, for my seventeenth birthday. I took one last look at myself in the mirror: *What are you doing?* Red lipstick. Tired eyes. *Do you even like this guy?*

At least he was hot.

The party at the Westin Copley Place entailed everything I'd imagined and dreaded: intimidatingly tall, beautiful, successful people; a multiple-course spread of unrecognizable fancy foods; loud, trendy pop music; grand, sparkling gowns; needle-thin stilettos; flashing cameras; little chance for real conversation.

As I shrunk into my polite smile, Austin whispered into my ear, "Wanna get out of here?"

"Right now?" The party had just begun.

He nodded.

We reclaimed our coats and bundled up to face the late November evening. A light snow drifted down and collected on the sidewalk. Faint yellow halos from the streetlamps lit the brick path. I pulled my coat tighter, blinked away snowflakes, found myself laughing and unexpectedly happy, surprised by the turn in the evening. Austin was not as predictable as I had supposed. When we got to the Public Garden across from the Boston Common, we stopped in front of a pond by a towering willow tree. I leaned against it and surveyed him.

Austin looked at me, *really* looked at me, his face thoughtful. "There's a dark side of you," he said after a pause.

My mother's words.

"What do you mean?" I pretended to laugh.

"I can tell you have a lot of depth."

My face relaxed. The comment might have felt presumptuous or off-putting had it not resonated with my past in a way Austin couldn't have known. His rendering dropped the evil connotations that had long haunted me, though I still failed to understand what darkness meant as a concept. Was it my tendency toward discontentment, the way I took nothing for granted and questioned simple stories? An intensity of feeling and a wellspring of sensitivity that rose from seemingly nowhere as I observed strangers on the sidewalk, studied handwriting in holiday cards, mourned every moth I'd seen dive into a campfire? Was it my restlessness, which

I'd internalized as bad yet also appreciated for every place it had brought me? Whatever this darkness was, I wondered if it was not so terrible, something a person could love about me, something I could love about myself.

Austin's comment made me feel seen, as if a layer of pretense had been stripped away. We went back to his apartment. Overflowing bookshelves lined his bedroom. We climbed into his twin-size bed: me in my red dress, Austin still in his suit. He had no pillows and instead used a few books swaddled in wool sweaters. He claimed this made reading in the evenings easier.

We cuddled and talked all night until falling asleep—no sex, no expectations of sex. Early the next morning, still in our formal clothes, Austin walked me to my car. My curled hair now fell in ratted knots. He brushed strands from my face, pulled me in.

For a minute he held my head in his hands, touched his nose and lips to my cheek. And what was it? A subtle sniff? An inhaling of my skin, a taking in of my scent? Beneath the obvious attraction, a pleasant current ran through my body, a feeling that said:

Stay.

I began drafting a letter for the Iquitos immigration office the next morning. The patchy internet mustered up Google Translate. I didn't want any mistakes in my Spanish and hoped to prevent any more mishaps.

"We left Santa Rosa before the immigration office was open," I typed, then copied down the Spanish onto a page ripped out of my journal. "No one stamped our passports or said anything before we boarded the boat."

"Write that we are on our honeymoon," Austin said. "Maybe they'll feel bad for us and let us off the hook."

"I have to focus," I said. I hadn't recovered enough from our argument the night before to tolerate his optimism.

"Esta manera es nuestra primera oportunidad," I wrote, trying to show we were attempting to do the right thing by coming into the immigration office at the first chance.

"Give them Miguel's contact information. He can vouch for us," Austin said.

I glared but added a new paragraph with his suggestion.

"It's not going to work anyway," I said.

"Do you *ever* assume things will go well?" Austin's patience wore thin. This was our first major fallout since the wedding. We were bone-weary; we were nervous; we were in another country illegally. The tension exposed the fault lines of our relationship.

I signed the note, "Gracias por ayudarnos," before folding it into fourths and stuffing it into my back pocket.

At the Oficina de Inmigración, we met with a slender woman in a black pantsuit. She nodded as she read the letter and stared down at her desk, speaking very slowly so I could understand. Regret shone in her demeanor, but there was no avoiding it; we had to go back to the Amazonian Trapezoid.

Borders. Boundaries. Rules. Confusion. Mistakes, no matter how honestly made, no matter how good the intentions.

After Holidazzle, Austin and I went our separate ways for Christmas with our families. Austin spent the break in rural Wyoming. I flew to Utah where all was not well. My siblings and I met with my mom's therapist to discuss her latest psychotic break. The delusional disorder diagnosis, and her inability to acknowledge her condition, pointed to a difficult road ahead.

That night, I felt like I had to tell Austin. I needed to talk to someone, but I also wanted to be honest. A few others I'd dated in the past were troubled by my family background—divorce, mother issues, mental health questions. I didn't want to play that game again.

"You there?" I texted.

Austin later told me that he'd received my message while driving with his family to the movie theater. They parked as Austin stared at my glowing words in the dark.

His intuition perked. "Go in without me," Austin told his family.

We talked until the movie ended about my mother and the likelihood of her long-term dependency on me, a premonition that would come to pass all too soon.

Austin must have felt concerned about my family struggles. We were mere weeks into our relationship and hadn't become exclusive yet, though we were well on our way. It wouldn't have been too late for him to come up with an excuse, to drift apart before things got serious. But Austin listened without judgment. He wanted to know if I was okay, what needed to be done, what he could do. But beneath the actual conversation, I sensed Austin's capacity to care, *genuinely* care.

"Can I fly to Utah? To see you?"

"Yes. I'd like that."

By the time we hung up, I think I knew he loved me. I don't remember the first time he told me those words; it's as if the love was always there, waiting.

Crates of chickens clucked overhead on the boat back to Santa Rosa the next morning. I stared at the white upholstery of the seat ahead, searching for shapes or interesting stains. Hours dragged by. I counted the number of orange life jackets. I tried reading *A Time of Gifts*, a memoir by Patrick Leigh Fermor who walked from England to Constantinople, but the romanticized travel tale worsened my mounting seasickness. My adventure didn't resemble his, not with his rosy descriptions written forty years after the trip. Austin flipped through his passport to read the quotes along the top. He started peeling off an old visa to Brazil.

"Stop doing that," I said. "Picking at the sticker will only make us seem more illegal."

"I want to read them all," he said. "Listen to this quote by John Paul Jones: 'It seems to be a law of nature, inflexible and inexorable, that those who will not risk cannot win.'"

His eyes were teary. Actually teary. He'd been moved by the quotes, emotion compounded by fatigue and hunger and stress and maybe homesickness. I'd only seen him cry once before, and heaven help me, that was about Jesus.

"Have you lost it?"

"The US is a good place."

Not for everyone, I thought, knowing full well how the US Border Patrol would have treated a Peruvian who'd illegally entered the country, even unintentionally, if our positions had been reversed. I didn't want to continue old debates. I wanted to sleep on Austin's shoulder, then remembered we were fighting. I leaned against the plastic wall instead. I knew by then this wasn't all Austin's fault, but I wasn't ready to admit that to him yet.

"You know I'm really Mormon, right?" Austin would say when we were dating, curious about my perspectives as we sat in my parked Ford Focus in the dark outside his apartment in Harvard Square. He lived a few blocks from the church we attended, a place where I simultaneously felt safe, at home, empty, and terribly alone. I took Austin's comment to suggest a few things: religious conviction and a strong belief in Christ's divinity, some loyalty to the institutional church, and the desire to have and raise children within that tradition.

When these tense conversations arose during our dating years, I would quickly shrivel into tears. Did I know if I wanted any of those things anymore? I felt I was "really Mormon" too, part of a distinct culture, something that existed alongside but also apart from religiosity, and dating non-Mormons had only made that clearer. But my religious landscape and the way I inhabited my faith seemed wildly, irreparably different—changing quicker than I could track. My childhood faith had ruptured upon my move to Boston, and I was still wrecked from the impact, blinded by existential grief, still collecting the pieces left, examining the fragments for what still felt beautiful and real. *What keeps the leaves on the trees?* I asked myself over and over as I walked along the Charles River or pushed a cart through the grocery store or pulled up to the church parking lot. I didn't have answers for Austin because I didn't have them for myself. The thought of losing my faith community, after losing my literal community and home at age fifteen, felt too heavy. I didn't want to lose Austin, either. Even the hint of a question probing into essential premarriage questions felt like a stab at the bruise left by past relationships when I hadn't matched the archetype of a Mormon woman worth marrying. Austin was moderate, wary of extremes, open-minded, and appreciated a healthy debate. But he was still a Mormon man and a product of a deeply conservative society. I didn't want to disappoint him or to be unfairly measured against these traditional norms and found to be not enough. Unable to answer Austin's questions about faith head-on, in a way that used to seem straightforward, I cried. Austin would reach over and hold my hand. The conversation fizzled.

While dating, Austin and I often joked about an old short film we had both watched in church as children. A Native American boy hikes through an arid mountain to prove himself as a man. At the summit, he encounters a rattlesnake in the sagebrush. The snake asks the boy to carry him down the mountain. The boy balks, "I can't carry you down. You'll bite me." The snake promises he won't hurt the boy. The boy relents and picks up the snake, wrapping it in his shirt.

But when they get to the base of the mountain, the snake sinks its teeth into the boy's skin. As the boy dies, he yells, "But you promised not to hurt me."

The snake slithers away. "You knew what I was when you picked me up."

As if anyone could be so immediately knowable. As if life provided little to no flexibility or margin for error. Though I rejected these ideas, part of me—like it or not—might have absorbed them, like venom.

Austin and I adopted the morbid slogan into our relationship. To remind the other of our differences, we'd manage a laugh or grimace and say, "You knew what I was when you picked me up."

For Mormons, the purpose of dating was to find someone to marry. To continue dating someone exclusively for more than a few months assumed an intention, so I do not recall Austin and I discussing the prospect of marriage for the first time. It's possible that we never did have that initial conversation, that it was assumed (as problematic as that sounds) the longer we went along.

Over our two years of courtship, I had us read books like *Things I Wish I'd Known Before We Got Married*, *The Five Love Languages*, *1001 Questions to Ask Before You Get Married*, etc. On the side, I devoured any book that seemed to present stories, *real* stories, about romantic relationships without lies or flowers or gild. Tolstoy's *Anna Karenina* struck me as the most honest account of marriage I'd ever encountered, however bleak at parts. I'd insisted on premarriage therapy for a few months before we got engaged, always searching the therapist's face and tone for a hint that we were making a mistake. But there is a difference between raising a question and deciding what to do with divergent answers. Where to draw the line? Some topics, pressing ones like if and when we would have children and what a life of faith together looked like, remained unsettled—not because we didn't think the answers were important and not because we didn't know we had to talk about them. We *wanted* things to work. We had a strong sense of what would be difficult. We each had concerns about the other. And yet neither of us could ever seriously consider breaking things off. We hurtled forward with the hope that love would be enough, that we would have enough love.

Sixteen
hours
later,
we pulled into the Amazonian Trapezoid again.

The Peru immigration officer wouldn't give us the coveted stamp because our exit out of Colombia had expired—a gap in our paper trail for a week. We caught a canoe back to Colombia, where we faced the same Leticia immigration officer who had warned us this might happen. He scolded me in Spanish, then stamped us in and out of Colombia. We were back on the map.

When we reached Santa Rosa again, the Peruvian officer acted as if nothing strange had happened. He gave us a form to fill out. I misspelled my own name and had to grab another one. The rubber hit my passport, then Austin's: a circle no bigger than a quarter with angular numbers and letters. I could barely make out the date in the faint ink.

"We could've forged that," Austin teased. I elbowed him back.

The boat for Iquitos left Santa Rosa at 3:00 a.m. the next morning. Similar to Iquitos, there were no roads, thus no traditional cars, in Santa Rosa. All vehicles were "moto-taxis," three-wheeled motorcycles topped with shells to seat passengers. Rather than hiring a moto-taxi to carry us to the dock, we decided to take our chances and walk the half mile ourselves. I want to say this was Austin's idea, but I must have agreed. On our first night in Santa Rosa—before this border snafu—our hired ride never showed. Our second driver had to be roused by our hotel owner who'd overheard our predicament. When my backpack strap got caught in the wheel of the moto-taxi, tearing my bag and causing the bike to smoke until Austin and the driver turned the vehicle onto its side to remove the ripped fabric, the driver's wife had leaned out of a window in a nightgown and shouted, "Esto no estaba en la cuenta." *This wasn't in the bill.* What a scene.

So we would walk to the boat to avoid any more fiascos, ignoring the advice of a stranger who'd stopped us in the street to say: "Don't go anywhere away from the light . . ."

Austin and I stirred out of bed at 2:00 a.m., but we were both wide awake. The fan didn't work and itchy bug bites kept us tossing and turning in the heat. Unfamiliar animal noises made sleep impossible. I put on my clothes and wondered if anyone lived along the path to the dock. Austin tucked our money into the bottom of his bag without prompting. He left the room key on the bed. This time, the hotel owner did not wake up to meet us. I didn't blame her. We were on our own.

We carried headlamps we'd purchased last minute before leaving the States. We'd agreed to keep silent to avoid catching the attention of potential attackers. Critters croaked in the shadowy brush. Total darkness engulfed us. The farther we got from the village streetlamps, the deeper I regretted our decision to walk. My heart raced. We tiptoed along the wooden planks in the mud in the general direction of the dock. If we followed the planks, we would reach the boat. I was aware of every cry, crack, and squeak as we crept along.

Then we heard a bark in the distance, followed by a howl in another direction.

"Walk faster," Austin said, breaking the silence. He grabbed my hand. My sympathetic nervous system awakened. The dogs grew louder.

"Faster," Austin said. We broke into a speed walk, trying not to trip, the light from our headlamps jolting back and forth.

Then a large white dog with bared teeth emerged. Its lip curled as it growled. The dog stepped in front of us with a wide gait. Austin pulled me to the side as we tried to move around it, off the plank walkway. My Chacos slipped in the mud. I couldn't run. Then another dog yapped at us from behind.

Soon, three more joined the pack. They were circling.

Austin and I drove across the country from Boston to Utah for our wedding. My thoughts spiraled. We'd stuffed my Ford Focus with the few possessions I had not put into storage in preparation for a year abroad. Long, straight roads stretched ahead. We batted away drowsiness after nights spent in cheap, creepy hotels. Our breath reeked of naps and gas-station nachos and peach ring gummies. The audio of Elizabeth Gilbert's *Committed: A Skeptic Makes Peace with Marriage* played through the car speakers. I had thought, with such a compelling title, that the book could quiet some of my fears about getting married. But it ended up having the opposite effect—a string of Gilbert's legitimate anxieties interwoven with historical research on the many ways marriage oppressed people, wrapped up with some final triumphant pages about how marriage could be viewed as subversive, a rebellion against the ways the early Christians valorized celibacy. It was an honest account of her own ambivalence, an ambivalence I could certainly relate to, but the down-to-earth conclusion was less comforting when all I wanted to hear was how everything was going to be magically okay.

An argument lasting days with no beginning or end ensued as we drove, trapped in the car with nowhere to go but forward. What did we argue about? What did I scream at him? I can't remember. I *do* know I swore, laid out my worst fears, played off of his. I felt that no one, including him, was listening—truly listening and seeing me. My reasonable concerns had little room to breathe. Subconsciously, I wanted to show him my worst, my very, very worst. I wanted to push him over the edge, wanted him to see how cruel, how terrible, how horrible I could be, as if daring him to explode. Austin rarely exploded. But I needed him to explode, to reject me, to stop this nonsense. Something. Wake up. Be real about the trap we were walking into. Surely he didn't want me. How could he? Then others would be safe from me in return.

For the most part, Austin stared through the windshield and sighed. "Well, this is an unpleasant conversation." Then he pulled over and made me drive for a few hours.

I continued to rage, poke, provoke, when what I really meant to say was: *I'm not ready for this. I'm not sure about this. Hear me. Please take me seriously.* Still, he appeared undisturbed. Years would go by before I would learn that Austin escalated plenty himself, but the process often stayed interior.

"We are making a mistake," I said.

"If that is the case, we should have the courage to call off the wedding," Austin said, calmly.

We drove a long time without speaking after that.

I recently asked Austin what he thought on this drive. "Why didn't you drop me off at the nearest curb?" I asked.

"I thought you were testing me," he said. Austin had felt a spiritual confirmation that our relationship was meant to be—a sense of peace whenever he considered our future, a sickening feeling at the thought of ending things. He believed I had a good heart, that my concerns were a sign that I cared deeply. He suspected that what I was pushing against was the utter vulnerability of marriage. He knew I had family baggage. "I appreciated your constant search for truth, the way you wrestled with your complicated faith. I saw how much you invested in friendships, your loyalty to them. Also, I never got bored with you. That had never happened before." As a self-identified "not overly concerned person," he felt good about marrying me. As we drove, a part of him thought, "Well, at least I know what I'm signing up for."

Our argument subsided for a few hours while we weaved through Canada, then morphed into casual conversation. The audiobook didn't work without cell reception.

At one point on the drive, Austin spoke up, laughing. "Listen, you'll need to remember this. I want you to know I'm sorry for everything. In advance."

"That's not how it works," I said, though I knew he didn't mean it seriously.

"Just remember!"

The dogs encroached. I could make out the illuminated dock in the distance where the boat would take us back to Iquitos. We were so close. I tried to bolt. Austin clutched my hand.

"Don't turn your back on them! Walk. Don't let go of me."

The pack snarled. Austin pointed his headlamp into their marble eyes, swinging it at each of them, like fighting off wolves with a torch. I didn't notice I was crying, couldn't hear myself screaming. We pushed our way forward. My heart hammered against my ribcage. The alpha white dog snuck in and snapped at my ankle, narrowly missing.

I tried to rip away again.

"They'll chase you if you run." Austin pushed himself in front of me just before another sprang. He shone his lamp into its eyes—pupils empty, dilated, angry. Another dog spun to attack from the front. Austin gripped my wrist and puffed out his chest, shooing the feral animals with a big body stance. Austin kept fending off the dogs with the small beam of his headlamp as we inched closer and closer to the dock.

When we got far enough from their territory, the dogs stopped stalking. I whimpered and broke away, sprinting through sludge.

Austin followed close behind.

I felt dizzy when we reached the boat. People were already boarding. This time, the attendants examined our passports thoroughly. We took our seats. My whole body quaked. I struggled to breathe and silence the haunting what-ifs: What if we'd been mangled, here in the middle of the Amazon, with no health coverage, no nearby hospital, and no family or friends back home who knew precisely where to find us, where to begin looking? What if my parents had to use the small life insurance policy my grandparents had gifted me as a peculiar wedding gift, afraid I "would perish" on this trip, a concern I'd dismissed like I had their frequent concerns about my travels?

"How did you know to use your flashlight like that?" I asked.

Austin shook his head, his eyes round as moons. "I don't know. Instinct or something."

I had those too, though clearly not the survive-in-the-wild kind. *Instinct*. Something older, deeper than whatever plotting and predicting I could throw into the mix. A voice that said *stay*. Or run. Fight if you have to. Grateful to not be alone, to be with him, I was no longer as interested in which of us was at fault.

I watched Austin lean back, close his eyes, and exhale. For a moment, I didn't recognize him. Who did I marry? Who did he think he married?

You knew what I was when you picked me up.

But maybe not. How could he, despite his best effort, have any idea who he picked up? Did I know what I would get with him either? We barely knew our own, changing selves. The farther we went into the uncharted future all relationships face, the more I began to question the premise of knowability. Finally, a muddy step in the dark, but a step pointed in the right direction.

CHAPTER 6

Trial Marriage

TWO MONTHS INTO MARRIAGE, I stood washing dishes in our rooftop communal kitchen in Cusco, Peru—a makeshift space with a tin roof, two aluminum counters, a sink, and a propane-powered, single-burner stove. To my left was a room surrounded by plastic windows, where hand-washed laundry hung to dry. Scouring a pot Austin had used to make something resembling spaghetti sauce from canned tomato paste and pepper (we were on a firm I-cook, you-clean rotation), I gazed out. The sun had set, casting a greenish tint to the night. The Andes Mountains flushed purple as specks of blue and yellow lights from Cusco—the capital of the ancient Inca Empire—flickered on, one after the other.

Austin and I had found this mustard-yellow, one-room apartment—our first shared apartment—near the city center. We explored backstreets where colorfully clothed women with long braids walked llamas on ropes. Sometimes we wandered through open-air markets in squares like the tourist-flooded Plaza de Armas. At 11,152 feet, many came to Cusco to acclimate before proceeding to

Machu Picchu. I ran my finger along the stone walls and felt the layers of history: the strong Inca foundations where carved boulders snapped together seamlessly, the plaster above added by the conquistadors, and the taped political flyers and "se alquila" ads flapping in the wind. Something about the exploited histories, the cool, dry air, the grays, the red-oranges, the silent mountains, and the language barriers (Quechua outranked Spanish as a first language) made Cusco, at least to me, feel walled off. As if beyond the two- or three-day tourist itineraries, its inner heart remained protected from foreigners like us. To get more involved, Austin and I spent several nights a week volunteering at English conversation classes.

There, I first heard about an evocative Peruvian tradition: trial marriage.

Trial marriage, called *sirvinacuy*, *pantanacuy*, *watanaki*, or *tincunakuspa* throughout the region, existed and has *persisted* since pre-Incan and pre-Columbian times despite the Catholic Church's repeated efforts to snuff it out. Trial marriage also allowed prospective couples to live together anywhere from a few months to a few years, though typically about one year, to determine whether or not they were a good fit before marrying for life. If the answer by the end was no, the pair could split without stigma toward them or any children born to them during the time. According to social science research done by Richard Price, Joanne Kay Haines, Miriam E. Berger, and Ward Stavig, trial marriage tested the woman's capabilities. Could she work and accept her responsibilities to serve well? Trial marriage allowed for a socially sanctioned sexual relationship before marriage, and it gave the couple an opportunity to examine their feelings and determine if they were generally compatible.

After finishing up the dishes, I dried my hands on my jeans.

Homemaking.

Sex.

Compatibility.

Using these three measures, I wondered how I would fare if I saw this trip with Austin as its own kind of trial period. Maybe not so much *trial* as in practice round (too late for that) but *trial* as in see-how-you-survive-twenty-four-seven-with-the-same-human-in-stressful-travel-situations.

First, take household skills. As our landlord had instructed, I wiped down the sink to erase any trace of water spots in the kitchen. I knew there was nothing inherently gendered, scary, or antifeminist about cleaning, but I had my fears. I could not pride myself on being a domestic goddess when, more accurately, I was almost-childishly opposed to housework and hypersensitive to any whiff of perceived imbalance in workload, though Austin had not yet displayed any issues in this realm. Now that we lived together, I wanted to establish fair habits. I weighed and tallied kind gestures and acts of service, perhaps because I knew that Austin, a BYU-educated man born in conservative Wyoming into a traditional family of boys, still sometimes said things like, "I thought catcalls were a compliment" and "Why do girls walk around with keys in their fists at night?" I shared my thoughts, and he changed his tune over the years. But for a while he didn't seem capable of saying he was a feminist without a string of caveats. This troubled me.

"We're on the same team," Austin would say whenever I'd get upset by his I-love-women-and-I'm-all-for-women's-empowerment statements, a vague stance on something deeply important to me.

Were we? What team was that, and what were the rules of the game?

My feminist awakening happened late. One night in my early twenties, not long after my move to Massachusetts, I sat on the living room floor with one of my soon-to-be best friends, Carol Ann, in her Cambridge apartment. We planned to watch part of a documentary on her laptop about the '50s and '60s called *Makers: Women Who Make America*. Carol Ann's place had beige carpet, the standard flooring in Utah but rare out East. I combed my fingers through the shaggy fibers while we listened to commentaries by Kathrine Switzer (the first woman to run in the Boston Marathon by sneaking into the race), Gloria Steinem, and Judy Blume. Other women discussed the danger of viewing college as a way to get an "Mrs. degree," the propaganda of the ideal wife and mother, the backstep women in the workforce took after World War II, the reactions following the landmark publication of *The Feminine Mystique*, the failures of the movement to include women of color, and the political battle to pass the Equal Rights Amendment.

Carol Ann paused the documentary. She'd recently "come out" on Facebook as a Mormon feminist. I thought she was so brave. Carol Ann moved to the Boston area to work in urban schools after becoming bored with suburban teaching in Utah. She had short, curly hair and teal-framed glasses. Her kitchen cupboard featured a "blue girl, red state" Idaho sticker. She said what she thought. She hosted parties, sang Josh Ritter songs, played the banjo, championed environmental stewardship, and rode her bike year-round. She was a total badass and unlike any other friend I'd ever known. I loved her immediately, though her past was not free of resistance. As a child, Carol Ann had once told her mom that she wanted to be an astronaut. "You have to choose. You can't be an astronaut and a mother," her mom said. Carol Ann's mother also told her stories about her own mom—Carol Ann's grandmother—accepting a volunteer church job to go door-to-door to ask people to vote against the Equal Rights Amendment. And when Carol Ann did get married in her late twenties, she nearly missed her flight to her wedding because she had to wait for a mysterious FedEx wedding gift from an old family friend to arrive. It was a wicker bassinet.

As the documentary remained on pause, the laptop screen

glowed.

"Whoa," I said, my head spinning. "The church is, like, *fifty years* behind." Though I'd obviously known my culture had been different from what I'd seen in the media and on my travels, and though I'd been primed toward feminist thinking from my liberal arts education, my life was not an exercise in textual analysis. Life was far too close to see critically. But explicitly placing myself within the feminist historical time line made things click. The documentary helped me realize I wasn't a freak for feeling skepticism; other women, decades ago, had felt the same and done something about it. It only took me twenty-three years to realize.

A few months after watching the documentary, Carol Ann and I backpacked through Turkey on a week-long break from teaching. At breakfast, Carol Ann noticed I pushed the tomatoes off to the side and focused on the boiled egg, wedge of cheese, and white bread.

"The vegetables are safe," she said.

"Actually, I don't really eat vegetables."

Wrong answer to give to a vegetarian. Or maybe to anyone who cares about your health and well-being.

My diet, as far back as I could remember, omitted vegetables, except for the occasional microwaved corn or canned green beans topped with ranch powder and bacon bits. In college, I prided myself on spending as little as possible on groceries and knew nil about nutrition. Most of the time, I ate at the restaurant where I worked or brought home "mess-ups" to eat as leftovers. I'd retrieve their unused bread loaves from the dumpster, then freeze them for later. I'd only grocery shop every one or two months, budgeting around thirty dollars per visit. My cart contained hint-of-lime chips, a block of cheddar cheese, peanut butter, canned chili, materials for butter noodles, Top Ramen, and a bottle of tomato juice for a dish I called "tomato mac and cheese" that I considered fancy.

Carol Ann taught me how to cook. We prepared meals that depended on veggies and spices that I began to know by scent: turmeric, cumin, rosemary. Cooked tomatoes didn't make me gag anymore. Onions, it turned out, were the foundation of everything. Watching Carol Ann wash spinach, slice cucumbers, or chop beets—a brilliant fuchsia seeping into the cutting board—soothed me. Slowly, I learned to not just tolerate but enjoy tomatoes and onions. I cultivated a few go-to recipes. My grocery-cart items diversified, and I began visiting the produce aisle.

I was always surprised that I enjoyed every meal Carol Ann prepared, the new, hearty ingredients melded into a glorious concoction. She was a good cook *and* a feminist. What a notion!

Carol Ann once asked me point-blank, "Why do you think you were resistant to learn to cook for so long?"

Cheap food and blatantly ignoring my basic nutritional needs supported my travel savings and my suffering, workaholic sense of identity when at home, but I knew that didn't explain it all.

Not learning to cook was, in some unconscious way, a refusal. I'd had plenty of chances. But if I didn't cook, didn't even know where to start, I was one step further away from being the ideal Mormon wife. No one could force me to cook for them, I imagined, if I didn't know how.

Austin's and my cooking proved *interesting* in Cusco, partly because of our strict budget constraints. For lunches, we often split a five-dollar plate of *lomo saltado*—a stew of beef, french fries, and sliced onions. Austin began to panic when, for the first time since high school, he discovered that he weighed five pounds less than his 165-pound baseline of lean muscle on his six-foot frame.

"I need more food!"

At the market, we stocked up on rice, pasta, Corn Flakes when we felt nostalgic, and packets of various sauces labeled in Spanish words I couldn't translate. We had the best luck with fruit. We purchased fresh-cut pineapple from a woman who pushed a cart outside the apartment each morning yelling, "Piña, piña . . .Uva, uva!" into a megaphone. Our first big feat was discovering cherimoya, a heart-shaped green apple with succulent white flesh that could be sucked out with a spoon, a treat so delicious that at one time it was illegal for anyone outside of Inca royalty to eat them; our second was an enormous wheel of white cheese that lasted almost our entire two-month stay.

If I'd had the luxury of a trial marriage with a scrutinizing potential mother-in-law overseeing my performance, I'm not sure I could have passed the test for maintaining a home. But for once, I wasn't too worried. I could make that Cusco kitchen shine like a new car. But Austin could too.

Another tenant of trial marriage? Sexual compatibility.

(Grandma, this is the part where you skip to the next chapter.)

In Peru, adolescents—even before trial marriage—could freely explore their sexuality. Historical accounts describe new wives being scorned by their husbands for *being* virgins. I, on the other hand, had been taught to "save myself" for my husband. Though I'd fooled around, it was also true that I'd always held a firm line when it came to traditional notions of virginity. I didn't want to risk rejection or "lose something," as purity had been framed.

Real-life married sex proved less thrilling at first than I'd anticipated during my extended virgin life. In truth, I'd spent most of my adolescence and young adult life feeling like I enforced the chastity line for the sake of guilt-riddled young men who shirked personal responsibility for their own sexual control.

The church's stance and its official *For the Strength of Youth* pamphlet from 2001 were clear about the importance of abstinence before marriage to "protect yourself from the emotional damage that always comes from sharing physical intimacies with someone outside of marriage." But the line of what sexual purity meant was not always clearly defined, or at least I pretended it wasn't. Keeping clothes on at all times? No French kissing? Never getting turned on? No horizontal cuddling? No back rubs because, as Austin's grandpa once joked, "a back rub in the front room leads to a front rub in the back room"? At what point was the transgression bad enough to seek a bishop to whom you could repent? These worthiness interviews with layperson bishops are now being called into question—for good reason, in my opinion. The one time I attempted a confession about masturbating, the sixty-something-year-old bishop (who was also my neighbor down the road) flushed red, did not ask any follow-up questions, and looked relieved when I left his office.

I would often be the one to call it quits on a passionate make-out session, the one responsible for stopping anything beyond "Levi loving," the one to listen with sympathy to shameful confessions about pornography. When a boyfriend once admitted he'd sexually molested two of his nieces as a preteen, I told him that I sometimes touched myself so we were even, both terribly flawed. To my amazement and horror now, the difference in severity did not register for years. I could not differentiate innocent exploration from abuse.

Many folks from conservative communities who marry young are accused of marrying for sex. Hormones and such. I get why this is the case for lots of people, but this was not the main reason I got married. I could have done the heavy make-out thing forever. I felt a power in my ability to *not* have sex, to be desired but never attainable. It gave me a feeling of control. Though repressing my sexuality in this way did put me out of touch with whatever reality lay behind the zipper, I felt terribly sexy. I thought I was the horniest thing that ever lived. And then I got married. Being able to have sex *whenever*

I wanted with Austin didn't seem as satisfying as I'd imagined, and after all those years of waiting, my hyped-up, imagined fantasy was probably more equivalent to tripping on LSD. Though my attraction to Austin remained unchanged, especially with his scruffy beard and long hair that curled around his ears, the intensity of my desire had waned. This, I would later learn, is a typical experience for women raised in sexually conservative communities who orient to being an object of desire, not around being embodied in desire themselves. The broader culture's sexualization of women didn't help.

Austin was the one to help me recognize what an orgasm was. Lying in the cool sheets of our queen-size bed in Cusco below a painting of bulbous figures carrying heavy loads strapped to their backs, I lamented that I'd never had an orgasm.

"Uh . . . I'm pretty sure something is going on down there."

Which would have been a jerk thing to say to a woman, except he was right. And I wasn't sure.

"Aren't you feeling some kind of release? That's an orgasm."

Though I'd been experiencing orgasm since before I could remember, from dreams or making out or rubbing a pillow between my legs, I didn't know *that* was what everyone was talking about. *That* felt good, but it wasn't rainbows and sparkler-carrying unicorns and total transcendence and scream-inducing the way movies had portrayed and promised. Though I felt eager to learn how to build our sexual relationship—Austin seemed thrilled with all of it—I felt disappointed by orgasm itself. Only after putting a name to the feeling in my body could I accept it, lean in, and learn to open myself up to the waves of pleasure.

Sex got better. But those acid-tripping unicorns had yet to show.

Then there was general compatibility, another pillar of trial marriage.

Soon after settling in Cusco, Carol Ann messaged me. "Has anything gone from cute to killer yet?" In other words, did I have any new pet peeves after *living* with Austin?

On the whole, Austin and I were getting on well. Maybe marriage, I imagined with a bit too much surprise, was not so different from dating. But as any couple that has just moved in together knows, there are differences.

Sharing a bathroom, for starters. He couldn't believe how much toilet paper a woman could use. We also had our first bout of traveler's diarrhea, which sent me to bed but didn't faze Austin. I'd knock on the bathroom door, "Are you okay? Are you sick?"

To which he'd assure, "I'm just acclimating" or "I'm building immunity."

We experienced our first earthquake together—a tiny one, routine along the Andes fault line. I leaped out of bed. The apartment walls shook.

"I think this is an earthquake."

"It's just the wind," Austin said.

Ignoring him, I scrambled to put on pants. I didn't want to be found dead without them. The next morning, the newspaper and a new crack running up our bedroom wall confirmed my suspicion.

We had arguments—one big one that sent me storming out of the apartment to walk around the city and clear my head, though I can't recall the details. I lost the memory, and thus, the sting. Forgetting, I would learn, could be just as useful as remembering in a long-term partnership.

With Carol Ann's question about "cute to killer," I remembered one habit immediately. Austin read himself to sleep every night. He ran his fingers through the pages and crinkled them repeatedly, fondling the paper and sometimes bringing the book to his nose to sniff. While dating, I thought this romantic, endearing, *sensual*. I loved watching him in the lamplight, thumbing through the pages of a novel. Now, however, it meant falling asleep in fluorescent light to the crackling sound of paper. Every. Single. Night.

Then there was the whole problem of mornings. As I tried to explain to Austin, I wasn't so much a morning or a night person as I was a *day* person, a detail that slipped his mind. He often tried to wake me up with a gentle kiss or an early cuddle. I didn't care how romantic this substitute for an alarm clock was; waking up remained miserable. Hollywood got that wrong too.

Austin seemed to have similar tiffs about me. Why was I always taking pictures instead of "enjoying the moment"? He wasn't pleased with my sheet-stealing habits or my long-standing opposition to making the bed (I couldn't fathom a more mundane and useless task). Meanwhile, when Austin watched me brush my hair and asked if *all* the hairs got caught in the brush, I smiled and said, "Yes" rather than "Mostly." Growing up in a house full of boys and countless Mormon roommates with missionary-short cuts, Austin had never lived in the world of long hair and all the shedding that comes with it. He was not particularly pleased by my habit of rolling stray strands into little hair spiders and depositing them on the floor either.

Cute to killer. But perhaps not so killer in the end, all things considered. We fell asleep cuddling, still wearing our ridiculous matching alpaca sweaters, in a bed we could call our own. We twisted our tongues over Spanish at the market and bought every unfamiliar fruit we spotted from the sellers managing makeshift stalls under overpasses. We went on aimless walks and followed hills that turned into mountains, stumbled through ancient stone citadels, held our arms out wide under stormy skies. We tasted the planet's best hot chocolate at a small restaurant without a sign, sipping in each other's company and pausing only to exchange eye contact, shared witnesses of this world wonder.

If I could do it all over again, I sometimes wondered if I would've preferred to live with Austin before tying the knot, doing something like actual and not just imagined trial marriage despite the religious pressures and curious stats on the correlation between cohabitation and divorce. But perhaps, as Dean John Coburn at the Episcopal Theological School wrote, "[m]arriage is a total commitment, and trial marriage is a contradiction in terms." I know this is a personal decision for everyone with no universal right answer. But is there anything Austin and I could have sorted earlier without such lofty stakes as eternity? Or, like Peruvians who have practiced trial marriage, would we have found ourselves among the vast majority (79 percent for the Vicosino highland community as recently as the 1970s) who did, in fact, move forward with marriage, but with more "paz, contento, y amistad"?

Patrick, our local friend and enthusiastic Inca expert who claimed to be descended from the Inca emperor Pachakutiq, said that *trial marriage* was not a phrase used by many modern Peruvians anymore, though the legacy remains with cohabitation. "Every person has their own mind about it," he said, adjusting thick glasses framing his small, dark eyes. Patrick guessed that 50 percent of his friends cohabit, living with their partner for three to four years. After two or three babies, they might get married by the church. Or not. Many people cohabit for life. Patrick's answer supported Peru having some of the highest cohabitation rates in the world. For women ages twenty-five to twenty-nine, a 2000 census showed that 69.8 percent were currently cohabitating.

"Nobody knows who will live with you permanently, right? There is not an understanding between man and woman." He could appreciate why people would want to try things out before committing.

I could too.

"In Peru, it's very complicated to get married," he continued. For one, it is expensive. Both the government and the church require a lot. *Why bother,* some people wonder. "You don't need to go to the church just to say 'cheese' and 'I want to be with you all my life.'" He claimed cohabitation was much easier.

"Why did you choose to go the marriage route?" I asked. Patrick happened to be engaged after dating his fashion-designer fiancée for three years.

For him, it didn't have much to do with religion. "If I were single, I could travel to different countries. But for me, this life is much better. It's beautiful because it is filled with people I love."

Why that dichotomy, always, between marriage/family and travel? I didn't ask. The question said more about me than it did about him.

Patrick claimed to be romantic and formal, thus in favor of weddings. "When I was younger, I dreamed of a classical, beautiful ceremony," he said. "A festival." Something like his Inca ancestors, who gathered once a year for an elaborate mass wedding. All upper-class Inca were mandated to marry. "I want to look at the woman who will be the mother of my sons. To me, a wedding is not a simple ceremony or event. It's a moment when you prove your love." He paused. "I don't know if you share my idea."

I didn't know if I shared his idea either, as lovely as it sounded. But I took some comfort imagining my own version of a global trial period with Austin and in reading Richard Price's research that claimed many who practiced trial marriage reported it to be "the happiest period of their lives."

A BRIEF LAYOVER

Advice Given at My Wedding

"Humor goes a long way."

"Never pet a burning dog."

"Buy two tubes of toothpaste!"

"Don't sweat the small stuff!!"

"Don't sweat the small stuff!!!"

"Don't sweat the petty things, and don't pet the sweaty things!"

"Name the first one Calvin!"

"Read *Middlemarch.*"

"Have a pillow fight every day and also have ice cube wars when things get too hot."

"Be good."

"Be Happy :)"

"Be Happy."

"Kiss for sixty seconds a day."

"Set your alarm fifteen minutes early and snuggle. Great for your marriage."

"Address the snoring issue now."

"Always hold hands even when you don't want to."

"The family that prays together stays together!"

"Our advice is to always hold hands when praying together."

"Pray together as a couple every night at least. Austin you take the odds and Rachel you take the even days (there are more odd days)."

"Remember, SEX IS FOR BABIES."

"Sometimes it is more important to be married than right."

"Learn to sacrifice and put your spouse first."

"Swallow your pride and fix things to get past the ugly parts and grow together . . . cuz it's for eternity baby, no goin' back!!!"

"Don't stop fighting, but don't stop making up, either. Make efforts to remember the other's preferences, especially in small things. Take all this with a grain of salt, because i am bitter and don't believe in love."

"Never give up and never surrender."

"Don't get mad at each other. But if you get mad, get naked. It's hard to be mad when you're naked :)"

"Don't do it."

"Enjoy it all!"

PART 2

ASIA

DECIDE | də'sīd |

verb

1. to come to a resolution as a result of consideration

Latin origin: dēcīdere

1. (original meaning) to cut off from something else
2. (later meaning) to make up one's mind

CHAPTER 7

The Danger of Dreams

I WOKE UP DISORIENTED. How long had I been sleeping? Why was it so dark? I smelled a faint whiff of car exhaust. A thin halo of midday light edged the blackout curtain. I rubbed my eyes. My leg brushed Austin's as he lay fast asleep. Then I remembered where we were:

Hong Kong.

October 24, 2014. Midway through the Umbrella Movement democracy protests, when more than one hundred thousand people had shut down major traffic arteries and camped outside government buildings to protest restrictive election reforms.

Austin and I had arrived the day protestors unfurled an enormous yellow banner which read, "I want real universal suffrage" over Lion Rock, a granite rockface shaped like a lion crouching over the Kowloon Peninsula. At the government's order, firefighters tore down the banner while Austin and I were sleeping. We had only the slightest understanding of the political situation outside our window.

We were staying at a friend's tiny studio apartment. In the bathroom, the shower head was fixed right above the toilet—to us, novel; to them, commonplace. Extra space seemed to be a luxury, not a necessity. Much of what I had, I was continually reminded, was a luxury.

I nudged Austin. "Wake up," I said, checking the time. "It's almost four in the afternoon."

He rolled over and swatted me away.

"Fight the jet lag. We're in *Hong Kong.*" We had fewer than two days before we would move on to Singapore, then Bangkok. Neither of us had been to East Asia before. "Don't you want to explore?"

He covered his head with a pillow.

I took the keys off the desk.

"I'll be back."

I flew down five flights of narrow concrete steps and slipped past a metal grate. Shops lined the packed street. A man with a pop-up stall selling infomercial fabric steamers blocked my path. I moved past him while a dozen onlookers watched the three-second "wrinkles-be-gone" demonstration, then I ducked under a rack of brightly colored shirts to reach the middle of the noisy street.

I like to walk without purpose or direction. My head felt hazy from jet lag and excessive sleep. There were no visible signs of the protest I'd seen in dozens of news headlines. I passed a market selling vibrant flower arrangements wrapped in plastic; pig feet hanging by a string from the ceiling while the pig's head was displayed on a table; a beauty vendor spraying perfumes as strangers leaned in to whiff; racks with three- to five-dollar T-shirts, pleather miniskirts, princess dresses, skeleton Halloween costumes, and hair accessories with glitzy rhinestones. With every other step, I inhaled sweets, artificial fruity fragrances, and body odor. A train a fourth the width of a standard double-decker bus teetered down an electric cable line. A Pizza Hut beckoned with a menu in Chinese. A cyclist edged by and I moved aside, back into the dense crowd.

I lamented not waking up earlier. *This* sensation, of taking in a city like none I had seen before, is part of why I loved to travel—what stretched my imagination, lit my curiosity, and heightened my awareness of being small and insignificant but also *alive* among other humans, striving in our own ways as we inhabited and made sense of this enormously diverse world. This feeling made all the discomforts worth it.

After an hour, I returned, bounding up the stairs to yank Austin from the bed. I wanted to share my joy. "You've got to see this."

Later that night, Austin and I walked the streets in the glow of skyscrapers lit with bold neons. One building featured shifting patterns of animated birds soaring through clouds with crescent moons floating along the side like shadow puppets. We were in pursuit of a ramen shop.

Our favorite Boston restaurant was an eccentric Japanese ramen shop called Yume Wo Katare, which roughly translates to "speak your dream." The small shop, which posts its erratic hours on a calendar taped to the front door, advertises itself as "an experience." After guests slurp the thick noodles swimming in warm garlic broth under slabs of succulent pork, the server examines the bowl before inviting each person to stand and announce their dream as onlookers clap and cheer. Though there was never an explicit connection between stuffing oneself with ramen to the point of feeling sick and the likelihood of your dream coming true, customers could link the two. *If I work hard, maybe I can have this unquestionably good thing.* But what if one person's dream clashes with another's? What happens when dreams conflict?

Each time Austin and I went to Yume Wo Katare, Austin's dream changed: he wanted to pass his CS50 programming class on one occasion and to build his own business on another. A few days before he proposed (I'd already picked out the ring), he'd told the Yume Wo Katare audience that his dream was to marry me.

Austin's firm footing in the present allowed him this flexibility, to find happiness in the tangible everyday without the weight of living in tomorrow's dreamscape, which, I imagined, he saw as unquestionably favorable. This anchor gave Austin the ability to collect or abandon some dreams without guilt if they lost their heat. Even his Big Dreams felt concrete and achievable, all very domestic: a house with big windows, a ranch or vegetable farm, children running around with a yellow dog. This sounded beautiful when described in Austin's honey voice, but less so when I began to sense these dreams would collide with my own, when I began to foresee the pain we could inflict on each other by harboring competing visions of the future.

On the other hand, my dream felt unchanging, tethered to a vague Yonder in some distant, faraway future that I would later come to identify as a place of spiritual, psychological, and intellectual freedom. At the time, what I had was a smaller, literal manifestation of that broad dream: I wanted to travel the world, forever if I could. This was what I always shared at Yume Wo Katare. I cared little about owning anything. I hesitated to probe into what this dream said about me and snapped at anyone who suggested my wanderlust could be reduced to a desire to escape from my constant dissatisfaction or the way I'd grown up. I became defensive. A dream so deeply felt, I imagined in my youthful fever, was not subject to questioning or compromise. I probably understood, though not well enough, that marriage was a string of constant compromises, evaluating one dream at a time.

It was my dream that brought us here. We walked through Hong Kong, scouting for ramen shops with the longest queues. This wasn't Japan, but we hoped Hong Kongese noodles would scratch our itch. We allowed ourselves to be mesmerized by the rainbow outlines running like rivers along a skyscraper's edge. The colors contrasted against the fuzzy, light-polluted sky. I took pictures. We followed our feet until we reached a cluster of tents on a barricaded road.

Austin and I stopped.

"It's the protestors," I said.

"I wondered if we'd see them," Austin said with admiration.

They had shut down a two-lane street. A young woman in a plaid scarf with a flushed face huddled in a camping chair as she chatted with two other women. They didn't look up when we passed. I wanted to ask questions. *How long have you been here? How long will you stay? What does democracy mean to you?* Why didn't I? Perhaps because I felt it wasn't my place to say anything, stare, or be there at all. Though effective political action requires observers, I didn't understand my role as an accidental witness. I worried about the consequences of their peaceful, brave actions. At the time, government officials in Hong Kong and Beijing had denounced the occupation and declared it a "violation of the rule of law," which had been influenced by the West. Officials warned of "deaths and injuries and other grave consequences."

Austin pointed to a sign written in English taped to a tent: "No pictures." Anonymity kept people safe.

I quickly put my camera away. The clear divider between me—the musing bystander—and them—the vulnerable, civilly disobedient—flew up like a wall.

Austin and I moved on in silence, sobered, but still in pursuit of the perfect ramen shop. We walked past more tents under a closed overpass. A traffic sign pointing toward Connaught Place Express Station had a yellow "Democracy" painted like a bullseye between "Place" and "Express." On another sign, a piece of paper had been plastered over the original words to read "Democracy This Way."

Eventually, we found a shop with a suitably long line. We waited an hour, then sat side by side at the bar where twin porcelain bowls of noodles, broth, greens, and pickled eggs appeared. The salty liquid burned my throat. The ramen tasted good but altogether *different* than Yume Wo Katare. I felt a rare wave of homesickness. My "dream" to wander forever, along with its elusive purpose, diminished. The tents in the garish underpass light were not far enough behind, nor the protestor I'd seen tightening her scarf, the same woman blowing into her palms to keep warm.

I nudged the remaining inch of noodles with my chopsticks. My appetite wasn't as fierce as I'd first imagined.

"I don't think I can finish."

"Me neither," Austin said, wiping his mouth with a napkin. "Not as good as Yume."

I nodded in reluctant agreement. Was it true? We didn't want to be Those Tourists who couldn't appreciate foods that failed to replicate the tastes from home.

A man took the plates away and left a tab, a spot of oil warping the ink in the total. We'd performed our simple role: buy something. No one asked me to declare a silly dream. No one spoke to us at all.

Austin and I tried to sleep without luck. By 3:30 a.m., we gave up and sprang out of bed with a sudden, fierce desire to find a McDonald's. *McDonald's.* Our bodies, still on Peruvian time, demanded lunch—and for some reason *American* lunch, though we both avoided McDonald's in the States.

We stood in the line behind an after-party group at a 24-hour McDonald's. A short woman in a yellow spaghetti-strap dress struggled to make a coherent order. She swayed and a companion caught her and laughed. The worker stared ahead, unmoved, her displeasure exaggerated by the harsh fluorescents. I was so entranced by the people ahead that I forgot to decide what to order. I didn't know what was on the standard McDonald's menu, let alone this one. The worker glared and tapped the register. I picked the first combo meal I saw on the board, ordering what Austin ordered.

"What drink? Coke?"

"Yes."

We paid. Austin turned to me with surprise. "You like Coke?"

"Not really." In all our time together, I stuck to tap water, sometimes lemonade, and the occasional mocktail at the bar. For me, this was more about being cheap than it was about being a Mormon. The Latter-day Saint church had been ambiguous about whether caffeinated sodas were compatible with the Word of Wisdom, the complicated health code Mormons follow whose cultural interpretations of scripture often baffle outsiders. Brigham Young University didn't stock caffeinated beverages in campus vending machines until 2017. Austin and I didn't subscribe to the dwindling myth of "caffeine is bad," but I also didn't crave soda. My mother, a self-proclaimed Diet Coke addict, told me to avoid all caffeinated drinks as a child, a habit that, for better or for worse, eventually shaped my taste.

I held the cola in my hand, amused and confused by my indulgence. The McDonald's dining area was so busy we had a hard time finding an empty table in the vast dining room, despite coming in the dead of night. McDonald's here, as in many other places, appeared to be something different—exported and then repurposed. The room featured a high ceiling and classy red barstools. We sat near a group of teen boys clutching cards around a red and yellow board game at a long table. The partiers took over the opposite corner, joining their other friends. At least ten other men, alone, slept with their heads buried in their arms like ostriches in the sand. A few used newspapers for padding.

"Are they homeless?" I whispered as I bit into a trifecta of greasy fries.

Austin glanced over his shoulder. "I don't think so. Maybe a few. I think they might be travelers." A strange comparison, an important distinction—rooted in opportunities, choices, and privilege.

I licked salt off my fingers and poked a straw into my all-American Coke. The plastic squeaked.

We walked from McDonald's back to the studio gripping vanilla ice cream cones. Again, the city shifted before us, showing us another face. The abundant traffic from the day had died out. Windows were closed up. The halter tops, cooking utensils, raw meat, and gadgets I'd seen earlier were all hidden from sight, stuffed away behind barred and shuttered doors. I wondered where all those people in the busy market went and who supported the Umbrella Movement. And who among them would become convinced, five years later, when those simmering embers of discontent flared again in the face of a new threat, a proposed extraction law, when the on-looking children of 2014 became the teens and students of 2019 that took to the streets with sure voices and a list of specific demands? I would like to know which side those people supported when, five years later, the bullets rained, the fire arrows flew, and the dyed-water cannons shot at the protestors, picked them out, forming rivers streaking the streets with a sickening blue. Who came to resent the protestors as their familiar spaces transformed into danger zones and the economy dipped into recession? Whose family divided? Who detested the violence that a dream like democracy could spring from a love for one's country? Dreams glow with an aura of individual conviction, with a sense of rightness. Not everyone gets to be right in the end. One person's dream can be another's nightmare.

The sun was rising by the time Austin and I climbed into bed. We closed the curtains, shut out everything. Blackout, once again, permeated the room. Austin fell asleep, his subconscious unspooling hopes and fears and joys that were not my own. I stayed awake, tracing his back with my finger, the unfamiliar pulse of caffeine galloping through my veins. But perhaps I only imagined the strength of its effect. Austin and I knew of our disagreements, we always had, though we were still measuring the depth and dimensions of our differences. For now, we had peace and (mostly) productive discussions. I only hoped it would last, that love could bridge the difference between our diverging images of a shared future. But was this its own kind of naïve dream? Somehow, the challenge felt enormous and, at the same time, incredibly—pathetically—small in the face of others' struggles.

In the dark, I squinted to make out coherent shapes in the plastered ceiling. Somewhere nearby, protestors slept in their tents, still waiting, still hoping, still dreaming dreams I had never had to dream.

CHAPTER 8

Never Again

A FOOLPROOF RECIPE for a marital dispute:

1. jet lag (worsened by watching bootleg horror films all night in our budget Bangkok hotel called Nasa Vegas, a mostly empty building providing pay-by-the-hour internet, real bars of soap, and silky crimson pillows but no bed comforter)
2. sleep deprivation (courtesy of two weeks of shoestring travel in hostels with noisy diaper-plastic mattress pads and fellow guests with night terrors)
3. candy for breakfast
4. a crowd

We waited almost an hour for a Bangkok subway to take us to the Hua Lamphong station. There, an overnight train would drop us off in Chiang Mai, a city in northern Thailand we hoped to call home for a few months.

Hundreds of other people gathered, ready to push their way inside when the subway finally came. The big screen on the platform ran a commercial on repeat of a red motorbike making impressive but unrealistic jumps for an average moped, over and over and over again. Austin sat on a bench, buried in a book. He crackled the pages as he fondled them, as usual. I glared at the large clock hovering above. The second hand. The red numbers flashing on the screen with the false ETA. The businessmen on their cell phones and the college kids chatting in packs. My blood pressure rose. I was aware of every person who'd arrived after us.

When the subway car squealed into the station, I heaved my bag onto my back and bulldozed forward. "Let's go," I said to Austin.

Austin took a few extra seconds to put away his book. Dozens had filled the space between us. The crowd pressed inside. My shoulders were stuck in the doorway. I searched for Austin, still several feet away from the door.

"Get in here," I said.

He shook his head. "There isn't room."

"Yes there is!" I elbowed the person in front of me while gesturing at the nonexistent space between us. My throat tightened.

A bell whistled. Austin didn't budge. So I pushed my way off the subway car.

I cursed at the top of my lungs as I marched past Austin, a word that did not resemble any of Austin's swears (which consisted of *criminy sakes*, *Jiminy Christmas*, *son of a gun*, *dad gummit*, *gosh dangit*, and *freak*).

"People here don't act like that," Austin said, suddenly quick at my heels.

That really helped.

We exited to find a taxi that, by some traffic miracle, might get us to the overnight train on time. A gust roared as the subway pulled away.

Surprisingly, or predictably, the hot-pink cab dropped us off at the train station with time to spare. Not seeing any local restaurants or street stalls frying hot noodle dishes on woks, Austin and I spoke the minimum words required to communicate that we were both open to settling for the nearby KFC. The Thai menu displayed chicken coated in spicy red dust. I slid into a booth with my pack next to me like a body bag as Austin set down the tray. We ate in perfect silence. I stared at the table. The culmination of weeks of stressful wandering, time zone changes, no solitude, and the absence of routine and purpose were stoking a bonfire. After the greasy meal, I licked my fingers and dared Austin to speak. He wouldn't. He continued to gnaw on a bone, oils glistening on his lip. He chewed and chewed.

Hadn't my dad always encouraged me to marry someone who inspired me to be a better person? I was not acting or feeling like a super great person, so my reverse logic told me this was somehow Austin's fault.

"You don't inspire me anymore," I said, the words reverberating like a bomb. I waited a heartbeat, maybe two. "I'm not happy."

Austin wiped his face with a napkin. He didn't look up.

"Did you hear me?" I choked. "This isn't working."

He sighed, long and heavy. Finally, he met my eyes.

"That's not my problem," he said flatly. He glanced at the clock on the wall. "Come on. The train is leaving soon."

"So?" I said, stung by his nonreaction.

"Aren't you coming?"

I didn't respond.

He emptied the tray into the trash before shouldering his bag and walking away. I watched it happen as if in slow motion.

Betrayal!

I'm not sure what else I expected him to do, but not that, even if I deserved it, even if a part of me was fishing for some strange form of validation or desire to be seen. I didn't understand why I sometimes said crueler things to him than anyone I'd ever known. Or did a part of me *want* him to leave? Hadn't I predicted all along this wouldn't work out?

For a long moment, I wondered if I would follow him, if the train would roll on without me and I would fly somewhere else, alone. I knew this was a real option. I kept the exit door cracked open in my mind with a full evacuation video reminding me that lights would illuminate the way in the event of an emergency. I needed to know there was always a way out. Better to leave than get left.

Never again.

I have something to confess, something I would rather not admit: Once, briefly, I suspended all inhibitions and threw myself headlong into the fairytale idea of marriage.

His name was Ethan.

Ethan and I met during our final years of college at BYU when I was twenty-one and he was twenty-three. We dated for thirty-three days before I left for a summer-long field study in Dharamsala, India, where I would live with a Tibetan host family and complete research for my undergraduate thesis, a collection of travel essays. In those whirlwind thirty-three days, we exchanged thousands of words over texts and letters. Our relationship grew out of a quick, easy friendship. I was taken with his smiling dark eyes with long lashes, his discipline and brilliant mind, his sensitivity and passion that vacillated between elation and moodiness, as well as his idiosyncratic fascinations with cipher languages, penguins, and numbers (someday, he hoped to write out all the digits from one to one million). He'd discovered my favorite song, "Konstantine" by Something Corporate—a ten-minute song with no chorus and no available sheet music—and listened to it on repeat, enough to transcribe each note by hand onto staff lines he'd used a ruler to draw. He'd bound the pages with twine and even made an ink sketch for an elaborate cover. When he'd played the song for me as a surprise, I sat beside him on the piano bench. Afterward, overwhelmed, I kissed him on the cheek but ached for more.

"We're in so much trouble," I said.

"I'm happy to know this is mutually understood."

Four days after our first kiss, he told me he loved me, which I reciprocated without my characteristic hesitation. We talked through nights until dawn, lying together in the middle of the intersection between University Avenue and 700 North. I whispered, "I used to sleep before I knew you."

"For the first time, I don't feel alone," he said.

As a pair of intense INFJs according to the Myers-Briggs personality test, we described what we had as "soul chemistry." He wrote me poetry. We sat side by side in restaurant booths rather than across from each other. I loved how he'd play with my hand whenever he held it, tap out songs on my body when we cuddled, skillfully hide his gum while making out with me, the damn perfect beauty mark on his cheek.

That spring, Bradford pear trees blossomed along the streets in Provo. But no matter how beautiful those delicate white petals appeared, the flowers reeked.

I didn't care. I picked the blossoms and pressed them between the pages of my journal, gathering them with our letters to make a scrapbook before I left for India. I didn't know that Bradford pear trees were a short-lived, invasive species, commonplace in the suburbs.

Ethan was leaving, too—moving across the country. Maybe part of my infatuation included his acceptance to Harvard with a generous PhD stipend to study musicology. This was before I realized Boston was just a city, Harvard was just a school, and Ethan was just a man. I'd never known anyone who'd been to Harvard, a vague dream I harbored for myself, perhaps imagining it represented the opposite of what folks expected of me. My family gushed over the Harvard detail and spread it around, a welcome change from the we-are-worried-about-Rachel narrative. Ethan made me realize, for the first time, that I might want to get married—to him. It felt like something of a miraculous change. For once, what *I* wanted seemed aligned with what my culture and family wanted for me. Now, everyone could be happy. I wondered if others had been right, if the travel bug had been a phase I would outgrow once I met The One, that elusive idea I had actively avoided yet also subconsciously absorbed. *The great love to prove I was wrong!* What a relief it would be to discover all my fears were silly phantoms after all.

Before parting ways, Ethan wrote me a letter: "I don't think I am a part of your big dreams. I really don't think they are a part of mine, either . . . I want, more than anything in the whole world, to have a loving family of my own. To find someone foreign and familiar and create the magnum opus of a lifetime. But Rachel Rueckert, please know that you would be worth every inch of the fight. Your ambition, your complexity, your adventure, your choices have made you into someone beautiful. Extraordinary. A kind of person I have only imagined. I would chase you until you stopped running away. If that is what you really wanted, I would wade through hell to give it to you."

To keep Ethan—which I wanted more than anything, I imagined, since I viewed this as a once-in-a-lifetime love—I had to stop running away. I had to want what he wanted.

I would be gone for almost four months in India that summer, according to plan. But within a week of long-distance, our fissures began to show.

"I hate traveling," Ethan spouted off during one of our Skype calls I took at an internet café. The call had dropped multiple times. He demanded to know why I traveled, like everyone else had. I responded with a ten-page defense, dripping with reassurances that this would be over soon.

We exchanged floods of emails. There was talk of picking out an engagement ring, a suggestion to look for a wedding dress. I baited him, fishing for assurance of his commitment to appease my insecurities. Ethan asked more questions about my faith, budding feminism, family, and restlessness. I did my best to answer, but in doing so, I deceived myself. The more it became clear that Ethan and I might not be the best fit for each other, the more I tried to convince him, and myself, that I was enough.

He told me his greatest desire was to "live a simple gospel family life." I said I wanted the same thing. He said I grew up in a split family, that my mom "did not provide and teach everything a mother should," and "if this weren't a deficit, then it's like telling Heavenly Father the family isn't important." He said he was "raised by a great homemaker," that he'd written many thank-you letters to his mother, that she was "a smart girl, but she was more than happy to let [his] dad work and stay home with the kids." I told him I took the idea of motherhood seriously. He said, "If I were a girl, I wouldn't be anything like you: I would not travel, I would not be a feminist, I would only go to grad school and have a career as a woeful plan B, and I would put my ambitions into developing mothering skills. You and I differ in these things, and pretty greatly. Why?" I begged him to be open-minded. "I want to be a good wife. A really good wife."

Reading these emails now, I squirm. They are hot with dangerous, youthful importance, still radiating with raw hope, a cracked-open vulnerability, and a capacity to love without reservation I have never felt since. They are, frankly, terrifying. I don't recognize myself.

"I'm going to attach a talk by Sister Beck," Ethan wrote. "I love it when the church talks about women. I feel strongly that the world needs more 'women who know.' Tender-hearted homemakers who don't care what the world's trends are."

Humidity clung to every particle in the stuffy internet café as I squinted at those words. The text of the email shimmied on the screen. I downloaded the sermon, "Mothers Who Know," clicking out of multiple pop-up reminders to renew the pirated software, and started to read.

Julie B. Beck, the president of the women's organization of the church, gave this conference talk in 2007 while fresh on the job. Though she went on to give more universally relevant talks throughout her term, this initial sermon sparked some outrage from circles of less conservative women. Beck cites a story in the Book of Mormon where two thousand young men had to fight in a battle but none were killed. They attributed this remarkable strength and fortune to their mothers' faith, saying, "we do not doubt for our mothers knew" (Alma 56:48).

Beck's thesis was that "the responsibility mothers have today has never required more vigilance. More than at any time in the history of the world, we need mothers who know" their priorities. She went on to clarify what this claim meant. "Mothers who know bear children" and "faithful daughters of God desire children," a statement I could not relate to. "Mothers who know honor covenants" and "bring daughters in clean and ironed dresses with hair brushed to perfection" while "their sons wear white shirts and ties and have missionary haircuts" to church. "Mothers who know are nurturers," which, to Beck, meant creating "a climate for spiritual and temporal growth in their homes" since "another word for *nurturing* is *homemaking*."

Then, "Mothers who know stand strong and immovable."

They are probably not restless. Probably not hanging out in sketchy internet cafés in India trying to convince their boyfriend-but-hopefully-soon-to-be-fiancé of their righteousness.

I replied the next day after taking some time to process. I sold out completely: "Ethan, I think that Sister Beck's talk was great, and I do not foresee any serious struggles on my account with any of the points she brings up."

When I wasn't lovesick for Ethan, I focused on my research and writing in Dharamsala, a vibrant town built along the edges of the Himalayas and home of the Tibetan government in exile. The rocky backdrop and stretches of oak trees, cedars, spruces, firs, and pines exuded a sense of sanctuary. People from wildly different walks of life came to this town for a few days, a few years, or a lifetime: Indian farmers who'd lived here long before the Tibetan exodus, older Tibetans who'd walked across the border with the Dalai Lama to escape persecution, second- and third-generation Tibetans who'd never seen their home country but didn't hold Indian passports, freshly arrived Tibetans with bulging scars on their backs from Chinese prisons, monks in maroon robes with prayer beads, scholars studying Tibetan culture or philosophy, Kashmiri and Nepalese shopkeepers, Indian tourists with cameras, and hippie Western tourists with dreadlocks.

On a typical day, I would say goodbye to my host family and attend an early morning yoga and meditation program in a studio with big windows overlooking the vast valley below. Afterward, I might circumnavigate the Dalai Lama's red and yellow temple with my host sister, always going the auspicious clockwise direction along the narrow path. Then, I would volunteer as a tutor at any number of the local organizations offering immersive conversation labs. Tibetans strived to learn English so they could tell their harrowing stories of national and religious persecution to a broader audience, as the Dalai Lama had encouraged.

Amanda, a middle-aged British expat, ran the certified English classes for monks, nuns, and recent Tibetans who'd escaped from Tibet via Nepal. I had never met a woman like Amanda before: a woman choosing a life of long-term travel. Each day in class we discussed a topic, such as natural disasters. The international sampling of volunteers made learning difficult for the monks.

"Dis*a*ster," Amanda would enunciate with smooth, round vowels.

"Fire," a volunteer from Germany would say.

"Aval*anche*," I would say, noting for the first time how ugly the word sounded in my American accent.

The monks in particular liked to discuss philosophy and religion. Part of their devotion included engaging in regular debates. These English conversation labs provided a great setting in which to practice.

"Attachments are dangerous," a monk named Geshe Sonam reminded me one day as we sat across from each other on thin, red cushions. "Attachment leads to sorrow."

Having talked with dozens of monks and Geshe Sonam many times by now, I was becoming better acquainted with some tenets of Tibetan Buddhism. The Dalai Lama also held talks during the rare moments he was in town. I would sit for hours on the tile in the crowded temple halls, pressing a radio to my ear to listen to a translated broadcast. *Attachment leads to suffering.* That message was loud and clear. The idea, I thought, conflicted with what I'd been taught and what I wanted with Ethan. I felt inclined to mend the troubling chasm, to smooth everything over.

"But Geshe Sonam, what about family? How can you love someone as His Holiness instructs without feeling attachment to them?" I asked, using the formal address for the Dalai Lama to show respect.

Geshe Sonam, with the equivalent of a PhD in philosophy, could probably have written a book on the subject. But he struggled to answer my question in English. After a long pause, he talked about "general love" before restating his opinion that avoiding marriage and family was the quickest way to nirvana, a release from suffering.

I nodded, understanding but not understanding.

Another monk, Geshe Lobsang, who was paired up with a different conversation volunteer, overheard our discussion. He leaned over to interject. "It would be better if no one married or procreated so that the human race would die off," Geshe Lobsang said, quite serious.

And with that comment, I found dismissing the wisdom about the relationship between attachment and suffering much easier. But also not. I sought validation from dozens of other sources for my premature decision to marry Ethan. No one told me what I wanted to hear.

The nuns in conversation class laughed at my questions. "Marriage is when all your troubles start, the beginning of all suffering," one said. As nuns, they were free to study, travel, and practice their religion without the pressures and difficulties of being wives and mothers.

Pamela, an opinionated Tibetan who wore a striped *pangden* apron over her black *chupa* wrap dress, was one of the few women her age who had a love marriage rather than an arranged one. She got to know her husband after eight years of letter correspondence while they both served in the military. I told her about Ethan. "Do you love him?" she asked me. I did. She eyed me closely. "Okay. Build a relationship on trust and respect."

Rita, an Indian woman I'd befriended, skirted my questions and instead talked about her own marriage as she held her crying infant. "So much change, so much jewelry. It makes you feel like a prisoner."

"But how do you feel now?" I asked.

"Tired," she said with a wry smile.

Mahinder, an elderly Indian man in an unhappy arranged marriage who lived down the road, asked me, "How long have you known each other?" After I told him, he took my hand in his. "Wait.

Five or ten years. You're so young and sweet. There is no need to rush."

Ram, a Nepalese shopkeeper, sold hand-carved flutes on the side of the road. I often talked with him on my walk back to my host family's house. I liked him because he talked to me like a person and not a generic tourist. When I offered to help carry his bags of instruments home, he never demurred to hospitality culture. I shouldered the weight, and it felt good to feel useful.

I stopped by once on a slow sales day. Ram was bored. He offered to read my palm.

The first thing he noticed was a freckle. "You will inherit a fortune," he said. I laughed. Maybe I had a long-lost rich relative I didn't know about.

He ignored my response and traced another line.

"You are like water."

"Water?"

"Your feelings are like water. Always on the move, going from one place and relationship to the next whenever things get difficult."

I stopped laughing, even though this is exactly what someone could expect Ram to say to me. At least he said water, not wind.

"Do I get married?" I blurted.

Ram switched his reading to my left palm. "You have had two men in your life. There is another on the way."

I could only guess at who the prior men might refer to. And he'd said nothing about the man I had now, a man I didn't "have" at all.

One afternoon, Amanda announced her imminent departure for Tibet. She had traveled to sixty countries by then and claimed to "shed friends the way a dog sheds hair." Her abrupt announcement caught me off guard and awoke something in me, *about* me.

We went out for a goodbye coffee—a cappuccino for her, a

mango lassi for me. She'd spent weeks teasing me about my strange religion and "vile American accent," the lines around her eyes deepening as she smiled. And yet, I looked up to her more than she would have found comfortable. She was the first woman I had seen who'd made a life on the road a long-term reality. The marriage convert in me wanted to discover her secret dissatisfaction, to declare her someone who was running away from her problems as so many had labeled me. I hadn't told Amanda about Ethan. A part of me sensed it wouldn't be wise. Her existence made me question my own choices, reminding me of loyalties to myself I'd tried to ignore. But I spilled the news over our coffee.

"Oh really," Amanda said. I could taste her thick skepticism. "How old are you?" Then, "*Really?* Marriage?"

I flushed with embarrassment.

A week before I left India, Ethan messaged me over Google Chat to say he wanted to take a break, that he wasn't sure he loved me anymore. The shock tore a hole in my universe. I barely ate for weeks. I called him once I got back to the States after a long layover in Europe. We tried to make it work. I flew to Boston for a week with borrowed SkyMiles, the city I would place as my top preference on my Teach For America application during my final semester at BYU. Ethan broke up with me over the phone the following weekend.

The Buddhists were right. I suffered from my attachment and illusions. Relationships, I would come to learn, depend on two separate beings partnering in solidarity while acknowledging aloneness and exercising responsibility for their own perimeters. Or, as poet Rainer Maria Rilke describes it, a love that consists of "two solitudes" that "protect and border and salute each other."

I fell into a blinding depression for six months and barricaded my heart—turning down dates, leaving the apartment only to go to school, erupting into tears over the smallest reminders of our thirty-three days together, such as the bald Bradford pear trees. *Never again*, I promised myself. And I meant it. Giving up important parts of myself to sacrifice on the altar of love, even as a thought experiment, shook me. Though I was, in theory, ready to curb my desires and career ambitions to be the "good Mormon wife" I thought I was supposed to be, it wasn't enough to keep Ethan around.

Ethan and I saw each other a few more times once I moved to Boston, but my fierce affection had waned. The hurt went too deep. I began dating someone else, a non-Mormon guy, and Ethan went on to embrace atheism and marry a feminist. I imagine that if he were to read through our old emails, Ethan would cringe too. We were both playing out roles that didn't quite fit. Years later, while biking through Central Square in Cambridge, Massachusetts, after work, I almost crashed into Ethan. He didn't notice, his face scrunched in concentration as he darted across the street. I thought to call out to him, but didn't. Maybe I couldn't. I've since replayed the scene over and over in my mind. I adjusted my helmet, biked away, and imagined I felt nothing but the terrible awareness of that nothingness—that we could go from such heat to something akin to the indifference of strangers.

I wallowed in the KFC booth for several minutes before my body acted for me. I dug my one-way, second-class ticket to Chiang Mai from my pocket and cinched up my backpack straps.

Austin stood outside the train, watching for me.

Relief spread across his face. I refused to catch his gaze. We stepped aboard without speaking and found our seats in a compartment with orange curtains where a middle-aged Thai man sat across from us, texting on his Nokia phone.

I took the window seat and folded my arms. Austin and the Thai man, who introduced himself as Chaow, started a conversation. I listened with mild interest, my heart still thumping with fury and destabilizing terror. I gleaned Chaow was from a small village in the North, five hours outside of Chiang Mai. He had been to the US once for work. Now he lived in Bangkok to make money, but his family still lived and grew rice in the village.

"You are lucky to be coming to Chiang Mai at this time," Chaow said. "Yi Peng is soon."

I turned from the window. "What's Yi Peng?"

"Yi Peng, Loi Krathong. The lantern festivals."

We would arrive just in time.

The railroad workers interrupted the conversation to transform our seats into fully made beds, a mesmerizing process that took all of about five seconds.

"It's been nice talking," Chaow said. "My stop will come sooner than the sun."

We said goodnight as he drew the curtain. Austin started to do the same. I took the taro-flavored chips he'd purchased at the train station from his backpack and smuggled them into my top bunk. The tube made a soft puff when I opened it.

"Are you going to share those?" Austin said from below.

I paused, took a handful, then passed the can. A peace offering.

"Thanks." He grabbed a stack, then gave it back. Our hands touched. He squeezed my wrist. "Goodnight. I love you."

"I love you too."

I stayed awake long after the crunching of chips stopped underneath me. Crumbs littered my industrial blanket, still warm from the dryer. Lying down, I could look out the window at the dark greens passing. Dusk dissolved into blackness. I didn't want to believe I had expended all of my youthful ardor on Ethan, the constant worrying and convincing and assurances. What had been so special and alluring about all of that anyway? The instability, I knew, stoked the heat. I wished I could forget the intensity of the feeling, the power of the feeling. Hadn't I witnessed, for myself, that heat fade? Feelings seemed dangerous, untrustworthy.

Though my relationship with Ethan had taught me to accept differences, that passion has limitations, that emotion is a tempestuous, windy ruler, that seemingly good things can end or become less beautiful in hindsight—all important realizations for maturity—I also wondered if I'd placed more meaning in my experience with Ethan than merited. Our story had been more about youth and first love than any specific lesson. I didn't want to believe that all I had left was a protective cynicism toward love, as if anticipating the punch line to an age-old joke. Austin offered love freely, as I was. I chose him more than I fell for him. Was there something so wrong with surges of feeling, moments of quiet calm, a space big enough for thinking? I had a budding sense of the power of my selfhood and individual choices to shape my world and relationships.

Perhaps more than anything, I distrusted stability or associated it with stagnation. But maybe stability was exactly what I needed to grow. Even passion, if it survives, evolves, as poet Amy Lowell wrote of her relationship with actor Ada Russell in her erotic poem "A Decade":

> When you came, you were like red wine and honey,
> And the taste of you burnt my mouth with its
>   sweetness.
> Now you are like morning bread,
> Smooth and pleasant.
> I hardly taste you at all for I know your savour,
> But I am completely nourished.

I wondered how a more vulnerable me would look and act in a healthy relationship—a stage less intoxicating but perhaps more sustaining. What would it look like to be completely nourished? And was it that easy? I wanted to know how much of this I could feed myself.

Maybe it was time to revisit those lessons on broader love and attachment that the Tibetans had tried to teach me years earlier. Until I took more responsibility for my choices and happiness—independent of someone else's dreams or affirmations, positive or negative—I risked seeking assurances from everyone but myself. Nobody could replace that personal quest for satisfaction and contentment. No matter what happened with Austin, I would never lose my me-ness and my perimeter. In the end, as for all of us, my infinite-yet-temporary self was the one true thing I had. But that self didn't want to spend life, however ultimately lonely, alone. Happiness, and maybe marriage, was a lived process, not a state of being to tack down, frame, and perpetually examine.

I pressed my face to the Plexiglas to make out unfamiliar shapes: a smattering of huts with glowing windows, occasional streetlamps, groves of trees leaning into each other like reunited friends, a clear sky with thousands of stars. The train surged forward.

CHAPTER 9

The Lantern Festivals

NITA, THE ENTREPRENEURIAL LANDLORD of Nature's Way Guesthouse—our home base in Chiang Mai for the next three months—insisted we make our lanterns for the Loi Krathong festival. She had the supplies ready at her restaurant down the road.

"There are two kinds of lanterns," Nita explained while watering the garden, her silky ponytail falling over her shoulder as Austin and I waited for her son, Tom, to lead us to the restaurant. Tonight, there would be sky lanterns *and* floating river lanterns. These were for two different festivals.

Yi Peng is the event most people recognize for its *khom loi* floating sky lanterns, the incredible event that has been copied all over the world in various forms. Yi Peng is celebrated on the full moon in the second month of the ancient Lanna lunar calendar—*yi* meaning "two" and *peng* meaning "full moon day." A khom loi sky lantern is made of tissue-thin paper with a crossed base that supports a wax heat source. Often people write a wish on the outside before sending the khom loi into the sky as a way to release negative energy, ward off problems, and invite good luck.

Loi Krathong, though less known to foreigners, is a huge celebration that occurs on the evening of the full moon during the twelfth month of the Thai lunar calendar, which is why these two festivals overlap. A *krathong*, or water lantern, is made by adorning either a banana tree trunk or a bread-slab base with leaves and floral garlands. People place a candle and a stick of incense in the middle before launching the lantern into the water.

"Loi Krathong is our way of saying sorry to the Goddess of the River for everything we do throughout the year," Nita said as she placed incense inside the spirit house, a miniature Buddhist temple nestled in the garden to draw positive energy. "We take so much."

I wasn't sure how putting more things into the river showed appreciation, but Nita spoke with a conviction I didn't dare question. Austin and I would make a krathong to launch into the river as a way to reset our relationship and symbolize a fresh beginning, per Thai tradition. This was our way to say sorry, in our own way, for what happened a few days before on the train.

"Ready to make a krathong?" Tom said when we got to The Nature's Way restaurant. He had his mother's generous smile and wore a maroon V-neck shirt on his slight frame.

Austin and I sat across from each other. A pile of tropical flowers and banana tree cores covered the table. We'd reconciled a bit—holding hands again, sharing fresh fruit smoothies, tag teaming to get rid of ants in our bedsheets—though the memory of our argument remained sharp.

"Here." Tom handed us a banana tree base. "It floats. We also eat them sometimes. The hearts of the banana tree are sweet." Tom handed Austin a few toothpicks and shiny leaves, then modeled how to fold them like ribbons to cover the base. We took turns weaving until no parts of the pale bottom showed. Next, Tom showed us how to pierce purple lilies and marigolds around the base in swirling patterns. I snipped stems and handed them to Austin, who pressed them down like hairpins. I took my turn placing daisies around the edges. We left room for a candle and incense. The candle was especially important, as light is a way to revere Buddha. The lantern festivals served as a reminder of Buddha's teachings to rid oneself of negative feelings, like selfishness.

Tom folded his arms and scrutinized our work. The sloppy difference between our skills and his showed. "Not bad for your first time," he said.

The wait for nightfall felt like ages. At dusk, Austin and I walked with our krathong through the unfamiliar Chiang Mai streets lined with lush trees and vivid flowers. *Plumeria* wafted like ripe peaches as eager kids lit off the first sky lanterns, unable to wait until pitch black. Rows of tea lights flickered in front of buildings and temples. Nita told us that the candles "light the way when we do not see a path but want good to come." I appreciated that image.

The crumbling wall of Chiang Mai's Old City, a relic from the Lanna kingdom that lasted from 1292 to 1775 CE, was decorated with lanterns of all shapes, sizes, and colors. Near the Tha Phae Gate, Austin and I made our way into a thick crowd as a parade began. Floats covered in nāga dragons, bells, and shiny plaster passed by, some bearing statues of Buddha. Some carried framed portraits of the Thai king and queen. Musicians in fringed costumes banged drums, the beat reverberating. Dancers holding paper umbrellas donned traditional silk skirts and gold headdresses—as elaborate and spiked and bejeweled as a Buddhist temple—as they extended their slender fingers so far they curved backward. Our bodies pressed against thousands of others speaking many languages. My gaze locked on the sky. A few more sky lanterns appeared. Austin and I would send off our own khom loi, but we needed to wait until it was darker, until after we launched our water krathong. We wanted to do it right.

Peeling away from the noise and shoulder-to-shoulder mass, we headed toward a nearby riverbank. A few others were already there. A man wearing Converse sneakers squatted low to the ground, his palms pressed together in fervent prayer. When he finished, he lit the incense that stuck out of his krathong like an antenna. Next, he placed a coin in the center as an additional offering to the water spirits and then pushed it out into the Mae Ping River. A family with two kids launched their own, shrieking as the krathong narrowly dodged a fallen log and tree branches. Nita had said that the way a lantern traveled reflected how well the hopes and wishes and apologies had been received, perhaps an indicator of the year ahead.

Austin and I made it to the water's edge. We looked at each other in the dimming light, then breathed. I held the krathong and faced him.

"I'm sorry for blaming you for things that aren't your fault," I said, thinking of the train, but also other incidents that brought out this critical side of me.

Austin nodded.

I continued, "What I get out of this experience isn't so dependent on you. I don't know why I act the way I do when I feel stuck or powerless. I know I'm not. I'm going to take more responsibility. Not just for my happiness on the trip but also in our marriage."

Austin kissed my forehead. I felt the heat of his body. He pulled out a lighter and lit the krathong. His face glowed as smoke began to spiral off the incense.

"I'm sorry too," he said. "I don't always listen. I'm slow to trust you. Sometimes I feel like you are stepping on my freedom." He paused. "But you're not. I know you're not."

A silence followed. For a moment, I saw Austin's own fears. In the tunnel vision of my own, I wrongly assumed he was fearless. But I wasn't just the scared, crazy partner while he was the brave, sane one. I was more than that, and he was more than a caricature too. I was beginning to see how our fears intersected and interacted, how they could fan and fuel each other. But one thing we held in common: neither of us wanted to feel trapped.

By now the sky was all ablaze with lanterns following wind currents, like enchanted orbs in the indigo sky. The flame of our krathong fluttered in the breeze. I held one side, and Austin held the other. We crouched.

"Here's to a new start," I said, the cold water touching my fingers.

"And letting go of negativity."

Though vague commitments, the mutual gesture felt healing and exhilarating. Together, we pushed the krathong into the river, our lantern finding the current to join the others. The krathong pushed forward until it grew smaller and smaller. We tried not to lose sight of it, as Nita told us this led to good luck. Austin and I wrapped our arms around each other's backs, our eyes glued to the candle until we could no longer tell which one was ours glittering in the distance.

Hand in hand, Austin and I walked back to the bustling main street. Hundreds of people were launching sky lanterns. Most of the lanterns were pale white, but a few were shaped like *Angry Birds* and *Minions* characters. We overheard a dad tell his daughter, "Keep an eye on it. It means your wish will come true."

The khom lois made a fiery S overhead, illuminating the air current like a vein in an unknown life force above, like mythical jellyfish in an inverted ocean. The lanterns outshone the stars. Even the moon looked embarrassed. I'd never seen anything more beautiful. I have never seen anything more beautiful since.

Austin and I bought a khom loi from a vendor. We stood on

a bridge overlooking the Old City's moat. Flames reflected in the channel below.

I unfolded the delicate white tissue and Austin broke up the wick.

"What should we write?" I asked. People wrote on the outside before lighting their sky lanterns. From what we could observe, many notes mentioned mothers, fathers, siblings, children.

"Maybe something for both of our families?" It seemed like a nice, appropriate thing to do.

He reached into his pocket and pulled out a pen. I used his back to write, "For our families. We love you!"

We ignited the wick and waited, holding the edges until our khom loi gathered enough heat to fly. Meanwhile, people around us let off their own. One man tied fireworks to the bottom of his khom loi, which sparked and snapped as it ascended. Others in the street lit fireworks haphazardly—the big aerial kind. (Some Buddhist locals criticize the pyrotechnics for drawing attention away from the festivals' main messages). A teen with black pigtails let go of her khom loi too early, which sent it into the canal without ceremony. The crowd clapped to cheer on lanterns as they dodged trees and power lines.

Our khom loi fought our restraint. "I think it's ready," I said.

We let go.

Austin and I knew something went wrong the moment we released it. The khom loi faltered, took a sharp right, and, to our horror, lodged itself into a tree. People shook their heads with sympathy. I groaned and covered my eyes.

Austin leaned forward for a better view. "Wait—it might free itself! Look!" he said.

When I opened my eyes, the lantern erupted into flames.

Austin winced. "That can't be good luck."

We thought we could laugh it away.

CHAPTER 10

Bad Luck

WITHIN THE NEXT WEEK, the following things happened:

First, my sister came home to find our Labrador retriever dead in the living room.

Then, my grandmother had a fatal stroke. My family and I made the difficult decision that, given tight timelines and last-minute-flight prices, I would stay in Chiang Mai.

Finally, my dad had news. "We're getting a divorce," he announced to Austin and me over Skype. Lisa, my stepmom, hooked her arm through his elbow and nodded.

I tried to hide my shock. "When did you decide?" I asked.

"Last week," my dad said. He looked like he hadn't slept in about as long.

They told us some of the reasons.

"I love your father, but I am no longer in love with him," Lisa said. She didn't like herself, who she was becoming, or how she treated my dad. She'd lost some trust and respect for him in return. It was time for a fresh start.

"We care about each other enough to make this decision, hard as it is," my dad said. "We are in mutual agreement, so the process should go fast."

"It won't change anything about our relationship," Lisa said, squinting with compassion into the camera. "I will always love you."

My most meaningful first *I love you* didn't come from any of my life's romantic relationships but from Lisa. She told me on a day I knocked on her and my dad's bedroom door to announce I was headed into work at Arctic Circle, a fast-food burger joint that hired fifteen-year-olds like me. She examined my too-big uniform and black visor. My jeans sported stains from mixing countless milkshakes a day. She liked that I never complained and saw a quiet strength in me. I was more resilient than she'd taken me for. Lisa, who'd spent periods of her childhood dumpster diving for food and fending off her alcoholic mother's violent lovers, valued hard work and resilience.

"I love you," Lisa said, almost like a confession. She burst into tears. Then, like a dramatic movie, I wondered what I would do next.

"I love you too," I said, startled yet sure of what I was saying. We hugged, then off I went to contemplate this change as I washed tables and cleaned poop out of the children's playground. What did it mean that Lisa loved me and that I loved her? In the beginning, she'd been my enemy. I'd been Team Mom, and my loyalty prevented me from seeing any beauty or goodness in the non-Mormon, tall, lipstick-wearing, pencil-thin woman from work my dad had started seeing suspiciously soon after my parents separated. "You used to just stare," Lisa said. It creeped her out and made her feel judged, but I must have stared in part to understand. Who was this woman who drank coffee (coffee!) and left it in the microwave? Who wielded a credit card without shame to buy another pair of black pumps? Who quoted the lines to all the PG-13 and R-rated movies Mom had never allowed me to watch? Lisa enchanted any audience with her vivacious personality, spoke with her hands, and had this way of throwing her head back when she laughed. "You had no idea what to make of me."

Now that I lived with my dad—my relationship with my mother recently shattered—I sought love wherever I could find it. I'd written Lisa a card that said, "My dad calls you his angel, but I wonder if you are mine." I had a mom-sized hole in my chest, and I felt desperate to cover it up. Over the years, Lisa did the best she could while helping me grow into a woman—a *strong woman*. Like her, I'd hoped. She taught me that, yes, actually, you should change your underwear and shower daily. That's a thing. Doing otherwise is not healthy for your *vagina*. She said it! Also: feelings. Apparently, I had them. Those were good to talk about, to acknowledge.

"You're restless," Lisa would say. She nicknamed me Restless Rachel. Perhaps she recognized a bit of herself in me. She stood at my side as I searched online to learn about programs like the Peace Corps and less familiar, (probably) ethically irresponsible volunteer opportunities abroad. My budding desire to see the world terrified my mission-bound boyfriend, much the same way dyeing my hair or contemplating buying a moped set him off. Lisa, on the other hand, took me seriously. She married her first husband at nineteen and had a child by twenty. She'd never had a chance to go to college to study psychology like she'd longed to do. She had never left the North American continent. But she ached to go to Italy. Maybe Greece. She had a hunch that her heritage came from there, that all that sun and olive oil must be the reason for her enormous dark eyes and curly hair. Her past haunted and eluded her. She had no idea where she came from. Her absent father had died in a mental institution, leaving behind a legacy of unanswered questions.

Lisa exuded confidence. Lacking confidence myself, I lapped up hers. She seemed to relish my admiration. I made Lisa, quite unfairly, into a Greek oracle of sorts.

"What should I say?"

"Which shirt do you like?"

"How should I cut my hair?"

"Tell me what to do."

A woman of many opinions and effusive generosity, she answered them all. Since the age of fifteen, I counted on her strong, ever-present intuition to guide me.

My dad and Lisa said more reassuring words over Skype. I bobbed my head in a daze and thanked them for telling us.

"I'm so proud of you," my dad said, eager to deflect any pity. He always said that. Though he often worried about my resistance to marriage (regretting his own example) and felt concern about me on my travels, he also admired how I went after my dreams. "Let's talk again soon. Love you both."

Austin closed the laptop. The air evaporated from my lungs. My eyes watered. I crawled under the Fruit Loop–patterned duvet of our Chiang Mai apartment. He placed a hand on my shrouded, curled-up form.

"I'm sorry, Rach."

I took a moment to respond.

"They seemed to be doing better. Didn't you see them at our wedding? I thought they were doing better. I'm just surprised." My dad and Lisa had long reassured me that their blow-out arguments were a signal that they cared deeply about each other. If they didn't fight so loudly, so dramatically, it would be because they were less invested that a couple who did.

"I'm not surprised," said Austin, folding me in a hug.

The summer I returned from India, I sensed something was awry the moment I stepped through the door. A shift. The air felt cold. Can people smell grief? Does a dying relationship have a scent? The walls seemed to echo. People kept to separate rooms. I cried, begging my dad and Lisa to tell me what was wrong. They assured me nothing was wrong. Why did I ask?

In her early 40s, Lisa went to bed at six o'clock every night, sometimes sleeping in until noon. I'd go into her room to talk about my many problems, but she'd be curled under the billowy white comforter, incapable of waking up. She missed work. She cited chronic pain, arthritis. Sleep issues. ADHD. Mental health struggles. I overheard screaming arguments from the other side of the house. Fury at my dad's inability to love her children the way she loved me and my siblings. How he didn't understand her, his calculating mind. Webs of lies. There were credit card receipts, Kleenex, and orange medicine bottles on the nightstand, more scattered in the bathroom among anti-aging formulas and samples for expensive makeup.

The outbursts continued, becoming more frequent, more cruel, and sometimes belligerent. Anything could set her off. Everything exhausted her. The shock devastated them both, each convinced they were soulmates. I must have absorbed some of that notion of souls. Sure, I had a rough example with my parents' marriage, but with Dad and Lisa, I'd hoped I'd found a better model. Sure, there was fighting involved, but at least there was love. Love was something. They'd been married for almost ten years, after all.

My dad and Lisa separated briefly, then moved back in together a couple of months before my wedding. If anything, they seemed more unstable than before the separation, but I pretended otherwise.

After moving to Massachusetts, I talked to Lisa less and less. Still, I valued her opinions. I trusted her with every major decision, and I wanted to talk to her about Austin. We'd dated for almost two years by now. He felt ready to move forward. I wasn't sure.

"What do you think?" I asked on the phone, describing my relationship. Lisa had met him many times before and had a sense of our dynamic. Though I knew I loved Austin, I felt wary of the extra leap in commitment, in part because I straddled disorienting, contradicting contexts with loud ideas about the right choice. A remarkable thing happened each time I boarded a plane from Utah to Boston, a total transformation, much like the leap in political ideologies. In Utah, friends and family teased me for not being engaged yet: "Two years of dating!" they'd say. "You're almost twenty-five. He's *thirty*. What are you waiting for?" But five hours later, I'd land in Boston, where friends and coworkers had the opposite reaction: "You've only known him for two years. You're only twenty-five. Why the rush?"

I wanted to please everyone—an impossibility. The noise of everyone else's expectations and concerns drowned out whispers of my own inclinations. But I knew Lisa would have inclinations. I could borrow hers, even though I'd observed that Lisa's gut feelings sometimes had the benefit of being right in retrospect, even if it meant a shift in her memory of her original stance.

"It sounds like he's the one," Lisa said on the other end of the phone.

He's *The One*.

I didn't flood with relief when I hung up the phone. I didn't feel joy or sadness either. I simply took my cue, or what I took to be a cue, in assembling the puzzle I'd already been piecing together for myself. Now, I could say yes to Austin's proposal. I'd found a great guy, gathered up the evidence, and vetted the relationship, and Lisa felt he was The One.

Austin didn't see the point in waiting. He subscribed to the idea of *When you know, you know*. A four-month-long engagement rolled forward.

I flew to Utah over a long weekend to find a wedding dress with Lisa. On that trip, she cornered me in the kitchen.

"Are you sure you love Austin?" she asked. I detected a hint of skepticism.

I set down my cup of tap water. "What do you mean?"

"Are you *in* love with him? You know, do you want to rip his clothes off whenever you see him?"

I *did*, in fact, often want to rip Austin's clothes off. But that didn't seem to be the point.

I can't remember what I said in response, processing her good intentions but also taken aback by this definition of love. Wasn't there a difference between lovers and long-term relationships? Also, how could she contradict her earlier declaration when she'd sounded so certain on the phone? A chill ran through me.

What if Lisa wasn't the expert on love I thought she was?

Or, what if she was, and now she was suggesting Austin was *not* The One? I'd already dropped hundreds of wedding invitations into a box at the post office, heard the THUNK when they hit the bottom with a beat of finality.

In Utah, I'd booked appointments at bridal shops all over the Wasatch Front. This was not a moment I'd fantasized about all my life, and I preferred to have it done in a day. I'd done the research and saved pictures of dresses for Lisa to get a sense of what I was looking for: something bohemian and wild but that still fit the strict modesty standards for a temple wedding—with sleeves and a fully covered back.

"What do you think of this lacy one?" I asked Lisa, showing her a picture of my top choice. "This is my favorite so far."

A pause. "The sleeves are weird."

I made note. No lacy sleeves.

At a Salt Lake City boutique, I fell for the first dress I tried on—whimsical, simple, and within my budget. Lisa admired it but said we had other shops to visit. Also, she wasn't feeling well.

In the car, she dry heaved over a grocery sack. While baffling to both of us, this had happened before—after picking me up from the airport when I'd returned from one of my long trips or whenever something big seemed to be happening for me.

We stopped at a gas station for saltine crackers. "Are you sure you feel okay enough to keep going?" I asked, wide-eyed.

She insisted she did.

At a dressmaker's shop in Orem, I tried on a sample dress made of plain satin material with a price tag that was double what I'd planned to pay. Lisa gasped when I emerged from the changing room. Her hand flew to her mouth.

"That's *the one*," she said. Lisa began to cry. The dressmaker swooned. I examined myself in the mirror, my face wrinkled with concern.

I told Lisa my reservations. "I liked the other dress," I said, thinking of the whimsical option I'd tried on that morning.

"This is better," Lisa said when the dressmaker went into her office to process a receipt. "I feel better about this one. The other would have required too many alterations to meet the temple's rules."

On the way out, Lisa paused to admire a lacy dress on display by the door. I recognized it as my original top choice, the gown I'd shown her a picture of earlier.

"That's the dress I would pick for myself," Lisa said as she touched the lacy sleeves without a hint of irony or recognition.

I went to the dressmaker's shop alone three more times for measurements leading up to the wedding. She had a no-return, no-refund policy. I left on the verge of tears each time, feeling a loss of control. The dress, though pretty and classic, was emerging into something I didn't want, didn't mean to sign up for. The sleeves poked out too much. The satin fabric didn't flow like the chiffon I'd imagined. I made suggestions, tweaks where I could. But what could I say? Though I was old enough to get married and obviously old enough to change my mind about my own dress, I didn't want to be fussy. I didn't want to hurt anyone's feelings. I believed, given our short engagement, that I didn't have enough time to find a different one. Worst of all, I feared disappointing or offending Lisa, whose love and approval I clung to like a hypersensitive child wrapped around her mother's legs. Lisa had been sure about the dress like she had been sure about the groom. I needed both, somehow, to be enough.

Uncanny, that our wedding photographer would email pictures of our wedding day a few hours after we got the news of my dad and Lisa's divorce. I scoured the collection of images, searching their faces and body language for clues. Lisa had taught me how. "You can discern so much about a relationship by how people pose in pictures."

Austin and I looked happy—really happy—and comfortable with each other as we kissed, linked fingers, laughed. The satin, in the end, photographed well and looked elegant. The fittings and shopping memories no longer stung. In the end, it was only a dress, one I wouldn't wear again. And the dress was fine, more than fine. Austin was also far more than fine, and my decision to marry him, of course, had been made on much more than a whim or someone else's suggestion.

I examined a photo of Lisa and me, heads tilted toward each other, smile lines, affection pooling in our eyes. Next, a family portrait. She and my father stand on opposite sides of the formation, the August sun highlighting their fixed grins.

Did he know then?

Did she?

Did *I*? Sometime after their divorce, my dad wondered aloud what Lisa's motives may have been: "Sometimes I wonder if she moved back in for that short time for you. So we could be a family for your wedding."

I came across a candid shot from the ring exchange ceremony we'd held after our temple sealing. My dad, holding Lisa's hand in his lap, squints at a speaker out of the frame. Lisa gazes down at nothing in particular, frowning. She appears more human than a saving angel—and beautiful in her vulnerability.

Contemplating my good luck, I reached up to touch the necklace around my throat—a gift from Lisa for my college graduation, before I'd moved off to Massachusetts to build a life far from home—a silver, rectangular pendant that read *FEARLESSNESS*. She'd known that fear was my biggest obstacle and believed I could move forward, despite it, alongside it.

CHAPTER 11

The Northern Hill Tribes

THE KAREN VILLAGE OF BAAN MUANG NGAM glowed in the golden light when we arrived. Outlines of workers dotted the distant rice fields, fields divided into clean rows against a muscular mountain backdrop. My T-shirt clung to my skin in the humidity.

"This is my wife's village," said Anan, our local expert, as we hoisted our bags from the truck. He lived with his wife and her family—Karen families are matriarchal. Anan wore a purple, fringed tunic over his small torso that his wife had woven. Chickens clucked near our feet as we walked.

Austin and I were on a four-day tour with his parents, Clark and Lu, who had flown out from their small town in Wyoming to see for themselves what we loved so much about Thailand. During our two months of living in Chiang Mai, Austin and I had visited a hill tribe village as part of a locally championed service project organized by our Thai, Mormon congregation (there are over thirty thousand Latter-day Saint congregations found everywhere around the globe). We'd delivered armloads of blankets and jackets to the mountain regions suffering from record-breaking temperature drops. Austin and I noted how different their customs varied from Thai culture, from the living arrangements (we slept on the tile floor, grouped by gender rather than couples) to the foods and earthy spices. We had hoped to learn more. And, given his parents' appreciation for agriculture and small-town life, we thought this excursion would fit everyone's interests.

The tour with Anan aimed to educate us about northern Thailand and the seven main hill tribes: the Akha, the Lahu, the Hmong, the Mien, the Lisu, the Palaung, and—the majority group—the Karen. Approximately one million hill tribe people live in Thailand. The phrase "hill tribe," translated from the Thai term *chao khao*, refers collectively to the ethnic minorities living in the North. The Karen make up an estimated five hundred thousand of that number. However, exact global Karen populations are hard to measure. Most remain in Myanmar, formerly known as Burma, where they are indigenous. Anan wouldn't consider returning to Myanmar, a country battling continual conflict and the horrors of ethnic cleansing.

As we traveled the dusty path toward the village center, Anan said, "One hundred and seventy families live here." Most Karen villages in Thailand contain somewhere between ten and two hundred homes. "Our tribe works together. We often borrow. The village is self-sufficient." The Karen across the globe seem to value the collective and making decisions based on group consensus. Villages are democratic. Elders and mediators settle disputes. Above all, they value harmony.

Anan drew our attention back to the stretch of rice fields and the specks in the vibrant green distance where villagers were harvesting the crop. From closer, we could make out their hats—some straw, some fabric with neck flaps. "Right now, we are growing rice. When we are not growing rice, we grow soybeans. We have many different herbs and vegetables for cooking as well." Anan labored in the fields instead of working as a guide during the busiest harvest months. He spoke five languages—Karen, Thai, Lahu, Akha, and English—and was learning Italian through a phone app. He seemed at home in the role of tour guide and showed tremendous respect for different cultures, as he did for his own.

Clark squinted into the distance and asked Anan about rainfall and harvest techniques. As a large-animal veterinarian and stoic cattle rancher, Clark wanted to know more about how the crops and grass grew compared to home. Lu—the woman from whom Austin had inherited his bright blue eyes, friendliness, zest for words, and unfailing optimism (characterized by her valiant gardening efforts in northern Wyoming)—listened with enthusiasm.

I adored my in-laws. Clark and Lu had welcomed me like their own daughter. They'd married in their early twenties in the Provo Utah Temple. Lu gave birth to Austin two years later. When I once pressed Clark for more details about the courtship, like describing their first kiss, Clark said, definitively, "That's private." I'd never been around a marriage that had lasted so long, one that appeared peaceful and contented. They had a quiet, loyal bond, a marriage of thirty-three years. Their joint commitment to The Church of Jesus Christ of Latter-day Saints provided an anchor. They understood each other and gave the other the space they needed. Once, when I was talking to Lu about our travels, she'd laughed and wondered aloud, "I don't know how you two do it." To her, Austin and I spent an astonishing amount of time together.

Anan continued, "Our heritage is to care about the land. If you care about the land, it will take care of you."

I imagined Clark herding steers into a fresh pasture of wild grass, Lu tsking at the deer and rabbits nibbling at the zucchini and bell pepper plants in her resilient garden. As I listened to Anan and Austin's parents talk about the land, I couldn't help but think about long-term relationships in general, what grows given enough effort, time, patience, and a little faith.

Did such a metaphor fit Austin and me?

We passed families gathered around open fires with pots of stew brewing on the coals. We greeted them the way Anan taught us, saying *o mushopa* in Karen with a slight bow. Each family owned a pig, tied to a post, to eat on a special occasion. Two children followed us, giggling whenever we looked over our shoulders.

Anan lived in a concrete, rectangular building. A green parrot outside squawked "o mushopa" at us. Inside, a few of Anan's extended family members met us, including his wife, Lucky, a round-faced woman wearing a woven indigo shirt. She greeted us with a shy head bob, then returned to the kitchen. A small TV sat on a stool in the main room. A colorful rug lined the cement floor. On the other wall hung dozens of photos in thin metal frames. A few I recognized as a celebration. Anan, wearing a red tunic, stood at the center of a large group. His forehead appeared a little less lined, less sun-weathered from farming.

"Was this your wedding?"

"Yes. My second marriage, actually. Those are my wife's nine siblings," he said. "I have been married to this woman for ten years. My first wife died of cancer."

"Oh, I'm sorry."

Anan nodded. "My first wife gave me my daughter. That's how I met my current wife. My daughter was lonely. She would go and visit this other woman in our village. I started talking with the woman too, then decided to marry her." Anan paused. "Too bad you can't meet my daughter. She's thirteen now and away at school in a nearby town. I can show you a video of her later. She is a wonderful singer. She makes music videos for our village."

"That would be great," I said, scanning the pictures on the wall, my eyes glued to the wedding photos: red-patterned cloth, no smiles.

The four of us sat on the living room rug as Anan's gracious family served us a feast of the local food. We ate a celebratory main entrée called *tai pow pow* with rice, fresh turnips, and baby rattan shoots from the garden—all spiced with chili, lemon grass, tumeric, garlic, coriander, and spring onion. This was paired with a fried rabbit meat dish called *pu daiya*, flavored with lime leaves and galangal (essential for wild meat, particularly if the meat has a strong smell to offset). The vegetable side was a dish called *pow pladou*, ferns plucked from the nearby river, then seasoned with garlic and soy salt. The earthy offerings tasted nothing like the creamy, sweet, spicy flavors we'd encountered in the Bangkok and Chiang Mai cuisines.

Anan offered more stew.

"Want to try some mouse?" he asked as he held out a plastic dish. The family members in the kitchen chuckled at the gesture as they ate from their own bowls.

After an awkward silence, Austin agreed. He took a spoonful with reluctance. His lip curled in subtle reaction when he swallowed, but he gave Anan a thumbs up and thanked him.

After dinner, Lucky emerged with an armful of bold, bright clothes and fanned them out on the floor. She said something to Anan without looking at him.

"My wife wants to show you the clothing she makes," Anan said. "Women in this village weave shirts for wedding presents." Each shirt took two months to make. "Women spend years of their lives creating shirts so they can offer whoever marries into their family a complete wardrobe." He laughed. "Our son is five. But we start making them early."

Quite early, I thought.

We marveled at the shirts—square in shape, short-sleeved, and adorned with a wide stripe of embroidery across the torso, layered with vibrant threads and intricate beads. The stitching of the garment near the arms and V neckline resembled bird tracks in the snow. The bottom of the tunics cascaded into fringe. Lucky held esteem in the village as a talented seamstress, clothing designer, and sewing teacher. What she didn't keep, she gave away to family or sometimes sold. Lucky took trips to Chiang Mai for additional materials and modern colors, but she still took pride in dyeing some of her own cotton thread. Her mother had taught her how to weave. Weaving kept her culture alive and present. I imagined each stitch as a way to sew herself into the fabric of her heritage, reaching back through the generations, despite so much political upheaval and loss from migration.

I thought the shirts were gorgeous. They reminded me of quilts my mother and the Utah pioneer generations used to make, the handiwork of women. Artifacts left in place of women's words and histories. Physical objects that insist, *I was here.*

"Do the colors mean anything?" I asked.

Unmarried girls wore white sack dresses, signaling virginity and cleanliness. "That is why they need all these new shirts after the wedding," Anan said.

This sounded familiar—the color white, the emphasis on virginity.

"Look at these for men," Anan said, pulling a scarlet slice from the pile. "The groom wears red. It is a color of power and shows he can provide for the family." He pointed to the lavender shirt he was currently wearing. "Most Karen men wear red, but I don't like that color. My wife makes me others." Anan wore purples, dusty greens, sky blues. He was one of the few men in his village to do so. When pressed, he said his reason for avoiding red had more to do with politics than resisting the symbolism. While studying in Bangkok years earlier, Anan had hated a particular candidate who sported red. However, for special occasions (like his wedding), Anan wore the traditional red as expected.

Anan returned to the pile. "The blue and black ones here are traditional for married women. It is also the color worn at weddings." He explained that bridal blue represented respect and submission to their husbands and black represented sadness.

"Sadness?" I asked. But perhaps I shouldn't have been surprised. Hadn't I been married long enough to know that some sadness was part of the marriage deal?

"I don't understand all of these things. Maybe they have to learn to be strong on their own, with themselves."

Anan consulted Lucky, who stood nearby. Together, they struggled to come up with an easy explanation. Blue and black represented the past and signaled that a Karen woman was married. Historically, few options existed outside this color palette. Black, red, and blue came from the dyes of local plants and tree barks. These colors indicated a readiness to cook, clean, and take care of the home.

Everyone offered their compliments on the stunning craftsmanship. I nodded and placed the shirts neatly back into the pile.

The next morning, Anan took us to see the Lahu, another hill tribe.

The Lahu used to be hunters in the Yunnan province of China, but now they also live in eastern Myanmar, northern Laos, Vietnam, the United States, and northern Thailand. They came to these regions as refugees and political asylum seekers in the wake of the Laotian Civil War. Like the Karen, the Lahu spoke dialects similar to Tibeto-Burman languages. Culturally, however, the Karen and the Lahu remained quite distinct.

"The Lahu are the most conservative of the hill tribes," Anan said as we walked down a dried mud trail to a cluster of dilapidated homes. A fenced enclosure stood on our left. A small, barefooted girl in a tank top ran past us, kicking up clouds of dirt. "We'll stop in to see one of my friends who lives at the end of the road," Anan continued. "You'll notice the Lahu build homes to face the sunrise since their shaman says it is good luck."

After paying the customary respects to the shaman, we visited the stick home. We removed our shoes. Clark hunched to fit through the door. Hot coals simmered on the floor. Padding for twenty or so beds lined the room and light shone through the gaps in the wall panels. An eighteen-year-old woman with dark eyes rocked a baby in the far corner. She smiled when Anan greeted her in Lahu. Anan introduced us.

"This is her first child, a baby boy," Anan said, admiring the bundled infant. "She has to stay inside because the Lahu believe that after you have a baby, you should remain indoors for a full moon." Lu swooned and we smiled politely back. But something caught in my chest. I felt uncomfortable standing in her living space, imposing on her in this way.

Anan said girls marry around age eleven or twelve, boys at thirteen or fourteen. The Lahu faced tremendous economic and educational challenges despite the government's efforts to provide them with more educational resources.

I did not feel neutral about child marriages or children having children. Yet I also didn't want to burden this young woman with my misplaced pity.

Anan, however, did not share my hang-ups. He said that of all the hill tribes in Thailand, he admired the Lahu the most. "They are true to themselves."

No one spoke after we left the home. Heat scorched the backs of our necks. On the way out, we stopped in front of the fence surrounding the circular enclosure we'd spotted earlier.

"This is where they dance," Anan said. "Remember, the Lahu are very traditional. They still practice the old religion. Each New Year, there is a big dance ceremony. There, you can change wives if you end up dancing with someone new."

Did I hear him right?

"Really? What happens to the original wife?"

"They switch partners. Men and women do it. The husband of the new wife would then become the new husband to the other wife."

Was this the safety outlet—the way the insular community could function, according to Anan, more or less harmoniously? Marriage seemed to mean something different here, something fluid and impermanent. A part of me admired it, another part of me felt resistance—an old, reactionary piece of me that had been taught the badness of divorce, the tragic "failure" of a marriage dissolving. But my admiration and resistance came from a shared root, the piece of me preoccupied with not just marriage but its potential *end*. Fear stared back at me from both sides. Without an option to exit (though there was always that option, however impossible it seemed to me), marriage might feel less like a continual, deliberate choice and more like the projection I'd feared—a one-way trap.

In a reversal, if the Lahu woman with her infant would have barged into my home and learned about my culture in passing, would she have felt pity for *me*? For committing to a single person for not just a whole life but for *eternity*?

I had a lot of questions about this New Year's dance of the Lahu. I have continued to press Anan for years since but cannot get more specifics. "Come back to Thailand!" Anan says. "We'll talk to them again." Yet he doesn't waver. He knows what he knows from growing up near the Lahu village, asking their elders about their community. Living near the Lahu gave Anan the chance to learn their language, why not their culture? I wanted to trust his information, but I needed more. I *still* need more. My outside research has failed to either verify or contradict Anan's claims. The Lahu New Year's dance seems to be a way to reestablish good relationships and forgiveness between Lahu communities with merriment and dancing and feasting. Adultery itself isn't seen as offensive unless a house spirit discovers the couple or the rest of the village finds out. "Chopsticks only work in pairs," according to a Lahu proverb.

"What did you think when you first heard about this spouse swap?" I asked.

Anan appeared unfazed, with no trace of judgment or awe. "It's their culture. I understand."

I surveyed the arena. Would it be dark, under a starlit night? Would lovers plan ahead or sneak into each other's arms at the right moment? What was the role of consent, and how terrible were the fallouts?

Perhaps the best metaphor for marriage was not a field of crops but a dance—full of different rhythms, individual movements synchronized with another's, swaying to a song with varied lengths for different couples.

After Anan's explanation, Austin flashed me a smug look. "Don't get any ideas."

Near the end of the four-day tour, I found Anan alone at a picnic table outside our guesthouse in the Chiang Dao district. Clark, Lu, and Austin had stayed inside to unpack and rest before dinner. I joined Anan in the twilight. I couldn't get the Lahu dance out of my head, nor Lucky and her collection of bridal shirts.

"Do you mind if I ask you a few more questions?" I asked.

"What do you want to know?" Anan said, amused.

"Can you tell me about how Karen decide to marry, maybe from personal experience?"

"The Karen used to have arranged marriages." Anan explained that engagement periods run for about two months. He was twenty-five and his first wife was twenty when they married. Marriage transitions Karen people into adulthood. Anan claimed "love" marriages were becoming more common, though he didn't consider himself a romantic. He didn't know how to define the word *romantic*. "How can say . . ." he stumbled, before deciding it had something to do with "sweet words" and celebrating special days. Like other Karen—a community that valued modesty and a certain quiet—he displayed shyness. No one encouraged public kissing, not even at weddings. A bride and groom linking arms might cause embarrassment.

"Most years, I do not even remember my wife's birthday. I think most Karen men are not romantic. Both times I was married, the decision was made by the two of us talking about it."

I asked him more about the low divorce rates.

"Karen people are very easy going. Romance is not the most important thing. We are also a strong community." As part of the Karen wedding tradition, the parents wash the feet of the bride and groom with purified water, a bottle with a stone at the bottom to symbolize unity and strength. Only after the stone-water washing do they split two bottles of whiskey to share and celebrate.

Anan did, however, acknowledge that there can be difficult marriages. "Marrying outside of the tribe is a big source of conflict." He considered this a natural consequence of people getting more education and going outside the community. But each tribe values distinct traditions that take a lifetime to learn. In his experience, couples who marry outside the tribe exhibit higher rates of divorce, around 50 percent.

"It is easier if you are from the same tribe," Anan said. "That way you understand the language and shared culture. Obedience also helps couples. The elders have lots of advice. I think if people listen, they will be happier."

Despite our immense cultural differences, these sentiments felt familiar. My dating of non-Mormon men had never progressed into anything serious—I felt I had too much to explain. I'd married inside my spiritual and cultural community, someone who spoke this strange language with me, though in a different dialect.

Obedience? Elders? Those concepts, too, sounded familiar. Who were my elders? Maybe my parents, whose examples of partnership offered some insight into what *not* to do. But that wasn't all. The word *elder* also evoked oodles of religious meaning for me. It is an office of the priesthood in Mormonism as well as a role and responsibility for certain men in the highest ranks in the church hierarchy. The word brought to mind images of older men in dark suits and white shirts and ties, men with authority who presided over the meeting in pews behind the podium. Spiritual leaders and gatekeepers who served on a volunteer basis.

Before getting married, I had to meet with the equivalent of my village elders—first, with the bishop of my congregation, and then with the stake president, the man above him. Each interviewed Austin and me to determine if we were worthy to be married and sealed in the temple. The first went fine since our bishop, who favored bow ties over traditional ties, knew us; the second interview still makes me grit my teeth.

I'd never met with President Rigby before, but I'd heard stories. A successful businessman, he once gave a dating lesson to the male twenty-somethings in my Boston singles congregation. He drew a flowchart on the chalkboard. The goal: marriage in six to twelve months. He listed the stages of courtship: dating, exclusivity, meeting the family, then engagement. Each stage should take one to two months. He reminded the young men, ordained with God's priesthood power from the age of twelve, that it was their sacred responsibility to be dating.

Women, on the other hand, he viewed as victims: wonderful and lovely and just waiting for some knucklehead to wake up and realize their greatness. President Rigby had also offered one-on-one marriage coaching for women. One friend of mine met with him for a few weeks until he told her to start wearing makeup.

For our final marriage interview, Austin and I met with President Rigby in a church office behind a closed door. Goosebumps formed along my arms in the strong air-conditioning. Austin sat on my right as President Rigby faced us head-on, a hard side part in his silver hair. He outlined the sacred promises I would be making before God by choosing to get married in the temple. I nodded along, putting on my best Utah-nice-girl face to ensure the meeting went smoothly and our plans could continue without fuss. He recommended scriptures, asked the standardized questions about our spiritual health, then placed the official church handbook and script for these sessions on the desk behind him. Time to go rogue.

"Who's responsible for making sure family home evening happens?" he asked, referring to the Monday nights set aside for quality family time.

Austin and I exchanged a look.

"Both of us?" I said.

President Rigby shook his head, then pointed at Austin. "*You* are."

I squirmed.

"Who's responsible for making sure the family reads scriptures together?" he asked.

"Both of us," I repeated, this time a bit firmer.

Again, he shook his head and pointed to Austin. "You are. As the priesthood holder, you are responsible for the spiritual well-being of your family."

The meeting went on in a similar pattern as I faded. I waited until the car ride home to erupt.

"Can you believe he said that?" Not that I wanted to be in charge of enforcing any orthodox church behaviors, but I hadn't even been *invited* to be a spiritual coleader. The patriarchy was alive and well. I smoldered.

"But he had some important advice about other things, like loyalty," said Austin, who had left feeling peace and excitement about our temple marriage. He gave our lay ministry the benefit of the doubt. He'd always been generous toward church leadership, a tenant of obedience but also his personality—he felt allergic to criticizing generally, even when merited. In time, as I began to see my own reactions as valid, I would recognize this challenge to sit with the negative (especially when it came to church) as one of Austin's greatest flaws, the shadow side of his desire to see the good, always. My anger scared him for the same reason his tolerance scared me. When the rubber hit the road, could we be what the other needed, or wanted, the other to be? Sure, we shared this complex religion and culture in common, but how often would it be a liability?

"I saw what you did, and it was louder than what you said," Austin once told me when I asked him why he believed in our relationship despite my painful doubts about our compatibility. "You're like that, you know."

Though Austin had said those words to me, the same could be true for him. His actions and clear support for my personal and professional growth came to mean more to me than abstract debates about religion. Still, this was an area where we both experienced loneliness, seeking out conversations with others when it came to difficult spiritual topics. This fault line in our relationship never disappeared. Being from the same community might help, but it did not guarantee anything.

Sometimes I wondered if things *would* be happier or easier if I was more able to obey, if I heeded the counsel of my elders more. This becomes apparent in distinct, less-understood communities with traditions considered strange to outsiders, whether Mormon or hill tribe. Each disposition—to welcome the dominant structure or to reject it—offers pros and cons. If I felt more inclined toward the safety of obedience, my marriage might appear more ideal, perhaps less dramatic, more harmonious. Like Lu and Clark's. Like Anan and Lucky's. How easy it was to assume things about others' marriages from the outside, to project, despite the unknowability of any individual's experience inside a partnership.

But that standard obedience narrative wasn't me.

"Well-behaved women seldom make history." This famous quote found on bumper stickers and protest signs is often misattributed. Few know—though millennial Mormon women do—that it actually comes from a Mormon woman, Laurel Thatcher Ulrich, the award-winning Harvard historian who I'd later teach Bible study alongside and come to call my friend. She and other members of Exponent II, a community of Mormon feminists, taught me about the church's radical theological beginnings, the founding feminists and resurgent wave in the 1970s, and how to feel God and find community among conscious, engaged women of all ages. I could be authentically me—with all my voice intact—and deeply Mormon.

When it came to elders, there were options to choose from, even within Mormonism. I could decide on the balance between others' advice and my own intuition.

In the end, I preferred a difficult life over one without a struggle against the vestiges of my culture that contradicted my emotional truth. I would bravely travel that honest, individual, sometimes-lonely road as far as it would take me. For the time being, Austin seemed happy enough to walk his own beside me. Maybe our paths were parallel enough. Maybe they would cross at points, or maybe they would diverge. It was impossible to see beyond the next bend.

I guess I choose "the journey" as my preferred marriage metaphor. Perhaps that comes as no surprise.

"I think some of these ideas are common in my culture too," I said to Anan, circling back to the obedience conversation as I swatted away a mosquito in the dimming light.

"Some things are common to all people," he said.

We both acknowledged the challenges and the changes for the rising generation. Some millennial Mormons were resisting certain parts of church culture that felt problematic and dated. Karen youth were no different. What might become lost? That remains to be seen. Anan and I watched a YouTube video of a Karen wedding. The bride wore a blue shirt with a slash of red across the front. When Anan was born, you would only see black and blue. Girls still wear white, but usually only to church. For everyday wear, they enjoy colors like green, purple, and yellow. Anan showed me a picture of his daughter flashing a peace sign and modeling a shirt Lucky had taught her how to weave herself: the tunic had the same square shape and fringe, but the white base was overwhelmed with bubblegum-pink stripes. I admired the heck out of her, straddling tradition and change with that much love.

I continued asking questions. "What is it like when Karen people first marry?"

Anan furrowed his brow. "Maybe more romantic." He cited that Lucky was more romantic than him. "I have been married to her for ten years now. The kids bring us joy, but there are also challenges. Sometimes I don't always listen or want to listen to my wife, which causes some problems. Living with my in-laws in a crowded home also means that everyone knows everyone's problems, which does not make it easier."

I took a moment, again, to appreciate how much I genuinely enjoyed my in-laws, thankful for a dose of stable normality (if such a thing existed) in my newly acquired parents. I felt grateful they'd come all this way to share this experience with Austin and me. Clark and Lu took a laissez-faire approach to parenting and never told Austin and me what to do or how to live.

I said, "A Thai woman once told me marriage gets harder later in life because couples separate to take care of aging parents. Does that happen with the Karen?"

Anan crossed his arms. Darkness was now upon us. Someone flipped on some white Christmas lights to illuminate the porch.

"It happens. Sometimes a few weeks or a month, but never years. In fact, I think being married for thirty or forty years is sometimes like coming back to the beginning of a marriage."

"How so?"

"It is the last light of day. The man and woman take care of each other and listen. They know each other better than anyone and have both worked hard. They start doing what is best for the . . . wife or husband. Wait, no . . . That's not the right word." He pulled out his phone for a translation app.

"Sweetheart."

I beamed. "Do you think that's the happiest time in a marriage?"

"Maybe," he shrugged. "But I think the happiest time should always be whatever stage you are in at the moment. Don't you think?"

The rest of the group joined the table—Clark and his broad shoulders, Lu and her sun visor taming her blonde curls, Austin and his boyish grin. The guesthouse owner passed around menus with the two available items underlined on the front page. Lu was laughing about something Clark mumbled. Austin slipped in beside me and squeezed my knee. Perhaps—along with the challenges—there was something to savor, at every stage, no matter the imperfect metaphor.

CHAPTER 12

Test of the Tattoo

AS AUSTIN AND I WERE ENJOYING hot plates of *panang* curry in Chiang Mai, a man chased a Swiss tourist into Nita's restaurant. The Swiss man hurtled himself into the bathroom, slamming the door behind him.

"Do you want to go to prison?" the Thai man yelled after him. "You owe me 2,500 baht!"

All the guests froze and stared. Austin stood up. "What's going on?"

Oh boy.

We'd been in Thailand for two months. We'd also been together long enough for me to recognize the look in Austin's eyes, the same hero expression he wore when he instinctively broke up a fistfight in the middle of a movie theater in Boston while I shrank into a ball as an explosive battle scene from *Captain America* played on the screen, the perfect backdrop. Both men in the altercation sat down again and finished watching the film.

Austin's eyes narrowed.

"He refused to pay for his tattoo," said the man, who explained that he worked in a tattoo parlor specializing in traditional bamboo tattoos.

"What does he owe?" Austin asked, imagining the horrors of Thai prison.

I rose to protest Austin's involvement, knocking my chopsticks to the ground in the process. "Don't," I said. "If he didn't pay, that's his problem."

Austin ignored me. "Let me try talking with him."

I blocked his way. "Please don't get involved."

"I'm just going to talk with him," Austin said. He headed for the bathroom, where the Swiss guy cowered behind a locked door. Austin knocked, but the man wouldn't emerge.

I crossed my arms, feeling smaller by the second. The worker recounted the story and showed me pictures of a tattoo that made my jaw drop: thin circles outlining the puckered pink skin around each of the Swiss man's hairy nipples.

I blinked. "Wait. How many drinks did you say he had?" I asked.

"I don't know how many he had before, but he had three more in the shop." The tattoo artist waved a paper in my face. "But he signed *this*."

Austin came back and reproached the employee for giving a tattoo to a drunk person without cash. I stormed off when I heard them negotiate a payment: the equivalent of a week of living expenses for us in Thailand.

Austin derives immense satisfaction from helping others. I have never met anyone so generous; he amazes me. In the years I have known him, he has never turned down an invitation to help someone move. I might even argue that he *likes* hefting overstuffed boxes in and out of moving trucks parked haphazardly along narrow streets. He volunteers at the temple twice a month, bakes bread for neighbors on Sundays, and gets *excited* to babysit our friends' children for free. He never turns down a volunteer position at church, whether it involves teaching kids, teens, or adults. He visits the sick, scrubs the chapel's bathrooms, and will rent a car if someone needs a ride. He is involved with the Big Brothers Big Sisters program, taking his "Little" fishing, to concerts in the park, to Renaissance festivals, and to comic book shops.

Austin is also the best and only friend to a sallow, eighty-year-old blind man named Jim who hoards garage-sale finds and threatens suicide whenever Austin declines his frequent requests to buy him another radio. Jim was evicted from his last apartment due to health-code complaints. Over many months, Austin sorted through rancid foods and secondhand treasures without Jim noticing and stacked the boxes into organized rows in the new apartment. Austin precleans Jim's bathroom, wiping away the roaches and urine stains, to dissuade the state-hired cleaner from reporting another health-code violation. Austin drives Jim across Massachusetts for day trips and reminds him to take his Glipizide after Jim insists on eating McDonald's despite his life-threatening diabetes. Austin is aware of Jim's sadness, feels that Jim's particular loneliness is among the most tragic of experiences. Yet Austin, seemingly unshaken, can help Jim then continue on with his day in a way I never could.

Sometimes Austin's altruism means shirking other responsibilities or tasks. Overstretching himself. Avoiding a dull work project. Sometimes it means letting strings of people stay on our couch without enough notice or calling me to say things like, "I had a conversation with a Russian woman in the neighborhood. How would you feel about hosting her and her daughter for a few months since they are trying to get into the Cambridge school system?"

There is the initial "what a great, charitable guy" response from others. Then there is the second, deeper question. What does *he* get from all this service?

"I have to feel needed in a relationship," Austin once told me.

Was *I* an Austin rescue mission?

We met and dated during one of the most difficult, vulnerable times of my life. I'd felt drawn toward a career in teaching because I knew from my own experience how transformative education could be, but Teach For America proved all-consuming. I left for work before dawn and returned after dark. Once home, I changed immediately into baggy pajamas before passing out cold. At the end of the weekend, Austin and I went through a ritual I downplayed as "Sunday night blues": heart palpitations, spontaneous bursts of tears, pleas for pep talks. I made perennial, empty threats to leave a job I felt I could never quit without letting down kids who had far more difficult lives than mine. In the classroom, I put on a strong performance. I threw everything I had into my work to earn the trust of my high school students and shared my love for literature as they navigated their way through a broken school system with a less than 50 percent graduation rate. I strived to cultivate a fun-yet-rigorous classroom culture, could point to qualitative and quantitative data showing growth for my students, and passed performance reviews with high praise. I loved and believed in my students, in their incredible potential. But outside the walls of the school, I fell apart, my emotional reservoirs depleted. After calling my students' parents on the commute home to praise a positive development, I envisioned driving off the road into a concrete barrier or watching my blood swirl like a red tornado down a bathtub drain.

Austin would lie with me in my down moments, stroking my hair and listening. He never coddled, a trait I appreciated. He could make me laugh at myself and remain present without becoming bogged down in the spiral with me. Maybe he liked being a source of comfort. Perhaps my predictable behavior made him take me less seriously, see past what I was saying, as he gauged my actions instead.

Maybe I did need him, needed someone. But no one wants to admit they may have been a subconscious rescue mission, a damsel in distress—least of all me.

My mother was a damsel in distress—a genuine victim of real, terrible child abuse, societal failures, and later-life sorrow, but she also brewed drama. Her budding psychotic distortions didn't help. After my dad left, she took on the maximum height and width of our perceived tragedy and made sure the neighborhood understood our desperate circumstances.

"Your dad isn't paying child support," she would tell me, and others, though this wasn't true. Maybe in her mind, it was.

Frozen turkeys appeared on our doorstep during the holidays.

"We don't have enough money for food," Mom would say.

We began picking up our groceries at the Bishops' Storehouse, the church's food pantry. The bags stockpiled in the closets and lasted ages, my mother vastly over-budgeting for our needs. To this day, I cannot smell Honey Nut Cheerios without a gut-punch reminder of the off-brand version from the Bishops' Storehouse I ate for breakfast every morning. I still recoil to think of the shampoo scented like public restroom soap.

"Your dad is stealing from us. I can't afford to get you any new clothes," she would say when I wore my only pair of jeans, tissue-thin with a hole in the faded knee, rolled up in different ways each day to appear as if I had more than one pair of pants in eighth grade.

I internalized this scarcity mindset around money early, a mindset that made sharing with Austin—let alone a drunk Swiss dude—difficult.

For a short stint, I enjoyed this sympathy bestowed on my family. At first, the divorce made us special, and the aftermath made us warriors. Attention felt nice. But the novelty soon faded. I felt sick of answering questions without answers, annoyed by the pitying looks, concerned by the disparity between my mother's and father's stories of what was true. There was never enough money, never enough proof, never enough signs from the universe that we would be okay. I craved stability. At that age, all I wanted was to fit in. I burned with shame, then resentment.

Mom was often on the phone speaking in sharp, hushed tones to some neighbor or friend. She threw me a dirty look if I stared too long. Sometimes, if I didn't move, she locked herself in her bedroom, the sound muffled from under the door.

She must have been afraid, anxiety and suffering and the stress of single motherhood manifesting as criticism, complaints, and unquenchable bitterness. She'd trapped herself within the walls of her stories, all the wrongdoings of others, herself incapable of fault or insight. I have compassion for her now, for how these bricks have stacked up all the higher as her mental health has declined. But back then, all I saw was the cruelty. Challenging her stories of persecution became a swift way to become the enemy. Before long, I began making out the sound of my own name in those cryptic calls.

I pushed open the door of our studio apartment in Thailand and pouted on the queen bed that took up more than half of the room we were renting. The cheerful sunlight filtering in from the window felt offensive.

Maybe I shouldn't have run off like that. That's something my mother would have done. Wasn't it time to advocate for myself, to listen and talk through difficult things? Running away seemed like a violation of the recent marriage reset, both of us reverting to our former roles of "nag" and "ignorer."

I seethed at Austin for getting involved in this tattoo drama when we were living off of savings—*my* savings. But I didn't take off and hide somewhere else in Chiang Mai. I didn't pack my bag. I didn't take this single argument as foundation-shattering the way I might have in the past. Healthy relationships, I was beginning to accept, could weather the occasional spat.

Instead, I waited for him to come home.

Sometimes Austin shocked me with a rare, strong reaction whenever I struck a nerve under the category he called *micromanaging*.

"You sound just like Victoria," Austin could snap, cutting me off mid-sentence. I'd heard all about his former consulting firm manager: perfectionist, critical, icy, demanding. She expected nothing less than pristine, error-free PowerPoints for clients. She wanted Austin to be like her, to attend to the details. Austin was Austin. During his exit interview, she noted that he "has a strong tendency to undercommunicate." His performance review read, "Austin lacks judgment."

Once, we were running late to a friend's graduation when the traffic light turned yellow.

"*Go, go, go,*" Austin said. "You have to be more aggressive if you're going to drive in Boston."

I pressed my foot down and ran the light. Austin clapped and whooped. He'd been after me about my "grandma driving" for months. Then a siren, followed by the flare of reds and blues. I clenched my jaw and pulled over. By the time the officer left, the battery of my car had died. We pushed my Ford Focus off to the side of the road and caught a ride to the graduation, walking in near the end.

Another time, I had to do a month's worth of laundry. It would take hours.

"Don't bother separating the colors," Austin said.

"But they'll bleed."

"No they won't. Who told you that? Mine never do."

Despite over a decade of doing my own laundry, *knowing* the risks of washing reds with whites, blacks with yellows, I threw them all in together. I felt shocked—actually shocked—when I removed them from the washer: my white-collared shirt sported navy splotches from a pair of jeans, my favorite white tank top looked more like the canvas of a pink watercolor.

I called Austin. "But you told me!" He had been so sure, so unwavering in his conviction, not even a trace of uncertainty. And I believed him. I wanted to believe everything.

Austin apologized, but what was the point? *I* had made the mistake. I never forgot the sting, the memory of touching those damp clothes, of holding them up to my face with disbelief, even minor betrayal.

What I had not yet learned was that the first step to cultivating a stronger sense of self—to feeling more like an active agent of my life, less susceptible to the torrent of pressures around me—was to get in touch with my intuition, to believe I *was* capable of keen perception and making good decisions. I expected Austin to listen to me, to take me seriously. Yet I had not learned how to do so for myself. Without that confidence, I failed to validate myself or self-soothe. I outsourced this responsibility to others, like Austin, as another form of dependency, another iteration of an oracle.

"Why do you love me?" I asked Austin, over and over and over. Not for mushy reassurance so much as a compulsive need to dispel my suspicion that he *didn't* know what I was when he picked me up. Maybe what I meant by the question wasn't so much why he loved me, but *how* he could love me, given our differences. Maybe, given the instability in my life, I sought in him a phantom parent I had yet to foster within myself: unconditional love; constancy, even when my inner child threw a tantrum; the stability I paradoxically feared and craved.

Austin listed whatever came to mind, usually referring to something that had happened within the past twenty-four hours.

"Because the tufts of hair by your ears remind me of an owlet."

"Because you're cute, like a beluga whale's forehead."

"Because you have the same phenotype as Colin Farrell."

"Those aren't good reasons," I would say. "Those aren't even flattering."

"Because you're weird."

"Why do you love me?" I asked again, wanting something more substantial, evidence that he had truly thought about this, that I was what he wanted and not just the woman who happened to be around when he felt a crisis about turning thirty. (He'd once told me that if he wasn't married by age thirty, he'd know he'd "been doing something wrong," then call up a good friend—any good friend—and propose.)

"Because you're smart."

"Because you care about and advocate for the marginalized."

"Because I never get tired of spending time with you."

"Because you're the hardest worker I know."

"Because you weren't swayed by my romantic salesmanship and demanded to know the real me," he would say.

These things never added up, never pacified my insatiable worries about our incompatibilities or thirst for assurance. I imagined he might want a more traditional wife, like the dozens and dozens of Mormon women he'd dated for years. But he claimed he grew bored of everyone else within a few months.

"Why do you love me?" I'd ask again.

Austin, exasperated, would finally look at me, really look at me. Though Austin suffers from overconfidence at times, he also had an impeccable sense of intuition. There's a lot to be said for intuition, and part of me craved to cultivate and recognize it for myself.

"There is no why," he said. "I just *do*."

Austin returned an hour later. The door creaked open. There was nowhere to hide in the tiny room. We stared at each other, daring the other to speak first.

"I'm sorry," he said.

I folded my arms. "So you paid it all?"

"The guy was blackout drunk. He could barely say his name." Austin held up a tattered napkin with some scrawl. "I have his email. He said he would pay me back."

"We'll never see that money again. You know that, right?"

We talked it out, a conversation that would be repeated throughout the years: Yes, we had to come to a consensus on money things going forward. No, I shouldn't have assumed the worst. Yes, he needed to listen. No, I shouldn't have run off. Yes, we'd both behave better next time.

To my amazement, the Swiss guy sobered up and wired us the full amount of the debt by the weekend. "Thanks again," the note said. Sometimes, I'm grateful to find out that I'm wrong. But was I wrong? This answer seemed less about whether or not the man paid up. Austin could afford to listen to my boundaries, and I could open my heart to his way of seeing the world—a long, philosophical conversation.

In ways, maybe Austin did help yank me out of some of my darkest places. But maybe I also helped pull him out of the clouds when needed. At times, I might remind him of the Victorias of the world. I might say no, offer a different perspective, keep his idealistic feet on the ground, enforce a budget, remind him of the time, or beg him to arrive earlier to the airport to avoid missing a flight. He could roll his eyes, but a part of him recognized how much he benefited from structure, attention to detail, and *my* judgment. He'd be the first to admit it. Besides, without me, he wouldn't be here in Thailand on this trip at all.

I wonder where the Swiss guy is now, how he lives with that

tattoo, and what version of this story he tells.

CHAPTER 13

The Air I Breathe

A CLUSTER OF SHUTTERED SHOPS greeted us as Austin and I got off the Indonesian ferry. A lone massage parlor advertising foot rubs had its door cracked open, as did a snack stall. A few taxi drivers, absorbed in conversation, sat at empty café tables. Austin and I approached.

"Which resort?" one of them said, standing quickly. "Where are you going?"

"No resort. Is there a public beach nearby?" Austin asked.

Another driver, overhearing our odd request, confirmed there was a public beach.

"Need a ride?"

"How much?"

Resort prices. We hadn't brought enough cash.

"Can we walk?" I asked. "Which direction?"

The drivers exchanged smiles. *Foreigners.* Then they motioned to the right before rejoining the banter.

I couldn't tell you with any confidence what drew Austin and me to visit Batam, Indonesia—a small island a quick ferry ride from Singapore—on our twenty-four-hour layover at the Changi Airport en route to India, our next home base. Perhaps because, by this point, we'd already flown through Singapore twice and done the sightseeing. Perhaps because that sightseeing took a toll on our budget. Perhaps because we weren't feeling particularly pro-Singapore after we'd spent a sleepless night on the tile floor of the airport to avoid paying for a hostel (I'd promised Austin that Changi had earned its reputation as "best airport in the world"), only to find that the movie theater and famed butterfly park were closed, all the famous sleep recliners were taken, and what little shut-eye we managed under the harsh fluorescents with our Peruvian sweaters covering our faces was interrupted by security guards with machine guns who demanded to see our boarding passes. Perhaps Austin and I just wanted to get out of Singapore and see something, anything, in our daze of sleeplessness and interest in seeing another country. Perhaps we didn't need a reason to go at all.

Austin and I walked in the general direction the drivers had suggested. Hoping to find the shore, our arbitrary destination, we trekked through roped-off fields, waded through prickly bushes, and finally stumbled upon the ocean and something like a beach.

An abandoned stick structure held up by stilts teetered on the bank. Austin and I climbed the rickety ladder. Aluminum cans and bottles formed a thick layer on the coastline below. Waves crashed. Humidity glued my hair to my forehead. Austin and I sat side by side in silence on the wooden platform. He pulled out his book, then read as he picked at his peeling sunburn. I unpacked my Kindle, but I couldn't focus on the screen. My eyes scanned the horizon, the crashing dark waves, the moody clouds. We didn't ask each other who built the shelter, who left it, or whose trash was left behind. Instead, we welcomed the quiet, a sound so distinct it made me realize how long I'd gone without feeling still. I cradled my knees in my arms, feeling the salty wind burn my cheeks.

Always the wind. It never left me alone for long. Quiet and liminal spaces brought my past closer to the surface. I'd recently had another dream about my mother. I'd stood in a snowy intersection, waving my arms and screaming for her until my throat burned raw, then watched as she drove away.

My mind reached out to her.

To my surprise, Mom came to my wedding. She was in the Salt Lake Temple waiting room when I arrived, frazzled and late, with my bagged wedding dress slung over my shoulder. Her wavy hair fell to her shoulders, the natural, somewhat wild style she'd kept for as long as I'd known her, though now with strands of gray. She smiled nervously. Did we hug? I can't remember. I stood four inches taller than her, a testament to my father's genes. The rest of me looked too much like her to deny that she was my mother. She wore a coral cardigan over a white blouse—she'd remembered this detail, that my wedding color was coral, though she'd been unwilling, perhaps unable, to talk about anything else related to the event. Despite my efforts to buy her a dress, to help her feel involved, to help her feel safe, she had demurred.

I couldn't have cared less about what she was wearing; I was happy she was there. This gesture of love, the courage to attend despite her paralyzing reclusively and whatever lingering resentment she may have still held against me, said things she wasn't able to.

Mom followed me as I raced to the busy bridal room to change. Fragrant bouquets bound up with ribbon were lined up on a side table. Dozens of couples get married in the historic Salt Lake Temple each day. Of course, this was not just a wedding day for us brides. It was also the day when we would enter into the most sacred covenant of our lives. To be sealed, not just legally married, meant that we were committing not "till death" but for eternity. Any children born into such a marriage would be sealed to us forever. The sealing ordinance binds not just partners but families, children to parents, in an unbroken line, eventually connecting the whole human family. The sealing ordinance, whether performed here or "on the other side," is considered within Latter-day Saint doctrine to be a prerequisite for the highest level of heaven, the celestial kingdom, where God lives. Many people take comfort in the sealing ordinance: true love, forever and ever, bound to family in heaven no matter what tragedies strike in life.

But I wasn't banking on an afterlife. To me, despite having serious doubts about the hereafter, the idea of a sealing invited terror. That terror had little to do with how much I loved Austin. Forever—even the potential of forever—was a long damn time.

I flew into a changing stall, climbed into my silky dress, and flung open the door again in less than thirty seconds. *Late late late* was an easier emotion to grasp than *I'm getting married, I'm getting sealed, and my mom came.*

"Mom, can you help me with this?" I asked, I struggled with the clasp of a pearl necklace Lisa had given me for my sixteenth birthday.

"Sshhhh," said a temple worker with a puff of white hair, reminding us to be reverent.

Oh please, I thought. Mom and I laughed quietly as we stood in front of a mirror. How long had it been since we'd laughed together? If I'd had even a few seconds to pause, I might have felt what this moment meant, perhaps to both of us. The last time my mom had been in this same room was when she was a bride, getting ready to be sealed to my dad with so much hope and promise, doing the very thing she'd prepared all her life to do. She wore a dress with an enormous ruffled train that she and her mother had taken great pains to adorn with hand-sewn plastic pearls. That dress had haunted our living room, folded neatly in the cedar chest my great-grandfather made, until the entire chest disappeared without warning. As a kid, I'd put on the dress with Mom's help. The sleeves billowed on my tiny shoulders and the hem floated around my ankles like tidal pools. Mom had lamented how out of fashion it was, how the fabric was yellowing. Now, there was no dress at all.

Though my parents had divorced, my mom and dad are still technically sealed together according to Latter-day Saint doctrine. It can be extremely difficult and painstaking to get permission to break a temple sealing; it involves interviews and letters to the highest church leadership. Few people attempt it, in part because it would mean breaking the sealing to any children the couple had while married. My mother would never consider breaking her sealing to us. Yet she often made jokes about how awkward it would be to "wake up on the morning of the First Resurrection" next to the man she felt had betrayed her.

Other women, however, do fight for the right to cancel their sealing—with great difficulty and sometimes with little success. Men, however, can remarry in the temple after a divorce or the death of their spouse without breaking their first sealing, although the church legally ended polygamy (on Earth) in 1890.

Not women.

For us, our first shot is pretty much it. This has to be the one.

Just before I peeled away to find Austin, to prevent our guests from waiting too long or to avoid another grumpy temple volunteer's rebuke, my mom handed me a sheer, white bag.

"I brought you this," she said casually. The bag contained ceremonial clothing used in the temple, items I would put on over my dress for the sealing ordinance.

"This was your great-great-grandmother's."

I hadn't known my mom had this family heirloom, and I gave it back to her right after the ceremony. I would like to know to which grandmother it belonged. Unfortunately, my mom no longer remembers and claims to have never had any ceremonial clothes. But I still want to know this grandmother's name. Did she also marry here in this temple, perhaps right after it was built in 1893, three years after the church declared it would discontinue legal polygamy? What had her own wedding day looked like? What did "celestial" marriage mean to her, a term that used to be synonymous with plural marriage? Was it about love, or did she view her marriage as a necessary religious rite of passage, a ticket to heaven to be with everyone she'd ever cared about?

I wonder how this unknown grandmother might feel now, about me, her granddaughter with all the choices in the world, choosing to wear her clothes, choosing to entertain the possibility that through this action I might bind myself to her forever. I also wonder how *I* feel now, about being sealed to Austin while putting on this complicated legacy, weightier than playing dress-up in my mother's 80s wedding gown all those years ago.

My beliefs waver. And yet I *feel* tied to these women of my past. To a wind-fearing child, then chronic wanderer, I take comfort that invisible threads might tether me to something bigger than myself.

My extended family says I inherited my wanderlust from my mother. "She was so independent, always traveling before she got married," they told me at family parties with a twinge of loss, helping me remember a woman I never knew. I recalled my mother's tales of backpacking across Europe, a trip to the British Virgin Islands, a boyfriend in Spain. She looked proud when she told these stories, all from before her marriage.

For all the romance of the road, I also knew my mother ran away from everything. She got in the car and drove off at any whiff of confrontation. There was the day she flew away from the kitchen table when my dad brought up the credit card bills. The day she packed my little suitcase and explained we were going to Grandma and Grandpa's house, only to change her mind when my dad stood in the doorway with a look of total surprise. The day my dad tried to discuss marriage therapy and she fled the house, leaving my dad to tell the kids alone that they were headed for divorce.

I understand the urge to run.

On my first major international trip—a three-month anthropology field study in a remote village in Ghana—I took to writing poems. I hunched under a mosquito net and wrote in a lined notebook illuminated by a flashlight. In one poem, I expressed my reluctance to return to the US. "I can run and run," I wrote. I described my "laurel wanderings" as "poisonous." My wandering itch as "sirens that threaten to steal me away for good." I described myself as a "self the sea of faces knows me as, a girl too young to settle down, too old for these dangerous dreams."

I was twenty. From the beginning of my becoming, I sensed I was doing *something* wrong in traveling, though I knew the "envisioned life" I described in the poem was "not so plotted as my to-do lists." I honestly didn't know if I had the power within me to live that so-called "envisioned life," or what that might look like, even when, from all appearances, it seemed I was doing exactly that.

In Ghana, I wrote another poem that began: "My mother is the wind."

When I wrote that line, I thought I was describing myself as the offspring of some hypothetical, elemental mother. I was restless. I wanted it explained away, like those internet articles that come out every so often with titles like "Research Shows That Wanderlust Is a Gene."

Now, I think of that line in my old field journal differently. *My mother is the wind.* She is. My mother left me with a howl, like the wind whistling through trees during a storm. I look around but cannot see her, an unseen force of devastation.

Except she is everywhere, the air I breathe, the creator of my life. And what is wind if not disturbed or angry air?

From my temple sealing, I remember the beaming faces of family and friends on both sides of the white and gold room as Austin and I made our commitments while kneeling before an altar covered in crocheted lace. I remember my mother—or was it someone else?—getting up to smooth my dress behind me. I remember Austin's coy smile and my own face, reflected back many times, from the two mirrors hanging on opposite walls, two mirrors facing each other to visualize eternity. I remember how handsome he looked, his gentle hand squeeze, that I didn't feel so afraid in that moment. I remember the stranger officiating the sealing giving us the advice in his opening remarks, "Don't yell unless the house is on fire." And though I remember little of what was said, I do remember the miracle that nothing had seriously offended me, a better outcome than a typical Sunday at church.

After, Mom followed me to the bridal room. I can't recall our idle chat as I rushed to put on my crown of wildflowers: white roses, blue bellflowers, and yellow balls of *Craspedia*. The photographer was waiting outside the door. We only had an hour until the conventional ring ceremony a few blocks away. I had planned the wedding myself, and I felt I alone could execute it now. My mom stayed for the pictures and to watch Austin and me exchange rings. She didn't show for the reception. In my harried mind, I retained no memory of my mother before we left the temple. She must have stood there beside me, one of the last times we would be together, side by side, mother and daughter, before psychosis would take more and more of her.

Is it so wrong that I take a secret comfort that I am sealed to her, perhaps the best part of her, even if a temple sealing might be no more than a powerful symbol of love?

I lost track of time. Austin and I stayed on that Batam platform for twenty minutes. Maybe two hours. Eventually, the clouds began to cluster. My arm hair rose. I didn't know what I'd say if anyone in the future asked me if I'd been to Indonesia. Was *this* Indonesia? Yet this scene stayed sharp in my mind. I can still smell the incoming storm, see the way the waves blew this way and that. A piece of myself is left on that shore, something between a beach and a trash heap, a strange wilderness between a fancy resort and the Singapore airport. I find a sense of home in unease. This home does not feel like solace, but it does feel like mine. This was my inheritance. I lived somewhere in the borderland between Utah and as-far-away-as-possible, between loyalty and freedom, roots and wind, faith and doubt, mother and daughter, and now the married and regular-old me. Whoever that was.

"Want to go?" I asked Austin, pushing myself up off the wooden boards, ready to move again, ready to get to the next place. I studied him, this man who believed so much in the power of the temple sealing.

"Sure," Austin said, scanning the last paragraph on his page. He looked up. Our eyes locked. He didn't have to say anything, and neither did I. This belief in me, in us, was and remains one of the sweetest parts of his faith. After so much instability in my life, I appreciated the emotional safety I found in his constancy, his unquestioning devotion to me. It was a gift I hadn't anticipated.

I took his hand in mine. Sometimes I wondered if he really knew who I was—this restless woman he'd chosen—or how much he feared where I might be going. But he never seemed afraid and was always there when it mattered most.

CHAPTER 14

The Color of Doubt

"CAN YOU TELL ME A LITTLE ABOUT HINDU WEDDINGS?" I asked a bridal store manager on my first outing in Bengaluru, formerly known as Bangalore under British occupation. After Thailand (my top choice for a home base), we'd landed on India for Austin. Here, he could intern with a start-up that was building more affordable diagnostic devices for diabetes. Wandering took a toll on him. Now he went off to work every day with a grin, happy to be settled, fulfilled and grateful to have a purpose for being here. I felt eager to work on my marriage research project in our new neighborhood, Koramangala. Hindus—at least in the US—were the only religious group to marry at higher rates than Mormons. I wondered how much we had in common.

The bridal store manager laughed at my question. "In which region?" She was about my age with shoulder-length hair and a nose ring. Her shop sold stunning ensembles lining the walls like a mash-up rainbow.

"Here," I said.

"You have to be more specific. If you go twenty kilometers in any direction, people have totally different customs."

She gave me a whirlwind tour of some of the outfits: elaborate, two-piece *lehenga* gowns; flowing, abaya-style *salwars* with floor-length circle skirts; traditional silk *saris*; enormous, gold-laden *dupatta* shawls to signal modesty. Her nimble fingers ran over the bridal clothes, encouraging me to touch the fabrics and sense the quality of the delicate materials. When I left, I had a greater appreciation for craftsmanship along with a more accurate understanding of how naïve my initial question had been. India, I quickly reminded myself, was massive and diverse. States and regions had distinct and varied traditions, as different as their languages, religious beliefs, foods, and holidays. I would never be able to learn anything about something as broad as "Hindu weddings and marriages."

Changing course, I hunted down a library. Reading more, I imagined, might help refine my questions about marriage in the area, or at least help me learn more about India generally. I found a place called Easy Library Koramangala about a mile away. As I walked, memories from my first trip to India returned with sharp clarity; the smells—jasmine, diesel exhaust, incense, sewage, foods rich with chili spices, the tang of livestock, the acrid scent of carrion; the sights—rickshaws, interspersed temples, traffic following unfathomable rules, rubbish heaps, an occasional mall, marigolds, ruptured sidewalks, stunning fluorescent tunics, paper-thin *dosas* so long they hung off the tin plates at *dhaba* stalls. There was no place in the world like India.

When I entered the three-room library, a woman with sharp eyebrows looked up from her novel without speaking and then continued reading at the front desk. Her black braid hung over her strong, bare shoulder draped with a red shawl. She had a gravity. Though she had never met an American, she didn't say so. The only Westerner who'd come through her library had complained about how dirty Bengaluru was before taking three expensive books he never bothered to return. No Indian had ever done that. Starting a library had been her dream—a high-risk endeavor she began after quitting a grinding engineering job at IBM. But the new library hemorrhaged money. Business was not steady. So she had two minds about whether or not to let another foreigner have a membership.

None the wiser, I browsed the shelves. India didn't have free public libraries. This was no university library, but a couple thousand well-loved books lined the shelves. An enormous section was dedicated to Indian writers. This sold me. After snagging a few on Hindu mythology that caught my attention, I decided to sign up for a month-to-month paid membership.

"You don't have a phone number?" The woman said, reluctant to sign the membership card. Her voice was quiet but firm.

"I don't."

She paused. The library needed more members. I assured her I'd return the books.

"Hope to see you again soon," she said.

When I returned, the librarian had recommendations. She introduced herself as Chaitra, a name that means "beginning."

"Try *Five Point Someone* by Chetan Bhagat," she said, passing me a worn copy. "Indians love this one." I took it home and devoured it within two days.

On my next visit, Chaitra's good-natured husband, Krishna, sat in a chair beside the desk, balancing a laptop on his knees. He had his own start-up company, a public transportation tracker.

"My husband is also an entrepreneur," I said, telling them about Austin's internship and his research on disruptive medtech innovations in resource-constrained environments. In my head, I could hear Austin's infectious enthusiasm. *Can you believe the Narayana*

Health Hospital can perform open-heart surgery for $2,500? One surgeon can do up to fifty a day. This could change the world.

I told them how I'd made traveling around the world with me a condition of our marriage and a bit about my project. "Do you have *India in Love* by Ira Trivedi?" I asked, referring to a recently published work of nonfiction on the drastic changes love culture had wrought upon India over the past decade.

Chaitra checked her spreadsheets. No luck, but she said she'd find a copy. I hovered in front of the desk for a while, hoping to linger, talk a little longer.

"Holi is coming up," I said, grasping for something between us. "I celebrated it sometimes in the US. There was a Hare Krishna temple near my university. But I was wondering if you could tell me more about Holi from your perspectives."

Chaitra and Krishna exchanged a look. Maybe they recognized my genuine interest, whatever vibe I gave off that helped strangers feel comfortable asking me to take their picture or emboldened them to share their life stories with me on public transportation.

Or maybe it was just dumb luck.

Krishna closed his laptop.

"Sit down," Chaitra said, gesturing to a chair.

I went to the library regularly, and Chaitra and I became quick friends. Her ambition inspired me. When we weren't at Chaitra's flat, I volunteered at the front desk, shelved and logged new book purchases, or ran Saturday workshops on writing for children. She and Krishna had twins, a pair of energetic three-year-old sons. The boys ran around and squealed, showing me illustrated encyclopedias about insects and astronauts. Chaitra had her sons on the waitlists for all the best preschools. She wanted them to learn to read, and fast. Chaitra was one of the most well-read people I'd ever known, putting my English-major friends to shame.

Amid library work, we brainstormed business plans to attract more customers. Flyers. An ad in the newspaper. A discount marketing strategy. I could write an op-ed on the importance of libraries. Chaitra and I spent afternoons shopping for secondhand books and discarded magazines like *National Geographic* at a local market to stock the children's section. She had a gentle voice, but I'd never seen such a fierce haggler. I was as curious about her life as she was about mine. Other than the library, Chaitra told me she had four life goals: to learn to drive, to swim, to ride horseback, and to rollerblade.

Chaitra had an arranged marriage when she was twenty-two. Her parents told her to "think of [her] younger sister," as it is typical for older siblings to marry before the younger ones can be courted. Fortunately, she and Krishna had a good relationship.

Whenever I talked to Chaitra about my interest in marriage ceremonies around the world, she brought up her own. Sometimes she struggled to translate the specifics from her native Kannada into English. The ceremony had been performed in Sanskrit. More often, however, she forgot the words outright. The details, the countless details. There was *a lot* to remember.

"We should go to the temple," Chaitra suggested one day as we cataloged a few musty boxes of donated books. "A priest would know."

We went on a Tuesday, the day the library was closed. Outside the temple, Chaitra wore a stunning pink *salwar kameez*—billowy pants under a long tunic. She purchased some jasmine flowers, then touched a stone representing the feet of the god. When Chaitra and I entered, we removed our shoes and stood in front of a statue of Hanuman. Bright bells rang. The tile felt cold on my bare feet, and the room smelled of rice and incense. Chaitra placed her hands together and circumnavigated the god three times. I followed, curious, trying to show respect. A Brahmin priest wearing a traditional white robe with red and orange trim draped over one shoulder blessed a few people. We waited, then stepped forward.

The priest conducted an elaborate prayer, or *puja*. I watched Chaitra closely, trying to mirror her actions to minimize any offense caused by my ignorance. How beautiful and graceful she looked. She gave the fresh jasmine to the priest. He held a candle on a tray. Chaitra waved her palms to the flame, fanning them toward her, the smoke engulfing her face. The priest placed a silver bowl on our heads, then poured a little liquid made of milk, honey, ghee, and other substances from earlier offerings—called the *tirtha*—into our cupped hands, which we then threw overhead. Last, the priest pressed a dot of vermillion, water, and ghee mixture to our foreheads. He gave us each a jasmine flower, a tangible sign of the god's blessing. Chaitra tucked the white flower into her long braid. I did the same.

Now we could begin.

We sat with legs crossed on the floor. Chaitra, my expert translator, explained my interest in learning about Hindu wedding ceremonies in the Kannada-speaking region. The priest nodded with enthusiasm, surveyed me with dark eyes, then proceeded to explain the steps to marriage.

First and foremost, according to the Vedic tradition, people consult horoscopes to ensure compatibility. The horoscope weighs thirty-six *gunas*, a complex Sanskrit word difficult to translate into English that contains three "tendencies": *sattva* relates to traits such as balance, positivity, and virtue; *rajas* refers to passion, ambition, and ego; *tamas* encompasses imbalance, anxiety, and negativity. Many websites can read this horoscope for free as long as you have the exact time and place of birth for each person. According to the priest, this astrological test requires the couple to match on at least twenty of the thirty-six points. If the horoscope finds compatibility, courting begins.

A male suitor accompanies his parents to a prospective girl's home to meet the young woman and her family. Chaitra said they say "girl" instead of "woman" because children are referred to as boys or girls before marriage, which is the transition into adulthood. After the visit, the boy and his parents decide whether or not they want to propose marriage. "The process is quite painful," Chaitra told me. "Some girls have to see hundreds of suitors before a match is made." Luckily for Chaitra, she met her husband on the second try. If a match is decided, both sets of parents consult a Brahmin priest to set the Lagna, the ideal marriage time. Traditionally, couples could not see each other before the wedding. Of course, as Chaitra pointed out, "now, it never works how it did fifty years ago." There is usually a chance to get to know the fiancé before the wedding and the engagement ceremony. Once Chaitra's match was determined, she and Krishna dated until they were married a year later.

A week before the wedding, an additional initiation happens in their respective homes. During the initiation, each officially takes on their new status as bride (*vadhu*) or bridegroom (*vara*).

Finally, the wedding day.

The day begins with many pujas. The priest and Chaitra emphasized that in a Hindu wedding ceremony, the couple takes on the roles of two married deities: the goddess Lakshmi and the god Venkateshwara. "Except in the case of a Brahmin couple, who take on the roles of Rama and Sita instead," said Chaitra. Throughout the wedding ceremony, the couple will, in a sense, act out the wedding of these gods.

The Sanskrit wedding ceremony takes about two hours. At first, the couple stays in different rooms. The bride does pujas with other women. For some castes, the groom goes through a threading ceremony, reciting the Gayatri Mantra from the Vedas, showing initiation as a brahmachari, symbolizing the end of boyhood. The man is expected to wear this thread under his clothes—around his shoulder and torso—for the rest of his life. This prepares him for what comes next: the Kashi Yatra, which translates as "pilgrimage place."

"During this part of the ceremony, the groom gets up and pretends to walk away, saying he has mastered the four Vedas and six Shadangs," Chaitra translated.

Had I heard that right?

"Wait, what?" I stopped to clarify. "Someone tries to run away, mid-ceremony?" But I had understood correctly. An official part of the ritual is the groom resisting the call of marriage in favor of another, more alluring path. The groom pretends he wants to acquire more knowledge, power, and wisdom in the sacred city of Varanasi. Embedded in the ceremony is the acknowledgment of doubt, a re-examining of choice.

Granted, the Kannada wedding ceremony was gendered and ritualized, a kind of performance. That fact could not and should not be dismissed. But how different this felt from the brazen certainty and unwavering posture I felt I had to assume when I entered into marriage.

I cringe remembering the first time I announced my engagement to anyone outside of close friends and family. The silver ring with a blue topaz stone felt unnatural on my left hand as I sat near the back of a Boston University classroom. Jewelry had never really been my thing. I didn't get my ears pierced until age twenty-one, and when I did, it was more a haphazard attempt to achieve that ever-elusive "personal style." The thinnest necklaces felt confining. Bracelets rattled throughout the day and left weird welts on my wrists. Rings were likely to get lost, then missed.

My engagement ring, the one I'd taken great effort to pick out myself—careful not to exceed our budget of $150—felt loose on my finger, a half size too big. I preferred too big over too tight, something I could slip off. I'd had a happy weekend with Austin, celebrating with close friends after the romantic proposal at Walden Pond (Austin had known that was among my favorite places), but things felt scarier now. The theoretical was turning real. A part of me felt the irrational need to justify my choice—to get hitched quickly so we could travel as soon as possible—before an invisible jury.

In the cramped desk, listening to the professor talk about literacy strategies, I spun the band with my thumb. *You have to tell them. Shouldn't you have already told them, right when you walked in?* I anticipated what my peers in the class would think or say—the Teach For America cohort I'd been with for two years. They were my friends, weren't they? But most came from liberal, coastal cities, and I imagined them to be very cool, very sophisticated, very kind to put up with me and my Shirley Temple at the bar. Few of the two hundred were married.

Twenty-four is too young to get engaged, I could envision them saying.

And none, I assumed, had heard of a four-month engagement. *Shotgun wedding.*

"What are your plans after Teach For America?" the professor asked before class ended a little early. We snaked around the room. I don't remember what anyone said before me, just the hammering in my chest. *This was my choice*, I told myself. *I'm not some child bride. I'm ready, even old by Utah standards.*

My turn came.

"I'm getting married," I said, trying to sound confident and totally normal. But what was normal? I didn't know, but I desperately wanted to be it.

"OH MY GOD, YOU'RE GETTING MARRIED!?"

"WHEN!?"

"SHOW US YOUR RING!"

"ARE YOU EXCITED?"

The frozen smiles of surprise when I named a date.

With each wave of exaggerated shrieks, I reddened and shrank into my seat. They meant well. They were showing over-the-top support in the way we have all been conditioned in the cult of certainty. What I was choosing to do felt hard to articulate. I didn't know how to perform my part. Instead, I internalized the nervousness they mirrored back, mistaking my awkwardness for a lack of enthusiasm. The uh-oh look. My inability to enact engagement giddiness led me to worry that maybe something was wrong with me. Or my relationship.

I couldn't get out of that classroom fast enough.

I didn't know how to talk meaningfully, honestly, about what marriage meant or who to talk about it with. My templated love stories of passion—the oversimplification of Jane Austen's novels, the "I knew by the end of our first date" accounts over the church pulpit, the dazzling rom-coms—were damningly incomplete for me. Why was questioning romance such a taboo? Some folks harbor no doubts when it comes to marrying their partner; I was not one of them. I spent far too long envying those lucky people. But what other serious, long-term, possibly forever commitment could I make and *not* have the space to voice sincere questions?

I might have had a more honest conversation about whether or not to wear my favorite color, yellow, every day for the rest of my life than about deciding who to spend the rest of my life with.

I know you love that color, but are you sure?

I mean, as sure as I can be right now.

Why yellow?

Yellow is a good color: so warm, so bright.
I really do love yellow.

But there are so many other colors out there.

I know. But I think I could be really happy with yellow.

It won't match everything. You'll cut yourself
off from other opportunities.

True. But there may be something beautiful
and grounding about commitment.

Isn't yellow risky?

Uh, yeah.

How do you feel?

Afraid. But aren't I always? What is fear
keeping me from enjoying?

I support your decision. If you ever
want to talk, I'm here. Things can change.

Thank you. I know they do. I know I will too.

I scribbled away in my notebook as Chaitra and the priest continued to explain the Kashi Yatra. This chapter of the ceremony ends when the father of the bride goes after the groom and says, "Why are you going alone? Take my daughter with you on the journey of life." The father offers gifts, usually silver items, then washes the groom's feet as a sign of respect. He asks the bridegroom to come back and marry his daughter. The groom dresses up, puts on eyeliner, and looks into a mirror to admire his reflection. At the end, the bride's brother will open an umbrella, pouring out flowers to welcome the groom back. All is forgiven.

The couple gets into the same room. When the white cloth called the *anthrapatam* is pulled away, the couple can see each other for the first time. The bride and groom place a mixture of cumin and jaggery on top of each other's heads. Cumin is bitter, jaggery sweet. When mixed into a paste, they represent the bitterness and sweetness the couple will face. Chaitra said this has turned into a kind of race to see who can place the goop first. The couple holds the mixture in place on the other person while those present bless the couple.

The pinnacle moment comes during the Mangalya Puja. A white thread, dyed yellow from turmeric, is placed on top of a coconut, jaggery, and betel leaf, then taken around the room for people to touch the thread, giving their permission for the couple to marry. All must consent. This step is as critical to Hindu weddings as the ring exchange is to Western traditions. Once this step is over, the yellow thread is placed around the couple's necks and tied three times. The bride is expected to wear the yellow thread for the rest of her life, although it is often replaced by a gold necklace.

The knots are tied. The groom gently applies *kumkum* to the bride's forehead and the central part of her hair. The bride receives toe rings and they exchange garlands. This shows they are now married: husband and wife.

After an hour of describing the ceremony and the postfestivities, the conversation between the three of us quieted. My back ached from sitting in an unfamiliar position for so long.

"Is that all?" I joked, then thanked them both.

"I told you it was a lot," Chaitra said. She smiled and said something in Kannada to the priest. "There is more, so much more."

But not enough hours in a day, in a life, I imagined, for an outsider to understand. I was grateful for their effort. The complexity was precisely what fascinated me. Weddings, especially religious weddings, transmit cultural messages and symbols from ages ago. They are canonized into tradition, then passed on. Examining these ceremonies helps us better understand the legacy we inherit. This is the case for any culture. Look no further than a standard Christian wedding in the US. If you don't believe me, research the origins of the garter toss from the Dark Ages—creepy people ripping at the bride's clothes.

The next time I went to the library, Chaitra and I sat in front of her whirring laptop. Purple half-circles hung under her eyes. One of her sons had spent the night throwing up. Krishna's start-up was giving him a headache. There hadn't been a library customer all day. So we watched YouTube videos of Kannada weddings. She wanted to show me what the priest had been talking about. Chaitra pointed out the symbolism, and I nodded with recognition. In return, I played her the video from my own wedding. "Sorry for all the kissing," I warned.

"You look like an elf or an angel," she swooned.

I squirmed, never one to take a compliment well, then tried to explain what the temple towering in the background meant in my own culture: the significance of ordinances like the sealing, how this building was supposed to be the house of the Lord, a place to go and ask questions and receive answers. She didn't need me to explain the ring ceremony stuff. She was already fluent in all that.

We spent at least an hour gushing over more online wedding videos. Why? These videos were edited, angled, cropped, curated. We both knew that. What was it about weddings that remained universally intriguing, despite all the problems?

"Do you think marriage is hard?" I asked. I thought about Austin, thriving in Bengaluru, already talking about returning home to Boston and resuming his MBA with a newfound focus on commercializing healthcare technology. He felt ready now, filled with a passion he hadn't felt before. Returning home had always been part of the deal. The thought kicked up the familiar fear. Who would I be at home? What did being married mean for me there?

Chaitra sank back into the chair. "Go ask someone else," she laughed.

"But I want to know what *you* think. What makes this so hard?"

"Many things. Getting to know the person, figuring out who he is inside and out. The family dynamic. Adjusting to all his quirks."

I told her about Carol Ann's "cute to killer" theory and Austin's bad habit of crinkling book pages before bed, how something I used to love had soured. She understood immediately. Krishna was a morning person.

As we commiserated, Chaitra grew more serious. "Not sharing responsibilities, not enough compatibility, dowry issues, infidelity—these are all major challenges."

I wanted to know what she thought a good marriage looked like. I told her I hadn't seen many great ones.

"First, the children are happy," she said firmly. "Your family and friends are happy with it. It's also good to spend at least an hour together a day."

For a moment I thought of Austin, how much I genuinely enjoyed spending almost every waking hour together in a tiny, one-room apartment. Having more independence in India was good for both of us, but the thought of having just an hour a day with him in a future routine at home made me sad.

"What words of wisdom would you give someone like me in their first year of marriage?"

Her face scrunched. I was hitting her with hard questions. The laptop's tired fan whined in the background.

"When people are newlyweds, people tend to be too involved with themselves, like it is only the two of them."

Guilty.

"Things will slowly fall into place as you remember your other responsibilities. Remember that a good night of sleep can help with frustrations."

"That is the opposite of the 'never go to bed angry' advice everyone gave me," I said. Sleep helped things fall into perspective.

Compatibility makes the biggest difference, we agreed. We talked a bit about chemistry and the horoscopes that helped Indians make these difficult decisions.

"Krishna and I matched on thirty-three out of the thirty-six points on the astrological test," Chaitra said with pride, referring to the Vedic reading mentioned at the temple.

My jaw fell open. So many points. "Is that common?" How incredible, I marveled, to have such a strong external signal from the universe. And from all accounts of her marriage, they seemed to be a great fit. Perhaps these things are easier to judge, or misjudge, from a distance. Why do we try? Part of me still felt the hole, the bit of me that had never received a personal confirmation, a conviction of the rightness of my own decision. I hadn't mastered the vetted Mormon process: date someone, pray about whether or not they were the right one, go to the temple, receive an inspired answer. When was the last time I'd felt the comfort of an answer? When I asked Austin if he'd prayed about the two of us, he had his own response: "I think God lets us choose," he'd said. "I felt good about you. I knew we'd have a lot of challenges, but any time I thought about ending our relationship, I was flooded with emptiness. That was my answer."

"Can I find out my compatibility with Austin?" I asked.

Chaitra grinned, and we returned to the computer.

"Do you know the exact time you were born?"

"No."

Her eyes widened. "Guessing will not produce accurate results." How could I not know? From Chaitra's context, the idea must have seemed absurd, like not knowing my birthday or middle name.

But our curiosity won out. We entered a guess, a random morning time, then punched in the longitude and latitude coordinates for the respective places where Austin and I were born. We submitted the information and waited. I held my breath.

ERROR.

We refreshed the page and tried again. The screen flashed the same result.

"Maybe you have to be Indian . . ." Chaitra said.

I swallowed the minor disappointment. I thought I'd stopped oracle seeking, yet here I was, fishing in someone else's culture when the signs from my own failed to satisfy. Another point of external assurance had escaped me. After six months of navigating marriage and making it my own, I was still a little captivated by the alluring, comforting lie of certainty.

But certainty didn't exist, contrary to some of the religious frameworks I'd been taught. True faith meant exercising trust in something unseen, hoped for, believed in, felt, but something ultimately unknowable.

CHAPTER 15

Ugadi

FIRECRACKERS EXPLODED ALL OVER TOWN on my walk to Chaitra's apartment to celebrate Ugadi, the New Year for the southern states of Andhra Pradesh and Karnataka. Austin, held up in a work meeting, planned to join me there. Along the way, kids watched as women bent at their doorsteps with chalk to paint *rangoli*, dust patterns of geometric diamonds or flowers, on the sidewalks.

When I arrived at Chaitra's apartment, I hardly recognized the place: a white rangoli lotus covered the entryway. Red flowers lined the doorframe. Chaitra answered, and a wave of noise escaped. Her eyes shone with joy. "Happy Ugadi," she said, wearing her thick hair down and a breathtaking blush sari trimmed with pale yellow. She and her family had been up decorating since four in the morning. I greeted Krishna, Chaitra's in-laws who lived with them, an aunt and uncle, and Chaitra's two sons, who chased each other around the living room with glee. They only paused to watch the occasional snippet of a cartoon on the television.

"First, we will do a puja," Chaitra explained. The group gathered around a corner of the house with an altar featuring icons of Hindu gods. Rosebuds balanced atop the picture frames. A split coconut with dabs of vermillion sat at the center, cut open, the white flesh facing us. A banana, grapes, and flowers were laid out on a betel leaf surrounded by candles.

Chaitra led us through a series of rituals featuring sacred elements: kumkum, turmeric, *vibhuti*, and *gandha*. She placed a dot of red kumkum on Krishna's forehead, the head of the household, then all the adults did a quick puja. Next, Chaitra served everyone a dark liquid that had "all six tastes," representing the mix of experiences we would have in the new year.

A new year in most cultures offers a chance to pause, reflect, and give thanks. How different my life was from a year earlier: waking up long before the cold dawn to commute to a relentless teaching job, juggling graduate school night classes, turning down most invitations for fun to save money for this trip, managing (but not well) constant anxiety about my upcoming marriage without consciously knowing what, precisely, I was afraid of.

Though travel offers no lasting cure for everyday or big-picture stresses (there is no escape from ourselves), those memories felt far away, ages ago. It was as if someone had pulled a curtain and let the light in, cracking open my capacity to be present and feel joy, to feel gratitude like a warm morning sun seeping in through the window. And I had much to feel grateful for. Despite our nomadic lifestyle, I was beginning to feel more grounded—with myself and in my relationship. Austin seemed to be growing, too, healing from burnout and recovering his lost sense of direction. Our "break from reality," as many called our trip, gave him the space and needed perspective to decide what *he* wanted to do. His independent research and India internship ultimately inspired him to launch a medtech career to help make health care more affordable and accessible. Our time abroad, and the chance for me to synthesize my notes, was also nudging me a little closer to a dream of my own: writing.

Along the way, we'd made friends. Since the onset of our trip, we'd met people with different backgrounds and refreshing views. In India alone, we'd met many characters who reminded me of the value of community.

One of those news friends was Jay, short for Jayanti, owner of The Book Stop, which sold Western and Indian titles. If I had to guess (which would be dangerous with her), I'd place her in her mid-forties. Jay wielded strong opinions, a pixie cut, and hawk eyes framed with purple librarian glasses. Raised Catholic, she often gazed at the Hindu temple in front of her shop, able to gossip about who was and was not going to the temple, signaling for friends to go pick up free, tasty *ladoos* for her on festival days. Jay was sharp, witty, and would throw her head back and cackle anytime I asked a stupid question, which was often. I relished The Book Shop's air-conditioning while I scanned the spines—some familiar, most not, abundant reminders of India's vibrant literary tradition and rich canon with oral stories dating back to before 1500 CE. As much as I loved the store, the smell of paper and floor cleaner, mostly I went to talk with Jay and see her loyal companion, an old pug named Rosie.

And we were probably destined to meet Maithili and Ashish. Ashish found Austin online through Austin's blog about healthcare research. They were a couple our age who'd met in dental school and shared many of our interests: Ashish was a savvy guy transitioning to business school and Maithili was a book-obsessed artist working in illustration. Maithili created a calligraphy print of the word *Bengaluru* in Kannada as a gift for us on our second meeting. They introduced us to Blossom Book House, cute cupcake stalls, McDonald's spice-dusted *piri piri* fries, and Goan seafood cuisine. Though Maithili was a vegetarian, she'd grown up in Goa, where the fish was so delicious that her family turned a blind eye to seafood, considering it "the fruit of the sea." Maithili also taught me how to fearlessly cross the busy roads in Bengaluru, like Moses parting the Red Sea by holding out the "hand of God" the way her father had taught her—walking at a steady pace, palm outward, with a confident stiff-arm.

Alok and Radha, a family living in a region of Bengaluru called Whitefield, were relatives of one of my Teach For America friends. They invited us to dinner a few times at their lovely house on the edge of the city with a sprawling garden and offered a place to "play" Holi (though it wasn't a big celebration in Bengaluru like it was in the North). Alok and Radha also introduced us to Indians who'd moved from all over the country to work in the city. They often discussed women's equality, religion, high-level politics, and the lingering effects of colonization over drinks and veg appetizers. They were the first folks I'd met who openly resented Gandhi for not taking a stronger stance against the partition of India. A Sikh friend of theirs named Vic, after drinking eight beers, told us about a time he yelled at a hippie British tourist walking down the street who said, "I love this country," to which Vic scowled and responded, "What's new? A Brit loving India. Go home, go chill. Haven't you had enough?" Vic gave Austin and me a judgment-free pass we probably didn't deserve because a) I had been to Amritsar, the location of the Sikhs' Golden Temple, and b) we were not British. Vic's wife, Nas, asked me thoughtful questions about my project. "My marriage has changed a lot over the years," she said, not minding Vic overhearing her. "Sometimes it feels like an arranged marriage. I don't recognize my husband with how much he's changed."

All these people reminded me of the need for others, that sustaining outside friendships could enrich a marriage. Soon, this budding community would help me remember my own community back home.

At Chaitra's, I lapped up the strange liquid containing all six spices out of my right hand like I had seen others do at the temple. I tried not to recoil at the sharp juxtaposition of flavors. Chaitra looked proud. "You know what to do."

Austin joined us after the puja, falling into conversation with Krishna. We feasted on heaps of Chaitra's mouth-watering chicken biryani and endured her insistence that we eat four times what we normally would. Afterward, Chaitra took me to her closet to show off the sari collection she'd been telling me about. They were as vibrant and elaborate as she'd described—metallic-trimmed silks dyed red, cyan, charcoal, aquamarine, tangerine-orange, fuchsia, periwinkle, and lemon-yellow, one after another after another. She then pulled out her old *veena*, a traditional stringed instrument made of jackfruit wood with a golden scroll, that she used to enjoy before being swept up in exams and a rigorous science career. She'd always been drawn to the humanities.

"Can you play a song for me?" I asked.

"No," she said, half-laughing, as she stared down at the strings.

"Are you sure?"

"Yes."

"Can I at least take your picture with it?" The instrument was so beautiful, as was Chaitra, the day, everything, and I wanted to keep this moment forever. I did not want it to go the way of the rangoli sidewalk art, chalk subject to the wear of time, born to be ephemeral, though everything is ephemeral in the end.

She demurred, then relented, allowing me to take a photograph.

"Do you want to visit my mother with me tonight?" Chaitra asked.

She probably already knew my answer.

Chaitra's mom, a tiny woman with kind eyes, lived only a few blocks away in the same home Chaitra had grown up in, a one-story house with a carved door featuring the mother goddess, Cauvery. Continuing the festivities from the day, her mom applied kumkum to our foreheads and presented us with *tambula*, a banana, and an orange that were used in the puja earlier. If she was baffled or somewhat surprised at seeing a Westerner in her living room, Chaitra's mother didn't show it. Chaitra knelt, said a blessing, then touched her mother's feet. I'd never seen anything like this intimate gesture before, and the respect moved me.

Her mother said something in Kannada.

"Sit down," Chaitra translated.

We took a small couch and her mother perched on an adjacent chair. My bare toes felt cold on the shiny tile. After the two of them spoke for a few minutes in their native language, Chaitra's mother brought out a calendar, or *panchāngam*.

"It's the new Indian calendar for the year," Chaitra said, handing it over. The humongous book felt like a brick in my lap. The panchāngam is so complex that not even Chaitra can read it. "Too many numbers and references," she said.

But her mother could.

Chaitra and her mom passed the calendar between each other, discussing in Kannada what the book revealed about their upcoming years.

Chaitra looked at me, then said something to her mother.

"What?" I asked.

"She's going to look yours up."

I remained curious but skeptical given my latest failure with star reading. "Astrology doesn't work for me here, remember?"

"She can identify your star in the panchāngam using your name." From there, they could determine if it would be a "good year or a bad year" for me. Chaitra's mother thumbed through the enormous book. She and Chaitra spoke back and forth, Chaitra translating:

"Your star is the Swati Nakshatra," Chaitra said. "Second *pada*." My stones were diamond and blue sapphire, my lucky numbers 6, 9, 15, 18, 24, and 27. "Your good direction is northeast, Eshan."

I nodded, trying to absorb what they were saying.

"She is determining your fortune," Chaitra said. Then, the two of them erupted into giggles.

"What?" I moaned.

"The first line says that for your work to get done, you will travel a lot." Now it was my turn to join in the laughter. If I didn't trust them, I'd assume they were making things up for our mutual amusement. Her mother resumed the reading. "You will have a lot of expenditures this year, but you'll succeed halfway through the year. You will have help from family and friends, and a lot of good will happen to your relationships."

I couldn't argue with that one. Maybe some oracles still brought comfort. Maybe that was sometimes okay.

Years later, I researched the significance of Swati Nakshatra, otherwise known as Arcturus in the West. I was surprised. I knew Arcturus well, one of the brightest stars in the sky. I'd memorized its location in Boötes in my college astronomy course, easy to find off the handle of the Big Dipper.

Swati, translated as "independent one," represented balance and harmony, adherence to ideals, an ability to let go, and a thirst for freedom. People connected to this star were said to be sensitive, curious, creative, gentle, perceptive, spiritual, and truth-seekers. They were also said to be critical.

Apparently, Swatis "enjoy travel," yet it was also listed as an "unfavorable" activity. A perfect contradiction. But that wasn't what bowled me over.

The symbol of Swati is of a young sprout quivering in the breeze. This constellation is ruled by Vayu.

The god of the wind.

CHAPTER 16

An Invitation

AFTER BEING MARRIED FOR SEVEN MONTHS, Austin and I decided to celebrate. Why not? Six months may have been the more obvious benchmark, but we'd forgotten and the date slipped by. So seven it was, a number symbolizing completeness in several world religions, including Hinduism: there are seven days in the week, seven continents, seven oceans, seven colors in the rainbow, seven notes in an octave, and, according to some Hindu marriage ceremonies, seven sacred steps taken by the bride and groom in front of a holy fire as part of the Saptapadi ritual, a gesture symbolizing their unwavering commitment to walk the path of life together.

Or maybe seven remained perfectly arbitrary, mundane, a random moment to stop and reflect on time's rapid unfolding. Austin and I splurged on an Italian restaurant. We couldn't remember the last time we'd had noodles or tomato sauce. The nostalgia paved a road to minor disappointment: it was impossible to rival Indian food in India.

Another thing we couldn't remember: the last time we'd had a big argument.

We smeared crumbly sandwich bread through a yin and yang puddle of oil and vinegar.

"I think things are going pretty well," I said, relieved by my authentic positivity.

"Really well," Austin agreed. Bengaluru proved generative for both of us—for our work, our friendships, and our relationship. In a short period, we'd formed a sense of community. We'd even been invited to a wedding by Jasmi, a woman we barely knew from church, who had graciously included us in her massive guest list. Jasmi and her fiancé were Mormon and intended to get sealed in the nearest temple, in Hong Kong, as soon as they could arrange for passports. For now, they planned a local wedding with a fusion of Latter-day Saint and Hindu customs.

Austin and I split our mediocre pasta dishes and got swept up in conversation. Though we still bickered, we faced each other with more honesty, more openness, perhaps a little less fear. On some level, I was beginning to trust—actually trust—that I had a foundation in this relationship, something strong enough to hold the weight of our mistakes and blowouts and miscommunications and differences.

We both committed, again, to keep listening.

Back at the apartment, I received a message I had been anticipating, though not for a while longer.

"Nate and I are engaged!" wrote Jane, the same friend who'd supported me through my engagement and wedding. We'd traveled miles and miles in a crowded van without doors in Ghana, pored over our anthropology homework until closing hours at the BYU library, and learned to rock climb together. I had met Nate over a quick lunch before leaving the country, and I'd never seen Jane look at anyone the way she looked at Nate, the way she held his hand across the table and laughed so hard she snorted. Jane and I had helped each other scale out of the depths of heartbreaks throughout college. This relationship felt different to her, and it showed. Her happiness warmed me to the bones.

Then, in her message, she included her wedding date. It was just a few months out, typical for Mormons but sooner than I'd expected.

"They're getting married at the end of May," I said, deadpan, flopping facedown onto the bed.

"Where?" asked Austin.

"Utah."

We weren't planning to return until summer. Attending Jane's wedding would mean cutting our one-year trip short by a few months. Meanwhile, our savings slipped through our fingers with each passing week despite aggressive budgeting. We'd looked into WWOOF, an organization where lodgers exchange volunteer farm labor for free accommodation, and other creative ways to support ourselves in Europe. We didn't have the funds to fly to the wedding and then fly back to Europe to finish our trip.

"You don't have to go. I'm sure she would understand," Austin said.

She would, but that wasn't the point. Something pulled at me. There were about six, maybe seven people in the world whose weddings I'd fly across the globe for. And damn it, Jane was one of them.

"Don't you remember how much it meant to us who came to our wedding?" I asked.

"Yeah. But things happen. We're on the other side of the planet."

"But this is *Jane*." I stopped myself before saying, *I wouldn't miss it for the world.*

"We could go home early . . ." Austin suggested with caution. "A summer job might help me earn some money before starting school in the fall." Lately, he'd been describing a desire to "establish roots, build something."

A long pause. I didn't want him to be right. "I'll think about it."

On the day of Jasmi's wedding, I went to see Jay at The Book Stop to find a gift and gather advice on basic wedding etiquette. I found her talking with her pug, Rosie, an empress on a leopard-print pillow as she drooled onto the tile. Jay cooed and used a towel to wipe away the slobber traced with blood.

"Rosie has a cancerous tumor in her mouth," Jay said. "They told me to put her to sleep." She rolled her eyes. "I'm going to do everything to make her last days as comfortable as possible."

I looked at the dog with pity, her little tongue sticking out. "I'm so sorry."

Jay said nothing more as she pampered Rosie. Eventually, I told her about Jasmi's wedding.

"What are you going to wear?" Jay asked without hesitation. Some questions seemed universal.

"What about this?" I pointed to what I was already wearing, a salmon-colored salwar I had custom-made when I first came to India. "It's the nicest thing I have."

Jay eyed me with scrutiny. "This one is looking very old." I could always count on Jay to tell me the truth.

She talked me through other options. I had a long cotton dress with a floral pattern I'd haggled for in Thailand, but I had no formal clothes to speak of. That dress would have to do. I regretted not purchasing one of the thousands of silk saris Chaitra had shown me at the market: "This would look nice on you, don't you think? With some gold?"

"What do I bring for a gift?"

"Cash is good," she said, handing me an envelope from a shelf near the register. "Maybe 1,001 rupees. You always have to add one to make it auspicious."

Jasmi held her wedding reception at the enormous Latter-day Saint chapel in Whitefield, the largest church building this Utah girl had ever seen. Hundreds gathered and sat in rows of chairs. All the women wore silk saris with elaborate embroidery—edged with glittery, shiny threads—making my tattered dress look like cheap beachwear. Gold jewelry hung from their necks and earlobes, a few wore orange *Crossandra* flowers in their hair. I tugged at the bottom of my dress when I sat down, trying to cover my Chacos, the one pair of everyday shoes I had brought on the trip. Austin wore his typical church uniform consisting of a white shirt and tie, which seemed appropriate for the men in attendance.

Jasmi and her now-husband, Peter, sat on a swan-shaped sofa on a stage. Above hung an elaborate formation of daisies, carnations, and purple orchids against a sheer bronze curtain. Peter wore a tan suit and tie. Jasmi opted out of a white gown and wore a traditional sari, fire-red and orange. She wore sparkling yellow and crimson bangles stacked up her wrists, a long golden *hara* necklace, a matching gold *kundan* choker, heavy earrings, and a jeweled headpiece that ended just between her eyebrows.

A photographer snapped hundreds of posed photographs while a videographer projected footage of Jasmi's face, close and blown up, struggling to sustain a tight, forced smile under a blinding light. Sweat beads formed along her upper lip and collected on her forehead. Everyone in the room stared at Jasmi and Peter as if watching a live jumbotron at a sports stadium. I was reminded of something Chaitra's husband Krishna had said about weddings: "They are no fun for the couple or the family."

But if weddings weren't for the couple or the family, who were they for? Soon, the videographer panned away from Jasmi and Peter and onto the crowd, moving from person to person. I failed to keep a straight face as the camera and migraine-inducing lamp settled on Austin and me.

Watching the spectacle reminded me of weddings I'd photographed for extra money during college. Behind the lens, as I clicked away at these intimate moments, I gained insight into the day's stress. One wedding in particular stood out. I remember hovering my finger above the shutter button on my Nikon D700 as I waited for the groom to smile, to do so much as look at the bride with affection. He seemed shell-shocked as they stumbled out of the temple into the clatter of cheers. As the evening progressed, I captured more accidental moments: the bride scowling at her pestering stepfather, a sister rolling her eyes, a frazzled kitchen staff made up of volunteers. For weeks, I couldn't shake the dull pain I'd caught from the wedding, like symptoms of a pesky cold. What was the point of all this? Why subject ourselves to this charade?

But was that entirely fair? I asked myself as Jasmi squirmed like a bug under a magnifying glass for the crowd. There was something comical, almost cruel, about the absurdity of weddings, the impossibly lofty expectations and elaborate celebration. And yet, I believed there was something else here, a reason we slogged through them as guests and as awkward participants. All the staring guests, their own memories churning inside them, had shown up. They chose to be here.

Community, I realized all at once. Like the one I'd found in India, I had a robust community at home.

I could remember everyone who came to my wedding: people who flew in from out of state, future in-laws who painted the fence around the backyard venue, cousins who sewed flower girl dresses, grandparents who helped me iron tablecloths, an aunt who plunged a clogged toilet at the reception, siblings who knocked down a hornet's nest in the parking lot, professors who offered their hearty congratulations, friends who gave thoroughly prepared toasts until sunset, and parents who took care of the cleanup as they picked confetti from the grass while holding flashlights.

Community meant something new to me that day. Despite my best efforts, I couldn't do it alone. I *wasn't* alone. Their generosity and solidarity lit a bonfire in me, a feeling brighter than the list of abundant mishaps on one of the most stressful, weighty days of my life.

It mattered who came to my wedding.

It mattered to me that I went to Jane's. I wanted to support her the way she had supported me leading up to my wedding, through the good and the nail-salon ugly.

After an hour of watching everyone get photographed at the reception, Jasmi and Peter cut a small cake and fed each other. They were given maroon, rose-petal garlands before the guests formed a long procession to congratulate the couple. Austin and I presented the card and cash Jay had recommended as a camera flashed in our faces.

"Congratulations," Austin said, shaking Peter's hand with gusto.

They thanked us for coming.

"Thank you for letting us be here," I said, quickly hugging Jasmi before being ushered off to make room for the next guest in line.

Soon after, Austin and I talked through what to do about Jane's wedding as we sat side by side in bed with our laptops glowing with flight deals. We would return early. The benefits outweighed the costs: a chance to get jobs, to see family again, to support Jane. The real toll was psychological. Could I be flexible? Could I be willing to shorten what I'd spent so long dreaming up and let go of The Idea of it? Could I stop seeing the end of the trip as an irrational end of me, stop seeing travel as the only literal manifestation of my restlessness?

To save time and funds, we'd scrap Israel, Egypt, Jordan, and Greece from our itinerary. Instead, we would jump to Europe via Rome for Easter. From Rome, we had the vague notion that we'd travel around a bit before walking the Camino de Santiago pilgrimage across Spain. One of our friends recommended the Camino, and we'd seen a film called *The Way* that inspired us to take up the challenge.

I breathed deeply, feeling the rightness of our decision. As Austin searched for one-way tickets leaving India, I scrolled through social media. I stumbled upon a post from the same groom whose wedding I'd photographed back in college: "Does anyone have advice on fun things for married people to do? All we do is watch Netflix and post on Facebook."

My heart stopped. I showed Austin the post and took his hand. "Promise me this will not be the end," I said. Though we'd have plenty of boring evenings and relaxing Netflix nights in our life together, what I really meant was this: *Don't let us become stagnant. Don't let us drift casually apart. Don't lose your sense of adventure. Don't let me lose my wildness.*

"I promise," Austin said.

He kissed my forehead, then booked the tickets.

CHAPTER 17

Goodbyes

A FEW DAYS BEFORE DEPARTING INDIA, I went to Jay's bookstore. I found her waving an electric mosquito bat, grinning as the racquet zapped a mosquito with a satisfying pop.

"Jay, I'm leaving," I said.

"I know."

"Can I ask you those questions about marriage now?"

She knew this moment was coming. Jay had no problem leaning into topics most people politely sidestep: feminism in India, rape culture, racism, religion, the "goofs" in politics. She told me frankly that my profile picture with Austin from celebrating Holi, my chin covered in blue powder, made me look like a bearded man. She gave me lots of advice on my project and once swiped my jotting notebook, hiding it until I returned in a full panic. She talked at length about her time in the States and her critical opinions about the world. But for the life of me, I could not get her to talk about marriage—at least, her *personal* experience with marriage. I only gathered hints: a love marriage, a happy marriage, later in life.

Jay raised an eyebrow, then laughed and consented, taking a seat at her desk. I sat on a dinky stool next to Rosie, taking a moment to scratch the dog's head before taking out my notebook.

"Parents *expect* grandchildren and their children to look after them," Jay began. "It's wrong to pressure people, but we have created this society. At the end of the day, there are certain laws. Someone can die, but their long-term partner has no rights compared to an ex-wife. It's completely taboo to not get married and live together instead. Bollywood stars are the only ones getting away with open sex," she said, throwing up her hands.

According to Jay, the other reason people get married is because they don't want to be alone. As far as what made marriage difficult, she cited differences as well as marrying into another family. In India, where living with the groom's parents remains the tradition, this can be especially tricky. "Mother-in-law jokes are common in all cultures. But I'm lucky. My mother-in-law is a gem—soft-spoken, kind, a village woman. She came to visit us for three to four months at a time, but she never lived with us."

Jay folded her arms and sank deeper into her chair. "Have you read the book *Leaving Home with Half a Fridge* by Arathi Menon?"

"No."

"It's a good one about divorce. Write that one down."

I did. Jay was always ready with a book recommendation.

"What would you say are the good things about marriage according to your culture?"

Jay scrunched her face, thought for a moment, then broke into a three-part response: respect for each other, companionship, and moral support. "You can't let your spouse down, even when you may not agree with them."

"What do you mean?" I probed.

Her brown eyes surveyed me like I was a child asking for the thirtieth time why the sky was blue, then she launched into a story:

When Jay was a little girl, she lived on the top floor of a tall building. Her mother loved cooking with chilies. Somewhere along the way, her mother had the idea to throw the stems of the chilies out the window for easy disposal, "thinking she was some cricket star." But one day, a neighbor woman banged on the door. When Jay's brother opened it, the woman started screaming.

"WHY ARE YOU THROWING CHILIES ON MY BALCONY?"

Recovering from the shock, Jay's brother launched into a calm, logical defense. "You don't have proof," he said. "It could have come from anywhere. Perhaps a bird dropped it there."

Baffled, the woman went downstairs. But Jay's brother immediately went to confront his mother.

"WHY ARE YOU THROWING CHILIES OUT THE WINDOW?"

Jay sighed again, signaling the end of her story. "*That* is moral support," she said.

"Loyalty," I agreed.

We talked a bit about what new couples face. "The first year can be good or traumatic," Jay said, reaching down to pet Rosie. "I did *not* choose to get married young. I had a great fear of the future and wanted a false sense of control about any silly thing, an extra dose of fear compared to a normal person. I didn't get married until I was thirty-five. I wanted to marry someone I knew, not the men my parents paraded."

I nodded, resonating with that feeling of fear, as Jay wiped another glob of drool from Rosie's lips.

"When I was in my thirties, I thought about adopting a child. But my parents saw this and called me desperate for a husband, so they paraded more men." Jay balked. "I backed out of my ideas of adoption. I met my husband at an expo." Then she paused.

I waited for her to say more, but she didn't. "Did he get your number or something?"

"That's not how it works," she said. "Besides, this was in the days of landlines anyway." She didn't expound further.

I bought the book she recommended, then we said our goodbyes. I took one last, hard look at Rosie.

"Don't forget to write about The Book Stop," Jay called on my way out.

"I won't."

Austin and I said a fond farewell to Maithili and Ashish, Alok and Radha, Vic and Nas, and the folks at Austin's internship.

Then, it was time for the hardest goodbye.

The day before I left India, Chaitra and I spent hours cataloging books in the library. I'd miss these books: the new hardcovers, the glossy secondhand magazines, the musty romances. I returned the last of the books that I'd meant to read. The regret didn't sting. I suspected I'd spent my time well.

I handed Chaitra my laminated library membership card.

"It's time I turn this in," I said.

"You keep it."

When I tried to pay my final month of fees, Chaitra wouldn't take the money.

"You *have* to," I said, playfully throwing money onto her desk. "The library needs it." Despite Chaitra's devotion to the library—all her entrepreneurial skills and high-quality materials and engaging community activities—the subscriptions lagged. The library hemorrhaged funds. It could not last much longer.

Chaitra rolled her eyes and exhaled. "Throwing money offends the goddess Lakshmi," she said as she did a quick puja to purge my sin from the air. There was still so much to learn.

We closed up shop for the day.

"Are you ready?" Chaitra said, turning the key behind us. Before I left India, she wanted to take me to get bridal *mehndi*.

Mehndi, temporary body art known as henna in other parts of the world, is used for many occasions, the most common being Indian weddings. Chaitra had shown me a Pinterest board with images of decorated arms and feet in elaborate bronze swirls and complex patterns, a Pinterest board not unlike some of the ones I'd created for cakes and color palettes while planning my own wedding.

"It is said you can measure the bride's love by the shade of the mehndi—the deeper the color, the deeper the love. Actually, it's about skin temperature," she said. Often the mehndi artist hides the letters of the groom's name, which turns into a kind of game to find the letters on the wedding night.

We found an outdoor mehndi stall staffed by two men on the side of the road. Chaitra stood by as I hunched on an orange plastic stool, palms skyward, balancing them awkwardly on each man's knee. One took my right side, the other my left. I shot Chaitra an embarrassed look, but the artists didn't mind. To begin, they rubbed eucalyptus oil onto my skin to help bring out the color. They held iridescent blue tubes of paste and began at the crook of my arm, working swiftly, squeezing out the pungent brown mixture into intricate lines to create delicate shapes as if decorating a cake. It smelled overwhelming, like earth, dried leaves, sour like something fermented. A peacock emerged first, followed by lotus flowers, paisley shapes, checkered circles, and scallops. The movements tickled.

"Can I ask them some questions?" I asked Chaitra, who was busy snapping pictures. She seemed to be having more fun than anyone.

"Sure."

"How many brides do they do mehndi for?"

Chaitra translated. "About five in a month."

"Do the brides seem nervous?"

Chaitra hedged. "I can't ask that. It's too personal. You'd have to ask a bride." After two months in Bengaluru, and six months of my life now spent in India, I was still nowhere near fluent in social decorum.

The mehndi artists turned my wrists, beginning again near my elbow, working their way toward the tips of my fingers. Chaitra insisted they hide an *A* somewhere in the design. It was so well hidden that Austin and I both had a hard time finding it later.

"Well, what was it like for you?" I asked.

"I was a mess," she said, leaving it at that.

By the time the artists finished, my back ached and my feet had fallen asleep. I stood up, holding my stiff arms at my sides, careful not to disturb any of the drying paste. I couldn't scratch my nose.

"This is how it always is with mehndi," said Chaitra, grinning. "You look like a zombie." But the longer I could keep the scabs of dye on, the darker and richer the color would be. And I wanted it to last, wanted to *will* the mehndi to last—a testament to my love not only for Austin but also for Chaitra and all the people I'd met. In time, the mehndi dried and flaked off, dropping like chocolate sprinkles all over the apartment and into the seams of my journal, where flecks spill out each time I crack open those pages. The paste left behind a burnt umber masterpiece, a mark on my skin that would last weeks and weeks, long after the goodbyes.

A BRIEF LAYOVER

Advice Given at My Wedding (Continued)

"Remember, always, this day and let it help you work through whatever life holds for the two of you!"

"Celebrate! Celebrate anything and everything."

"Express your love every day!"

"Say what you mean, mean what you say."

"Best friends make it through anything! If you start to forget your best friend . . . put the world on hold. It can wait for you to remember."

"Stay friends! The best relationships are based on friendship."

"Never underestimate the importance of communication."

"Believe each other when you say it."

"For better or for worse but not for granted."

"Tell each other at least one specific reason why you love each other daily. Sometimes it's just simple, like 'I love you today because you cleaned the bathroom.'"

"Gordon B. Hinckley said, 'True love is not so much a matter of romance as it is a matter of anxious concern for the well-being of one's companion.'"

"Always make time for fun with each other."

"To quote Samuel Beckett, 'The creation of the world did not take place once and for all time, but takes place every day.' I imagine the same could be said of a marriage!"

"Don't listen to people; marriage doesn't have to be 'hard.'"

"Life is beautiful and hard! Enjoy it."

"Build trust with each other."

"Continue together in the pursuit of all that is good and adventurous."

"Live boldly."

"Encourage each other's dreams."

"Don't dream separately only; have shared dreams."

"I feel like you guys got this under control. Congrats!"

"Don't take my advice. <3"

"Don't pay much attention to advice."

"Remember that most advice is free and you often get what you paid for."

PART 3

EUROPE

PAY | pā |

verb

1. to give (someone) money that is due for work done, goods received, or a debt incurred
2. to suffer a loss or other misfortune as a consequence of an action

---

CHAPTER 18

A Pilgrim's Initiation

"WE'RE HERE." Austin nudged my shoulder.

I blinked. Outside the bus window, I saw mist and hills—purple hills, green hills, dandelion-covered hills with plump, grazing sheep. A river divided the town consisting of stone buildings with red clay roofs and wooden shutters. Saint-Jean-Pied-de-Port, the name of this small Basque village at the base of the towering French Pyrenees, meant "at the foot of the pass."

Austin ducked to merge into the crowded bus aisle with the other eager passengers, all clad in fancy hiking gear, the people beginning the pilgrimage from France across the northern length of Spain, a walking journey of five hundred miles.

I slung on my backpack—a black school bag, bulging with the possessions meant to last me a little over a month: a linen sleeping bag, two shirts, two pairs of pants, one extra set of underwear, merino wool socks, a toothbrush, shower sandals, a pair of minimalist mesh running shoes, a bottle of Suave shampoo, my Peruvian alpaca sweater, a flimsy poncho we'd purchased in Rome, my camera, my Kindle so we could download the Camino trail guide and—more difficult to justify due to weight—my temperamental HP laptop filled with all the pictures from our trip along with my field journals. I had refused to trust those last two items to the French postal system.

Days earlier, Austin and I had evaluated what we'd keep and what we'd ship home during our stay in Menton, a French Riviera refuge bordering Italy, where we'd spent two glorious days at a generous friend's guesthouse. The brief-but-lavish stopover made me feel like I was living in a Febreze commercial. From the balcony, we'd watched the sun sparkle over the aquamarine water. To the right, we could see the city center, a cluster of stacked buildings painted the colors of sherbet. We made love on the faux fur rug and took long, hot showers. The air smelled of lemons.

Did we have to leave paradise so soon?

The short answer was yes—a few nights of a brochure honeymoon would have to suffice. In Menton, Austin and I had lazily calculated the directions to the starting place of the pilgrimage. Since we now had tickets back to the US for Jane's wedding, we had to finish the walk before our pending departure from Madrid. We thought a few trains would allow us to arrive on the same day. To our surprise, the complicated journey to get to Saint-Jean took much longer; it required piecing together a flight from Nice to Bordeaux, a train to Bayonne, and then, finally, a three-hour bus shuttle to Saint-Jean. Upon realizing our error, we began packing immediately.

While waiting for the bus in Bayonne, I'd purchased a round, floppy-but-not-too-floppy woven hat I'd been obsessed with finding since envisioning the pilgrimage. I had to have The Hat, like a talisman. Somehow, The Hat, the act of wearing The Hat, seemed more urgent than some of the other, more essential preparations Austin and I were slowly realizing we'd neglected. The two of us had sat in a Bayonne café, gobbling up chocolate crepes with a side of traditional gâteau Basque, a local almond cake, when we pulled up John Brierley's popular book *A Pilgrim's Guide to the Camino de Santiago* on my Kindle for the first time. Austin bookmarked the important pages and noted the miles, copying each day down into his Moleskine and announcing them aloud, making me realize how long thirty-two days of walking was. My palms began to sweat.

Exiting that Bayonne café, we ran into an English gentleman with a white beard as he sat on a portable stool. He paused to look at us while balancing a sketchbook on his knee. He recognized us as fellow future pilgrims.

"How are you wearing your bag like that?" he asked Austin.

Austin looked down. He'd been wearing his pack on his chest to shift the weight and to have quicker access. He showed the man how to loop the straps to wear his bag backward.

"Brilliant," the artist said. "I need to be able to carry this stool with me, along with my travel bag." He waved a pencil at a nearby church. "I walked the Camino a few years ago. I do watercolors. But you shouldn't paint based off of photographs; the angles aren't right. You have to do it in person."

We spent a minute admiring his impressive sketchbook featuring buildings with meticulous lines shaded in with grays and browns, an occasional color splash for stained glass or curling ivy.

"First time?" he asked, looking us up and down.

How could he tell?

"Well, buen camino," he said. *Good way*. Or, *Have a good way*.

Hearing that phrase for the first time gave me pause, like observing myself on the stage of a fatalistic epic drama—unsure of my role, let alone my level of commitment to play it out. I'd grown weary of roles, others' roles. I'd carried the notion of "good" around for so long. The singular "way" implied one path, one direction, which I'd developed a kind of allergy toward. But "the way" was less a literal path and more the personal, individual variety. No one else could forge your way for you. No one else could evaluate whether or not it qualified as good besides you. All they could offer were good wishes on your solitary journey.

Buen camino. The phrase sounded kind of beautiful too.

Austin and I watched the man until he rounded a corner.

I didn't see the white-haired English man and his grandfatherly manner in the clump of people getting off the bus in Saint-Jean, though he must have been there somewhere. A few people about our age spoke to each other in languages that were unfamiliar to me. Many others were older than us, possibly retired. A light sense of competition hung in the air. I'd heard that bed space in the dormitories was limited. These people around us were fully outfitted in Spandex, Under Armour, sturdy hiking shoes, metal walking poles, and brand-name packs with waterproof covers.

I peered down at my clothes: denim cutoffs, a button-down checkered shirt, Chaco sandals. My hat began to feel a little less magical. Austin wore khakis, his typical J.Crew collared shirt, and a pair of once-blue Sperry boat shoes. Austin had to have known the shoes wouldn't support him much, but he pretended they were fine for what he saw as a long, leisurely walk (he stands behind his stubborn decision to wear boat shoes rather than bulky, blister-inviting hiking boots). Besides, moneymoneymoney.

We followed the others, who seemed to know what to do. They speed-walked up a hill to beat the crowd to the official pilgrim's office. We took the cue and picked up our pace. When we arrived, a single-file line had formed outside the rock building, where an arched entry covered a massive wooden door.

We waited in the April air, inching closer to the front. Inside, the office walls were covered with posters and charts documenting the numbers and nationalities of pilgrims who had walked el Camino

Francés (the French Way). In 2014, the year before we arrived, we noted a spike in the bar graph: 54,218 pilgrims from ninety-nine countries. The route had become increasingly popular in the summer, perhaps in part due to its appearance in dramatized films like Martin Sheen's *The Way* in 2011. Some critiqued the pilgrimage as a booming business.

Austin and I were taking the popular French Way, a five-hundred-mile/eight-hundred-kilometer path to Santiago de Compostela, a northwestern city in Galicia, Spain, near the Atlantic. But there were other paths: el Camino del Norte (the North Way), el Camino Portugués (the Portuguese Way), and el Camino Primitivo (the Original Way). All led to the same place. Technically, walkers could do the last one hundred kilometers of any path (two hundred for cyclists) and still count it as a bona fide pilgrimage by the Catholic Church's standards. But many, like us, preferred the original starting points. Tradition says that the body of Saint James, after being beheaded by King Herod Agrippa, was taken to Galicia by two other disciples of Jesus. Legend says that a hermit in the ninth century was led to the bones of Saint James by following a star. The site became popular amid the widespread worship of relics. Campus Stellae, or "field of stars," became the city of Santiago de Compostela. People erected a Romanesque church to house the bones of Saint James, a church that transformed into one of the most imposing Gothic cathedrals in Europe.

Santiago de Compostela has drawn pilgrims from all over the world since the Middle Ages, the reason why the Camino is often called the Way of Saint James. The first pilgrims to take the French Way were documented in the mid-eleventh century. Most of them were interested in penance. Now, people take the journey for many reasons: to heal, to adventure, to challenge themselves physically, to challenge themselves spiritually, to find themselves, to lose themselves, to prove themselves, etc. Austin and I were still sorting through our own motivations. They didn't fall into any single, obvious category. We just wanted to, or so we told ourselves. The Camino offered an affordable but culturally meaningful way to see Europe. At the time, that seemed like enough.

At last, we reached the front of the line. A man with reading glasses and sun-spotted hands prepared a credential for each of us, a collection of blank pages folded up like an accordion that would work as a passport on the walk. We needed stamps from two places each day to serve as evidence at the end that we had walked the full journey. Only then would we earn our official Compostela completion certificate.

"Your first stamp," the man said in English through a nasal French accent. He made a dramatic gesture, leaving a black imprint behind of a robed pilgrim holding a staff next to a crest containing a fireplace, a flower, and a lamb. I swelled at seeing the fresh ink, all the blank pages left to fill. Each location along the Camino would have a custom stamp, unique and difficult to forge if anyone, though it was hard to imagine, had the time or energy to do so. More likely, the stamps served as special souvenirs.

"Your first stamp," the man said, again, this time to the next person.

On the way out of the pilgrim's office, Austin and I noticed a basket of scallop shells next to a donation jar. He picked a shell with a rose-purple tint. I wavered in my decision but ultimately landed on an ivory one with blotches of buttery yellow. We tied them to our bags with string, a symbol to others that we were pilgrims. The shell tradition came from the earliest days of the Camino. One theory: a pilgrim had to bring a shell home to prove they had made it to the ocean, that they had completed their pilgrimage and been forgiven of their sins. Another: like the many paths to Santiago, all the shell's lines end at the same point.

For ten euro, Austin and I secured two of the last beds in a hostel, which were called *albergues* along the Camino. We grabbed dinner at an outdoor restaurant with picnic tables and listened to the click-clack of hiking sticks on stone as fellow pilgrims explored the streets lined with rock walls draped with vines. As we dug into our Basque-prepared chicken—fried drumsticks soaked with red chili sauce—accompanied by limp fries, a nearby German scooted closer to us. He ate his fries with a fork and had a bottle of red wine in hand. He was eager to talk.

Manfred introduced himself as a retired air traffic controller. He had been dreaming of and preparing for this walk for half of his seventy years of life. He had audiobooks, waterproof gear, and a coveted bed reservation he'd made weeks in advance at Orisson, a place we hadn't heard of, that served as a midway point to break up the difficult day's crossing over the Pyrenees. Manfred had a plan for everything, even for making friends. He'd practiced conversations for situations when he might have to leave a walking group without causing any "hard feelings."

The more Manfred talked, the more I began to bounce my leg under the table. If he represented the best-prepared people here, we represented the worst.

"Do you have rain gear?" Manfred asked, pointing at the gray sky. "It's going to rain tomorrow."

Austin and I exchanged a look. Earlier we had convinced ourselves that we didn't need any more gear. When I expressed concern, Austin said, "They didn't have Under Armour a thousand years ago." Portraits of ancient pilgrims depicted people sporting uncomfortable capes and powerful-but-awkward-looking staffs. We told ourselves we couldn't afford new gear. Even Austin seemed hyper-reluctant to spend. We'd debated whether or not the two euros we'd spent on carabiners were worth the investment. Austin: *What do we need to hang from our bags?* Me: *Laundry? Sack lunches? My new hat?*

The shoes we'd brought and our disposable ponchos would have to do, as would our lacking physical preparation. The most training I'd done was taking the stairs instead of the elevator to our second-floor apartment for a few weeks before leaving India.

"I imagine I will see you again. That's the way these things work," Manfred said before we parted, patting his mouth with a napkin. "But remember—it is not the pace that matters, it is *the Way*."

I was the last one to fall asleep in the albergue. I lay on my stomach, scribbling in my journal while holding a flashlight on the hard bottom bunk. Dozens of strangers, men and women, snored and shifted on squeaky mattresses around me. This Camino thing had seemed like a cool idea to us a month ago at the height of our abstract planning. Now, we faced the hard realities of our decision. I felt a mixture of excitement and anticipation, but mostly I felt a dull dread tinged with a greater sense of the true dimensions of what we had gotten ourselves into. Again.

I tossed and turned, waking to every unfamiliar sound.

CHAPTER 19

The Pyrenees

AUSTIN AND I HAD CONSIDERED 6:30 a.m. an early start for the 25.1-kilometer/15.6-mile hike up the Pyrenees to Roncesvalles on the other side of the pass, but the dark dormitory in Saint-Jean was mostly empty by the time we roused. We studied a topographic map of the day's journey: a jagged, steep ascent followed by a sharp descent. I strapped on my Chacos, the sturdier shoe for a rigorous hike. The mesh running shoes tied to my bag had almost no support or grip. Austin and I packed, then wandered into the kitchen. A basket of breadcrumbs remained from the hungry crowd before us.

"We're late," I said to Austin.

"We're fine," he said, sharing friendly smiles with a few less-calm stragglers rushing out the door.

Austin and I picked up water and a breakfast of green apples from a fruit seller on the side of the road. Then, we headed toward the mountains.

"The first steps of our pilgrimage," I whooped to Austin. The dawn sky was still fringed with navy as the sun slowly rose. The Pyrenees beckoned ahead. Gray clouds hung above but no rain. The excitement overshadowed whatever dread I'd felt the day before. My hat flopped above my forehead. I took a bite of my apple. Sixteen miles didn't sound too hard, though we'd understood this to be the toughest day of the Camino by far. This wasn't Everest. *We were young*, I told myself. *We were healthy*. *We had all day*.

We exited Saint-Jean through two brick pillars flanking the road. Austin paused in front of a sign. He could never help himself from reading every sign, including the ones in Spanish, though he understood about 7 percent of the language. This sign, however, had an English translation: "Even today, in the early morning, the cobblestones of the Rue d'Espagne still resounded with the noise of the pilgrims' footsteps. As in the Middle Ages, pilgrims leave town after a night's rest, resolute and prepared for the much-feared journey through the Pyrenees."

My eyes lingered on the words "resolute" and "much-feared." This summit had been passed by legends like Charlemagne's army, Ferdinand the Catholic, Charles V, and (much later) Napoleon. One mountain pass, one road, but so many layers of history—a violent history that up until then had seemed an abstract, faraway thing—the stuff reserved for strange tales in *The Song of Roland*.

"Hannibal crossed this same section of the Pyrenees with elephants during the Second Punic War," Austin said, ever the history buff. Austin failed to mention that almost none of the fifty thousand soldiers and thirty-eight elephants survived to return.

The brutal history dampened a bit of my earlier enthusiasm.

"We need to find rocks," I said, reminding Austin of what we'd read in our Camino guidebook. Pilgrims were supposed to bring a stone from home to place at the base of an iron cross called Cruz de Ferro toward the end of the journey to represent a weight to leave behind. Since Austin and I hadn't brought a rock from home, we decided to gather one from here.

We stared at the ground and picked a matching pair: generic gray things with specks of white and dirt.

The first hours went by leisurely. We followed yellow arrows that would lead us all the way to Santiago. We fell into a steady string of other pilgrims of all ages and nationalities. "Wouldn't it be nice to have a farm?" Austin said, inhaling the familiar manure smells from his childhood. My eyes soaked up the pastoral views outside of town. I stopped often, too often for Austin's liking (though I reminded him that he halted for every sign, statue, and bridge), to take pictures of the emerald farms against the dramatic clouds, the fluffy sheep, the white cows with caps of blonde hair and blanched horns, a neighing miniature pony. My photographs revealed my desire to linger in the short-lived romance. We played fetch with a collie who brought us a stick over and over again.

When I stopped to take more snapshots of the view below, Austin interjected. "We really do have to get going." He looked up at the sky. "You have your poncho ready?"

We put them on for good measure. I clipped my hat to my backpack.

Soon, the switchbacks began to ascend at a steeper rate. Before long, my lungs began to burn. Rugged older folks we'd passed earlier were now moving ahead while we took breaks to pant. The Kelly-green landscape rippled and sprawled. The wind began to roar so loudly that I couldn't hear Austin speak. The gusts ripped at our ponchos like sails until, eventually, they began to tear the glued seams.

At midday, an eagle circled overhead. We sat with legs folded in a treeless, grassy landscape in silence as we scarfed down a quick lunch of cheese and sausage. A chill settled under my skin. Austin massaged his legs. "This is fun," I'd said to him a few hours earlier, dizzy from the austere vista. That already felt like another person ago. Was this fun? And if not, what else could it be?

The rain came around the time we crossed unceremoniously from France into Spain.

Then, a little higher up, spring snow.

Snow heaped in banks. Snow coated the mountain. Snow slushed along the path with a menacing drop-off on the right side.

No one, not even Manfred, had mentioned the snow.

I stared at my sandals and grimace-laughed. "How much farther do we have?"

Austin had been unusually quiet. "I'd guess we are about halfway." In other words, we had a long way to go, a long way up. "Do you want to change shoes?"

"No," I said, looking at the slippery path ahead.

We kept walking. The snow sloshed onto my bare skin. The sting turned to a burn, then a needling sensation. Though the Pyrenees landscape was new and transfixing, the feeling felt all too familiar.

Somehow, somewhere along the way in my life, I had internalized the subconscious idea of suffering as currency, a necessary means to any end. I had to *earn* happiness. The harder the struggle, the bigger the payoff, the more valiant the short-lived triumph. Without pain, how could I afford or justify my undeserved joy? Without identifying closely with past trauma—the tissue-thin jeans from middle school, the sound the key made when I couldn't turn it in the lock of my childhood home anymore, the taste of Village Inn waffles with my dad and Lisa instead of the family Thanksgiving dinner I wasn't invited to, all the times I left church crying or had my heart broken for not being Mormon enough, a student throwing a desk across my classroom, my mother's humiliated eyes in the psychiatric ward, my anxiety about marriage—who was I? Resilience became an identity, a war medal. This scarcity mindset taught me that everything good was rare, a lucky blip of pleasure. Sooner or later, the happiness would run dry. I'd be sucked down into my boring, familiar misery again. To expect another hit of delight? Ludicrous.

Everything I did, every step I took, felt like a movement toward some kind of end. Not in the existential-death kind of way, though there was that too, but the end of my ability to make the kind of deliberate decisions that put me here to begin with. How dare I believe I could be happy, and not just happy, but drink deeply from the well of satisfaction? I didn't trust that good things would come again, and often, like a sunrise or a simple step forward.

For now, that level of joy remained elusive. But I was very comfortable and very at home with suffering, with carrying fears I still struggled to pinpoint. If I stopped enduring, I imagined I risked freezing.

It probably surprised no one when I finally slipped, my whole body horizontal in the snow and mud and slush. I stared down a cliff a foot away from my face. Jagged rocks cascaded down, down, down. Rain pelted my cheeks.

I could hear Austin say my name.

"Are you okay?" he asked.

I took his hand and yanked myself up. I didn't know when I'd started crying. I felt all shades of sorry for myself. My torn green poncho, jacket, and pants dripped with goo. My bag and hat looked no better. My feet felt numb against the stiff Chaco sandal straps. I tried to scrape the sludge off my hands on a bank of hardened snow.

"Are you hurt?"

"I don't think so."

A few other pilgrims who'd watched me fall continued walking once they saw I'd be okay. A few tsk-tsked at my shoe selection. One man paused and handed me his pack of Kleenex. He said something I didn't make out in French.

"Thanks," I said, overwhelmed with gratitude as I used a tissue to wipe the mud from my shaky hands while Austin took a pass at mopping up my sleeve.

Would it have killed me to prepare, at least a little? To buy gear and reasonable shoes, even if it meant taking out loans when we returned home?

Maybe it wasn't as much about the money as I then imagined. Perhaps a small part of me never intended to be ready, seeking another needless layer of challenge.

"I can't do this," I said, my voice wobbly. "I don't think I can do this." I began to hyperventilate.

"You can," Austin said. *This far in, you have to*, I imagined him thinking. "I know you can. Try the other shoes."

Austin held my hand as another mile or so passed. I'd lost all confidence. I stopped too often. The sun sank lower, threatening nightfall before we arrived. Panic pummeled me in gusts. Tears came and went without warning. My running shoes filled up with water and my feet began to chafe. I reluctantly switched back to my Chacos; I couldn't afford a blister this early in the pilgrimage. Austin remained encouraging, pushing me onward as we curved around the pass. I wanted to tell him to leave me there on the mountain, but also to stay—*please* stay. Though I didn't need him to be one of my oracles anymore, I still drew comfort from his faith.

"How much farther?" I moaned.

"I don't know," he'd say. We had no way of knowing for sure.

Howmuchfartherhowmuchfartherhowmuchfarther?

Idon'tknowIdon'tknowIdon'tknow.

"But we have to keep going."

This is the part where I want to write in a way that lets you know that this foolish lack of preparation and momentary suffering meant something, that somehow the conflict led to a more triumphal climax and greater reward, that the difficulty helped prove my worthiness of the goal. That's how the grade-school arc of a story "should" look, a triangular shape similar to the elevation plot of that first day through the Pyrenees.

But the me of that moment, the one covered in stiffened mud, toes red from snow, her swollen face flushed with sweat and windburn, was not a character experiencing growth along a predictable plot. She'd met her limit and knew it. There was no meaning in that instant. She resisted being trapped in a story. Her shaky motivation had hollowed out. The sound of the pilgrimage, the mere idea of it, could not sustain her, not on a journey like this.

I may have turned back if that had been an option. But the shortest path out of the Pyrenees was forward.

My heart palpitations didn't ease until we reached Lepoeder, the highest part of the mountain at 1,450 meters in elevation. Reaching that marker surrounded by flat grass and naked boulders meant we'd climbed 1,200 meters since leaving Saint-Jean. It was time to descend with 3.6 kilometers to go.

This too proved steep, though downhill made everything seem more possible.

The scene morphed into something like Sleepy Hollow, the gray trees bare with marshy orange leaves along the ground.

"This looks like a place where you would expect to see a pack of wolves," Austin said.

I caught his smile, present even now. Though only I could get myself out of the Pyrenees, I felt grateful that he'd been a literal helpmeet through the worst of it.

At one point, gazing down at the snowy slope, Austin and I

ripped off our useless, tattered ponchos. We placed them on the ground, using the plastic as a sled to slide to the next visible path. We bellowed with something like exhilaration.

At dusk, we were some of the last pilgrims to roll into Roncesvalles. I wanted to run with joy for the open door when I saw the massive albergue, but my stiff thighs and knocking knees demanded otherwise. A volunteer welcome staff greeted us. They stamped our credentials with an oval seal that contained flowers. I placed my mud-caked Chacos, the only sandals in sight, next to the rows of hiking boots and tennis shoes.

"You'll feel like a new person after a shower," said a middle-aged volunteer. Though he'd probably said this a hundred times that day, and the same number of times the day before, his words felt genuine, striking me right in the chest. The hardest day was now behind us. He gave directions to our bunks and the bathroom. "If you hurry, you can make the Pilgrim's Mass tonight," he added.

Austin and I were given two of the 183 beds in the albergue. We peeled off our clothes and took warm showers in the steamy communal bathroom, the water regulated by push-button knobs. I stood with my long hair under the faucet, my forehead pressed to the wall, my legs trembling, and hit the button for water again and again and again.

After settling in, Austin and I hobbled to the thirteenth-century church in the courtyard. We walked into the service late and hugged the stone wall behind the pack of pilgrims in the dim chapel, listening to what sounded like a prayer in Latin, or maybe formal Spanish, though I've since heard they conduct the blessing in many languages. A gold statue of Mary floated above on a high altar, surrounded by royal-blue glass windows. A priest read from a text dated back to 1078 CE:

PRIEST: O Lord whose word makes all things holy, bless we beseech you these emblems, rucksacks, and staffs to be used on this pilgrimage. May all those who carry them arrive safely at the shrine of Saint James the Apostle, the objective of their journey.

CONGREGATION: Amen.

PRIEST: Shoulder these rucksacks which will help you during your pilgrimage. May the fatigue of carrying them be expiation for your sins, so that when you have been forgiven you may reach the shrine of Saint James full of courage, and when your pilgrimage is over, return home full of joy.

CONGREGATION: Amen.

PRIEST: Receive these shells and medals, as signs of your pilgrimage. With God's grace may you behave as true pilgrims throughout your entire journey and be able to reach your objective, which is to visit the shrine of Saint James and gain indulgences.

CONGREGATION: Amen.

PRIEST: Lord Jesus Christ, you taught us through the Apostle Saint Paul that here below we have no lasting city and must always seek the heavenly city. Hear our prayers for these pilgrims we commission. May the Holy Spirit breathe his grace into their hearts; may he enliven their faith, strengthen their hope, and feed the flame of their love . . .

I didn't internalize this blessing with big words like *sin*, *forgive*, *joy*, *spirit*, and *grace*—though they were spoken and perhaps felt throughout the room. Despite claiming that I did not believe in penance (the word was not part of my religious upbringing; Mormonism, caught between liturgical orthodoxy and Protestant leanings, favored the term *repentance*), I wonder now if a hidden part of me did have some version of that impulse. Why else the constant need to prove myself, to pay through suffering? Why the incessant, almost-masochistic need to do hard things or to interpret everything as hard, marriage included? Why the overwhelming, constant compulsion to punish myself, to overcome, and to overcome what, exactly?

Dazed, I focused on the echoey quality of the church, a beautiful-yet-eerie space I didn't quite understand, though I sensed the pull of its gravity.

I remember how difficult it was to stand, how my legs still shook under the weight of my body.

CHAPTER 20

The Canterbury Pals

AUSTIN AND I SQUINTED THROUGH the welcomed sunlight at a sign outside of Roncesvalles: "SANTIAGO DE COMPOSTELA 790." It didn't have to specify kilometers. Pilgrims called them k's.

We had 790 k's until Santiago.

Somehow, that staggering number dazzled me more than it terrified me. Half-conscious, I'd dressed when the Gregorian chants on loudspeakers throughout the Roncesvalles hostel woke all the pilgrims at six that morning. I'd forgotten that I'd mentally given up. Maybe the boost in confidence came from knowing that we'd survived the worst day, evidence that I could move forward. Regardless, sleep had been a miracle drug. My body felt achy but remarkably restored after a night of rest and two Advil.

"Evolutionarily, we were made to walk," Austin had said while stuffing his bag at the albergue, as if ashamed by his own "pathetic" soreness. I'd sat on the bottom bunk and noticed his slight limp. "It's fine," he said, swatting away my concern. I wanted to comfort him. We inhabited hurt so differently. He treated his physical pain much like his psychological pain, an inconvenient weakness to endure until, eventually, he made a full recovery.

But I *knew* he experienced pain and fear, even when he claimed he didn't. "I don't get afraid," Austin often said whenever I probed about his stress levels before a big presentation or embarking on a wilderness expedition with friends. He'd shrug. "I'm not like you." My concern, particularly for his safety, sometimes annoyed him, *insulted* him and his Wild West childhood stoicism and lingering cowboy sense of masculinity.

Austin rubbed his muscles. I knew his incessant, almost-stubborn courage stemmed from his optimistic personality and idealistic worldview. His faith created a solid base of certainty, a secure and powerful narrative that supported his past and future and gave his existence purpose and a clear direction. He could absorb, question, and experience the world without falling into a pit of despair. Why waste energy on "obsessing" about "what could go wrong"? And if something did go wrong, he "took care of it." No complaints, no fuss.

But I also knew better than to take Austin at his word. Of course he knew fear. Of course he knew pain. I'd witnessed him wince and pace the apartment at night, exhaling loudly, struggling to make sense of a family member leaving the church or a friend calling off a marriage. To me, he said things like, "I don't say the d-word" (d for divorce). We had different approaches to addressing the fears about our marriage, but I believed we shared more in common than I'd initially suspected: the concern that I might leave him for reasons or forces he couldn't fathom. He couldn't afford to be afraid with me, listen closely, or take my omnipresent concerns more seriously. If my personality leaned into the wounds, his leaned out. He stayed safer that way, maintained his bravery and peace of mind. Better to make me laugh. Better to make me smile. Better to make me believe again.

I pulled on my socks and mesh running shoes, an attempt at trying different footwear since the day's walk had fewer uphills compared to yesterday's. Maybe it was okay that I understood, or at least guessed at, Austin's fears more than he did. I'd watch from afar to see if his knee would heal. I wouldn't stop asking about it either.

On the way out of the albergue, we'd rooted through a donation box. I uncovered a dank poncho, a poncho I desperately needed after the Pyrenees winds shredded my disposable one. As I held it up, a gray sock tumbled out of the blue sleeve. Austin laughed. I recoiled, then zipped the poncho away as my new treasure.

Today we planned to walk 27.4 k's from Roncesvalles to a tiny town called Larrasoaña. We wove through a few Basque villages and farms along the way—clusters of white houses with exposed rock corners, windows with pear-embroidered curtains, wooden doors, *pelota* wall-ball courts, the smell of fermenting hay and the tang of livestock, paths with purple stones paved in patterns like giraffe spots.

It was on our route through the Basque villages that we ran into two pilgrims about our age: a scruffy guy with an enormous pack and a woman with a straw hat and wooden walking staff. We recognized them from the pilgrim's office.

"Hello again," Austin said, extending his hand.

The man, Michael, greeted us in a Czech accent. His azure irises shone when he told us his bulky rucksack weighed twenty kilograms to account for a tent, a sleeping pad, and a propane stove for camping. He'd been hitchhiking for a few months after becoming disillusioned by the way hospitals cared more about their finances than about their patients and had left his paramedic job. Michael wore a skull T-shirt and a shark's-tooth necklace.

"It's cool to meet someone from the Czech Republic," I said. I told him we'd been in Prague briefly on a twenty-four-hour layover.

"No one travels from my country," Michael said with regret. To a small degree, I understood. So far—perhaps due to our spring departure—Austin and I were the rare millennial Americans on the trail, and we would be for a while to come.

Joanina, a twenty-three-year-old dancer, had honey-colored hair and smiling brown eyes. She practiced experimental art therapy back in Germany. A quarter-sized white shell dangled from her lime-green backpack. She told us she'd gotten her impressive stick in the Pyrenees and intended to use it all the way to Santiago. I kept my nerdy Gandalf comments to myself, though I knew Austin would agree with the image.

"Did you come together?" Austin said.

"No," Joanina said, reddening.

"We just met a few days ago," Michael clarified.

We walked with Joanina and Michael the rest of the way to Larrasoaña. I felt grateful for the new company, and I think Austin did too. He and Michael walked a few steps ahead, engrossed in conversation. My feet had begun to feel as if someone had taken hammers to the soles. Talking with Joanina distracted me from the dull throb.

"This is my second Camino," Joanina said, "I walked the Norte two years ago." She described how few people were on that trail, the up and down terrain, the cinematic views of the rolling ocean, and sleeping on the beach.

"Why are you doing another Camino?" I asked.

She took a deep, intentional breath. "It makes me happier."

I recognized her as a kindred restless spirit. It felt nice not having to explain or justify what I was doing. I told her a bit about me and my travels with Austin, and Joanina shared more about herself. She'd grown up in a small town in eastern Germany and had two older sisters, both vegetarian like her. She also had a boyfriend back home: a two-and-a-half-year relationship, turbulent at best. For this walk, she sought perspective on what to do about him.

"I see," I said, casting a glance at Michael and Austin up the trail.

Hours later, and a few k's before our destination as we crossed stone bridges over a gurgling river, Joanina and I grew braver with our questions. I would soon learn that on the Camino, one had time for the long version of any story, for conversations beyond the superficial. We talked briefly about the needless death of a German exchange student who'd been shot in a garage by a scared homeowner in Missoula, Montana.

A heavy pause.

"Are you proud to be American?" Joanina asked with caution and curiosity. I imagined what stereotypes she might be conjuring: guns, war, ego, racism. Then I remembered these were similar to what I'd been taught about her country.

"Are you proud to be German?" I asked with equal caution and curiosity.

We shared the ways we were, the ways we were not, our responsibility to make things better.

At one point, Joanina stopped when we saw a dead mole on the road. She crouched down on her knees and moved a few stones into a circle. I knelt and joined her in silence. We put aside our nationalities and the heavy histories we carried. For now, we were only pilgrims, and borders were flimsy dividers.

The four of us reached Larrasoaña in good spirits with achy bodies. We found a stone bench overlooking the river Arga and split a bar of chocolate, then toasted with red wine and juice boxes (for Austin and me). We parted ways with Joanina and Michael for the night but agreed to meet the next morning.

Austin and I settled into our albergue, joining a communal table for dinner. The yellow room had energy. I scooted onto a long bench, elbow to elbow with strangers, though some of them looked familiar.

"You made it," one voice at the table piped up, then, upon seeing Austin's checkered collared shirt, he hummed the lumberjack song from *Monty Python and the Holy Grail*.

Austin and I recognized him: the English painter we'd met in Bayonne. He'd managed to carry his bag and his artist's stool across the mountain pass. We came to learn his name was Austin. For the rest of the Camino, people referred to him as "Older Austin" and my husband by the sing-song "Austin from Boston." We learned Older Austin had been an architect, thus his obsession with straight lines and live painting.

We feasted on vegetable soup, juicy pork, fresh salad, and caramelized cakes while exchanging accounts of voyaging across the Pyrenees. For the first time, I dared to mock our lack of preparation and misadventures, including the snow and my sandals.

Then, we went around the table and introduced ourselves.

Kim was a writer and pilot from Nashville who'd also worked in local radio. She had Top Ramen–curly hair clipped up like cascading blonde pigtails. She asked a million questions about my writing and her curiosity seemed genuine. Kim was small but mighty, unfailingly sincere in her conversation and intense listening, water-blue eyes flashing behind her narrow, black-framed glasses. Kim confessed that, seeing us at the Bayonne bus stop with our unusual gear and my silly hat, she wasn't sure we'd last day one.

Hal—with his ever-ready, "Kim, did you try this? Kim, make sure you get some of that!"—was a private investigator, also born and raised in Tennessee. They'd met during flight school. Kim had been his teacher, and they married soon after. Their mutual affection was palpable. Hal had a barrel chest, a kind face grizzled with a charcoal-streaked beard, and a deep voice always on the verge of a pun. I loved the sound of his ringing laugh instantly. He documented everything with his GoPro, creating minifilms set to music at the end of each day.

This was Kim and Hal's second Camino.

Neil was a graphic artist from London with red hair and a flushed, whiskered face. An unabashed atheist, Neil was along for the adventure, none of this "spiritual rubbish." He laced his sentences with jokes that made the whole table shake. He wore a beanie no matter the weather, and his solution to blister prevention was gaffer tape.

James was a Catholic construction worker from Florida with Sicilian heritage. He was a gentle giant with enormous hands and long ringlets that he conditioned with olive oil. He often had to brush his dark mane with an occasional streak of gray away from his face or tie it back with a bandana. He showed us pictures of his beloved, recently deceased greyhound. James was completely enamored with Spain, save for the crooked lines and corners in all the buildings he studied, which ran contrary to his construction training. This was also his second Camino.

"Why a second time?" I asked, as I'd asked Joanina earlier. Humbled by how challenging the first day had been, and exhausted by the second, I wondered how so many of these pilgrims had braved another attempt.

"Because I did it the first time," James said, brown eyes unflinching, his voice heavy with gravitas. The others who had walked the Camino before nodded with silent approval.

Then James broke into a grin. "But no spoilers!"

CHAPTER 21

The Why

> What is the true object of Don Quixote's quest? I find that unanswerable.
>
> —Harold Bloom,
> introduction to *Don Quixote*
> (transl. Edith Grossman)

ON THE EIGHTH DAY OF THE PILGRIMAGE, Austin and I—along with our growing group of new friends who were quickly becoming a "Camino family"—checked into an albergue in Ventosa, an agricultural village with a population of 169 in the province of La Rioja. *Ventosa* means "sucker" in Spanish. As everyone waited for the full crew to arrive, we lounged leisurely in the back courtyard on chairs and swaths of lawn. Our colorful laundry fluttered like prayer flags. The afternoon sun graced us with healing energy. The mood felt light.

I sat in the grass and removed my sandals. I barely recognized my feet: bandaged with tape to prevent my toes from rubbing together, zigzag tan lines thanks to the straps of my Chacos, and bruised purple nails. My mesh running shoes had proved too tight to wear, even on shorter days. People warned me that my toenails might fall off. A blood blister burned on the bottom of my big toe.

But I couldn't complain, I thought, as I looked around at the others.

There was Neil to my right; his feet looked like they'd brushed against a meat grinder. The gaffer tape turned out to be a bad idea, making his skin sweat even worse. His blisters oozed yellow pus.

Enter Sheila, a tiny Swiss woman with a high-pitched voice. She sported cute tattoos peeking through her sports bra and was not afraid to show off the one on her hip. "Always I am undressing for pilgrims!" Sheila happened to be a burn unit nurse, armed with a first aid kit. She reminded me of a nymph, the way she tucked wildflowers into her black hair, a habit that earned her the nickname "Flower Pot." Her short, curly locks were often adorned with red spring poppies and bachelor button blue boys. "Flowers in hair make me happy." Her English was so-so, but it didn't stop her and Neil from effective, flirty communication, assisted by Google Translate.

Sheila took out her scissors.

"What are you going to do with these instruments of torture?" Neil said. His sunburned face seemed almost as red as his scruffy beard.

James hooted at the spectacle. His Sicilian voice boomed between puffs on a Marlboro cigarette from a carton that read *fumar mata*.

"A burn unit nurse just *happens* to be here when you have an infected blister?" James said. He insisted that Sheila was serving as a "Camino Angel" for Neil: the right person at the exact right time to make the journey more possible.

Neil squirmed as Sheila rested the metal scissors on his raw foot.

"What?" Sheila trilled. "Look, infection!" She snipped away flaps of dead skin on Neil's feet. He flinched and made jokes between shriek-laughs.

We were all a little injured, each in our own way.

Austin shielded his face from the sun with a book as he napped in the grass. His knee continued to give him problems, though less so. From what I could observe, the pain came and went. He refused to complain. I continued to worry.

Frida, another new friend, wore a knee brace. We adopted her the moment she offered us ostrich sausage, though maybe she adopted us. Frida was a muscular, fearless Swede in her early thirties with straight blonde hair and cool-kid plastic sunglasses. Her tales of traveling the world and working on a cruise ship never ceased to entertain us: being pounced on by a jaguar, slipping food from the ship captain's quarters, and skid marks left in guests' bedsheets. She had blisters so large we named them Thor and Spartacus.

Frida shrugged off her injuries, sipping a large glass of red wine.

Suzy, the tango dancer, yogi, and massage therapist from Australia who was "seeking closure for an old dream," used the handrail on the garden stairs to stretch out the strained muscles in her lean, long legs while Elise, a twenty-one-year-old medical student from Denmark with white hair and startling opal eyes, joined her in conversation. At one point, Elise had walked forty k's in a single day to catch up with the group after nursing a back injury. She wore pink socks her grandmother had knitted, but she was tougher than steel.

To my left sat Martin, a young, blond police officer from Berlin. The group adored his accent and often mimicked the way he said: "That's gReat!" and "I have to pack my rUcksack." He kept everything in his pack in plastic bags, each with a label written in three different languages: English, German, and Spanish. Martin suffered from bouts of private melancholy he didn't like to explain, often waking up long before everyone else to set out alone after receiving a "bad message" from home. He enjoyed securing albergue beds for the rest of us at the day's destination.

Perhaps Martin wrote his pain down. He scribbled away in a journal at a table where Kim also sat writing in a blue notebook. Hal sat next to her, making a video on his iPad to document the day. Though the Nashville couple had planned on a rest day in Pamplona, they'd changed course to keep going with the emerging cohort. I couldn't have been happier. I'd grown fond of Kim and Hal and felt eager to become better friends.

Then there was Joanina, resting on her back, her honey hair glowing in the sun. Michael had fallen behind but said he would try to catch up. Joanina had told him she wouldn't wait for him, "I never look back," though her heavy smile revealed her internal conflict. On the walk, she'd confessed to me that she was more confused than ever about her romantic life.

A few days earlier, the four of us—Michael, Joanina, Austin, and I—had settled into a patch of crabgrass atop a hill lined with swishing windmills outside of Pamplona. I had to hold my hat to keep the wind from knocking it off. The backdrop of moody clouds against the whirling white arms, long as airplane wings and sharp like knives slashing the air, reminded me of Don Quixote's rebuke to his travel companion, Sancho, who'd tried to convince his master that the windmills weren't giants: "'It seems clear to me,' replied Don Quixote, 'that thou are not well versed in the matter of adventures.'" To Don Quixote, it was a matter of perspective. I had a hard time *not* imagining Cervantes's groundbreaking novel *Don Quixote* as I walked the pilgrimage: A Spanish gentleman from La Mancha who'd been indoctrinated by tales of knights decides to prove himself a true knight, errant like the heroes of old. As he wanders, he sustains a passionate love for an elusive, completely fabricated woman named Dulcinea. Sancho, his loyal servant, serves as an everyman in the story—often the wise fool. Characters who encounter Don Quixote struggle to understand him. Is he irredeemably mad? Or does he understand something no one else does, seeing what others can't or won't?

Our picnic lunch beneath the windmills with Michael and Joanina consisted of fruit and Oreos. Michael had planned to stay in Pamplona longer to meet up with friends, but here he was still. He and Joanina exchanged foot massages, held hands, giggled, and took turns guiding each other while blindfolded—a trust exercise. Austin studied them, then looked at me with a smirk that said, *Do you remember?* Those early days when he'd installed a hammock in my bedroom, when I'd once read all of his middle school journals in front of him, when we'd cuddled and read Russian novels in his twin-size bed, when we'd leaped into a lake with all our clothes on, just because.

I looked at him hard with eyes that said, *I remember.* And not just the past but also the unfolding present.

The four of us plucked wild rosemary, rubbing the rough stems and crumbling the leaves over our bare, stinky feet. Michael pocketed some to improve the camp cooking he'd resume once he returned to Pamplona. I hoped we'd see him again.

In surveying everyone's pain in the courtyard, visible or hidden, acute or dull, a part of me wondered if we were all part fool. This trek made sense to those of us doing it, as irrational as it appeared to friends and family back home. Those conversations did not look so different from the one Don Quixote had with his niece before leaving La Mancha.

> "But Señor Uncle, wouldn't it be better to stay

> peacefully in your house and not wander the world searching for bread made from something better than wheat, never stopping to think that many people go looking for wool and come back shorn?"
>
> "Oh, my dear niece," replied Don Quixote, "how little you understand!"

But what, exactly, did any of us understand? We'd been walking long enough to burn through superficial motivations, making space for any deeper reasons—ugly or otherwise—to surface.

Earlier on the road, while walking with Joanina and Michael, we met another American, Lexi, from DC—the first twenty-something person from the United States we'd encountered. We found her while climbing up a steep part of the mountain. She dragged her right leg behind her, swinging it forward with dramatic effort, as she slowly heaved her body up the dirt path.

We slowed down.

"Are you okay?"

She pulled out her earbuds. "What?"

"Are you okay?"

No. She was not okay. Lexi was miserable, in fact. But she was obstinate. And this was supposed to be a "life-changing experience." She'd paid a lot of money to get here.

"Do you have internet?" she asked.

We shook our heads.

"I need to call my mom," she said between a string of complaints. We guessed some larger villages ahead might and suggested she stop and recover, maybe consider going home if that's what she wanted. One of the unofficial rules of the pilgrimage is that if you are seriously injured, *really* injured, you have to stop. That can be hard to gauge, especially if you've formed a solid friend group, especially if you've committed to your plans. But those pressures are not as important as taking care of yourself.

Or so pilgrims say.

After a few minutes, I went ahead with Joanina and Michael as Austin, in his usual kindness, paced with Lexi to try and lift her spirits. Her hobble disappeared immediately once she got talking.

The Camino was as much a mental challenge as it was a physical one. Many times in my life, I had been Lexi, careening myself into every hard thing I could experience, pushing myself to the limits until I burned out to a crisp, unhappy but busy with my Puritan work ethic and the project of being "successful"—getting good grades, earning accolades, maintaining scholarships, holding steady jobs, attending church, sustaining some kind of relationship with some kind of man, paying bills on time, not making anyone angry. It was hard to know when to stop, to jump out of the strong current of the status quo, to make my own choices regardless of what others were doing or saying, what I imagined they expected I should do. Challenging the "normal" incurs costs, as does wanting something others don't understand.

"Don Quixote's crazy, we're sane," says Tomé Cecial in Cervantes's novel, asserting the distinctions and placing himself among the well. "And he walks away healthy and laughing, while your grace is bruised and sad. So tell me now, who's crazier: the man who's crazy because he can't help it or the man who chooses to be crazy?"

Choosing to be crazy. What an idea. Actual mental health challenges are real—nothing to make light of or minimize, that is not what I'm talking about here—but I wondered if there was another category of unwell. Living according to what others explicitly or implicitly expected, ignoring the soft but steady pulse of my own desires, felt a bit like that. Given my mother's delusional disorder, I never felt I could afford to be "crazy." I, like Tomé Cecial, divided the world into groups, too eager to count myself among the "sane," the functioning, the normal. But what would it look like to live wildly? To stop caring or "keeping it together" so much? To give up on others' ideas of "good" so I could begin the project of nurturing my individual sense of satisfaction?

To others, that might look a little crazy. Like walking five hundred miles across Spain for the hell of it. But at least here we ditched some of the pretenses. On the Camino, we embraced our crazy.

At the top of the mountain, people paused by a little lake where a German wearing a feathered fedora strummed Green Day's "Time of Your Life" on a ukulele. Lexi refused to stop with us. "I don't let myself have breaks," she said before disappearing from view. We never saw her again.

"We're making dinner for everyone," announced Bob and Soyoung as they stood at the back door of the Ventosa albergue. They were a young married couple from Korea. Inspired by a video they'd seen of a homemade feast on the Camino, they wanted to share some of their traditional foods with fellow pilgrims. Bob and Soyoung had packed all the ingredients and sauce packets for a meal they'd planned to make for a special occasion. Why not today? The albergue had a dining room table.

Knowing how much even a pound of extra weight costs on the pilgrimage, Bob and Soyoung's effort demonstrated more than casual kindness. A few of us helped them in the communal kitchen as Bob and Soyoung prepared a chili stir-fry and a sweet-smelling stew over noodles.

The group gathered around the long table draped in a blue cloth. Everyone took a seat and ogled the home-cooked dinner. By day eight, we'd grown weary of standard pilgrim menus: canned soup and soggy spaghetti. Meals had become events.

As Sancho said, "Griefs are better with bread." But joys are too.

We held our plates to our noses to savor the smells of the sauces, the fresh cabbage and steaming carrot sides.

"How about a toast?" someone said. "To Bob and Soyoung." We raised our glasses, their surfaces reflecting the flickering candle on the uncharacteristically fancy table. A stick of incense burned nearby.

As we ate, Austin made a suggestion. "Can we go around the table and say why we are each walking the Camino?" Though we guessed and had shared substantial conversations, we'd never heard it directly from everyone before.

After a silence, Bob went first.

"To show Soyoung where and how I first fell in love with her," Bob said, earning a sly look from his recent bride, who'd spent the day hobbling on blistered feet. "On my first Camino, I realized something when I walked into Santiago. I knew then who I wanted by my side—in that moment and for the rest of my life." Bob proposed to Soyoung when he returned to Korea. They'd been married for about a year.

We all sighed. Hal wiped away a tear with a napkin. Soyoung blushed. She appeared more relaxed than I'd seen her yet. I wondered how much of this trip was her idea and how much of it was to make Bob happy.

It was a hard speech to follow, but James went next.

"Saint James has work to do on me," he said, casting a look at Neil, who'd laughed loudly throughout a cathedral service a few days ago in the dusty city of Los Arcos. "What a load of rubbish," Neil had said.

"I'm compelled," said Hal. Kim nodded in solidarity.

"To recapture happiness, to learn to not look back," Joanina said, then paused. "And to get over a bad relationship back home."

"To learn to live well with less," Austin said. He touched my knee: *your turn.*

I gulped. "To try and live a happy and successful life without sacrificing one over the other."

To my surprise, what I'd said wasn't explicitly about marriage (or so I thought); it felt bigger, truer, but also more vague and complicated. What *was* success? What *was* happiness? These ideas, like marriage, came with models I had inherited. But sometime within the past few months, without notice or ceremony, the stronghold of that primary story—all that fear feeding my obsession about marriage and failure—shrunk a little. I recalled it with more distance, a relief like opening a clenched fist. Maybe marriage had not been my most urgent concern after all. Fear itself can trick people into acting insane. Don Quixote said as much:

> "It is your fear, Sancho," said Don Quixote, "that keeps you from seeing or hearing properly, because one of the effects of fear is to cloud the senses and make things appear other than they are."

Yet, there *are* realities to face. Life must be lived among other people, after all. Windmills are windmills at the end of the day, and bills are still bills, acknowledged or not. I didn't know how much I admired Don Quixote by the end of Cervantes's novel—all his violent, irresponsible outbursts, his blind romanticizing, his willful abandon of objective realities. Fear teaches, keeps people safe. Knowing which fears to listen to and which to conquer remains the difficulty.

As others went around the table, sharing their compelling motivations as best as they understood them, I noticed the disillusioned hostel worker, the one who'd earlier told us her plans to sell the albergue. She stood behind the cracked door with her ear to the gap, listening.

So much joy, so much beer and wine to pair with Bob and Soyoung's generous feast. After cleaning up, Austin asked if I wanted to go for a walk.

"Seriously? *More* walking?"

"Why not? Right now, before it gets dark."

Not everything needed to be tied to a goal. Within minutes, we had circled Ventosa to see what lay beyond the albergue: an empty bar with red plastic chairs, green fields, simple framed houses with white, rust, or orange-red walls and pointed clay roofs. We had enjoyed ourselves, appreciated each other's company, and witnessed the scene around us. That seemed reason enough.

When we returned, we were shocked to spot Michael standing outside the albergue. We rushed to greet him.

"You caught up!"

Michael flushed. We didn't have to ask why he'd changed his logical plans again.

"I'll go get her," I said.

Joanina showered Michael with such passionate hugs and kisses that we had to turn away. They spent the night in his tent, as they would for many nights to come. People are fools in love—everyone knows that. But perhaps we are all fools, period. Fools in our own way as we navigate our footing along the map of who we thought we are, or who we think we're supposed to be.

> "There are many who are errant," said Sancho.
> "Many," responded Don Quixote, "but few who deserve to be called knights."

Errant used to mean "to search for adventure, to travel abroad, or to go on a quest." That usage fizzled out. Now, most understand it only to mean "erring, failing, or straying from the proper course or standards." I felt grateful to claim the former for a while, no matter how deviant that may appear. On the Camino, I liked to believe that the fools, the wounded, and the fearful alike could find their way.

CHAPTER 22

A New Story

THE SKY ON THE THIRTEENTH DAY looked like a picture taken with a fish-eye lens: so blue, so big, vast enough to prove that Earth really was round and bulging. The cartoonish clouds looked as if they had been mass photocopied and taped into place. Flat green fields with occasional piles of bleached rocks lined the path.

On my right walked Kim. On my left, Frida. We wore matching earrings—silver scallop shells dangling below a single bead—a gift from Kim's mother who'd made hundreds for Kim to pass out along the Camino. Kim and Frida's walking poles ticked against the stony path as we played a new game to pass the twenty-one k's:

"Pancakes or waffles?" Frida began.

"Pancakes."

Things escalated.

"Black plague or cholera?"

"Lick your own diarrhea or your enemy's vomit?" Frida continued.

"Gross."

Today was a ladies' day, more needed than I had realized. We hadn't experienced any more "buen camino" taunts or catcall whistles since leaving behind some of the industrial edges of Burgos, where we'd stayed for the night, the historical capital of Castile. This was the first full day I'd walked without Austin, and one of the rare days we'd spent apart since getting married. He'd left a note behind in my backpack: "I don't know where you'll be or what you'll be doing when you read this, but I am sure that I'll be missing you. There's no better company for me than you. You're still the light of my life."

I would miss him too, but sometimes it's nice to miss someone.

In Burgos, our group had heard a rumor that beds were hard to come by in our next destination, Hornillo, a village name that translates as "stove." Hal, Austin, and a few other guys had volunteered to walk ahead to secure beds and make dinner, allowing us to sleep in. Though some pilgrims adamantly argued that the Camino is "no vacation"—and it certainly wasn't what I'd leap to describe as *fun*—we'd allowed ourselves this one morning to be blatant tourists.

Kim, Frida, and I slept until eight in the cushy beds with clean sheets at a hotel that offered discounts to pilgrims. During my twenty-hour stay, I'd taken three showers: two by necessity, one for fun. My eager hands relished the automatic soap dispenser with its satisfying buzz. The morning felt lavish. I savored a plate of sugar-dusted churros paired with a mug of viscous hot chocolate. After slathering each churro with the molten sauce and dipping just about anything else on the table in the chocolate, there was still half a cup left. I tried to drink it, but it was pudding-thick. No one could explain to me, there or anywhere else along the Way, why the absurd proportions for this common treat.

Before leaving, we also toured the Gothic cathedral, an iconic center to the city of 180,000 people. My neck ached from staring up at the ceiling—intricate like a crystal snowflake—while the audio guide claimed: "It looked more like the work of angels than men." Burgos radiated history amid the modern realities of brightly painted apartment buildings with large square windows, chain grocery stores, ATMs, and beckoning *pinchos* shops. El Cid, buried in the cathedral with full honors for his efforts to protect Spain's "Christian identity" in the eleventh century, remains one of the most established legends of the area. Yet, there is room for other stories. Burgos was founded as a city in 884 CE. I wondered how many once-outsiders inhabited the city now and how they felt about its version of history. The beauty of the Camino is also its greatest loss: you move on, always, without looking back, without learning the complex narratives aside from the one you first encountered, perhaps on a sign or in a guidebook or from a friendly local. Then you move on to the next town.

But stories matter, however casually consumed. To tell a story, any history, is to assert a kind of power. *This is how it was. This is what we're about. This is who we are.* To interrogate or reframe a story—to realize we are enmeshed in stories—is to reclaim part of that power, a power I was beginning to consider for myself given my own histories.

Kim, Frida, and I didn't leave Burgos until noon. As we walked, my jeans fluttered off the side of my bag to dry, like a shameful banner. Austin had made me laugh so hard the day before that I'd peed my pants in the middle of a busy intersection. "Imagine a rushing waterfall," he'd teased. "Imagine the sound of a running river." I hadn't had time to find a bathroom, much less "drop pants" as Kim called it. Pedestrians gawked. I burst out laughing. Austin's face immediately changed from mirth to remorse. Like many people, the constant physical exertion did a number on my bodily functions. I had washed my jeans in the hotel shower with shampoo. From that day forward, Frida was sure to make an announcement each time I wore my "pee pants."

I looked at Frida as her plastic sunglasses glinted in the sun. Strong, resilient, blister-covered Frida. She had been the first person to help me with my blisters. When one made my pinky toe swell to twice its size, she offered to poke it with a needle. I'd never stabbed a needle into a blister before, and many pilgrims preached you should never pop them. But I couldn't continue to walk with a toe that size. The thought of metal jabbing into the epicenter of my pain made me dizzy. Austin wouldn't help, wanting me to learn to do it myself and toughen up. Frida stepped in, put on her headlamp in order to look like a doctor, and pricked the bubble. Two Korean women weighed in, instructing me to leave a thread in the blisters overnight to absorb the liquid. To my enormous gratitude, it worked.

There was one day when Frida had insisted on staying behind. Her hiking boots had torn holes into the soles of her soft flesh, like someone had taken a cheese grater to her skin. She needed a rest. We felt gutted to press on without her, but we all had schedules. "We'll see you in Santiago," we'd said. Then, that night, she arrived at the albergue an hour after us. Everyone smothered her with wine and hugs; we would never leave her again.

Kim and I often fawned over Frida's vitality, her adrenaline, her seeming lack of worry. Kim and I had more than enough anxiety and self-doubt to spare. We wanted Frida lessons. Frida told Kim to "stop apologizing for everything." She told me to "stop giving a f— about what other people think." Frida curated her own stories, stories of adventure—ice skating across pristine lakes in November, biking across entire countries on a three-speed, or gathering golden cloudberries in the forest near her home in northern Sweden.

We clipped along toward our destination of Hornillo. At one point, the three of us stopped to look at a mound of white rocks. A single hiking boot, similar to the ones that had chewed up Frida's feet, sat on top of a pile of rocks. A flower was growing out of the top of the boot, like a planter. The sight resembled a shrine. But to what? Who left the boot? How could a plant grow in those conditions?

That, too, was a tale I wanted to know—with no one around to tell it.

We walked on.

Kim moved alongside me with her swishy athletic shorts over black leggings. Kim knew the power of stories down to her bones. As a writer, she knew what a narrative could do. I was ready to begin creating my own. Perhaps this was one of the many reasons why I had felt drawn to her since the start of the Camino.

On another day, a downpour of a day, Austin and I had gotten into a morning squabble over his burst of spending on roadside treats—enough to fill an entire plastic bag—putting us over our daily budget.

"We can't eat chips and licorice for breakfast, lunch, and dinner. What were you thinking?"

"I thought you'd be happy. You're *welcome* for getting you snacks."

He became fed up with my criticisms and stormed off, leaving me to hike a miserable ten k's alone. Without snacks. Why did things still have to feel hard sometimes? I hadn't meant to push him away. I wondered if a difficult marriage appealed to me, the way difficulty had appealed to me in so many other areas of my life given my pull toward complexity, my never-ending quest for truth and meaning. The thought left me exhausted, like the exhaustion of this constant walking and walking. I didn't see Austin again until I arrived at a lunch spot, a bar where Hal and Kim were also huddled away from the rain, stealing a few moments before braving another increase in elevation. Austin's eyes said *I'm sorry* and *forgive me* and

I missed you, and mine did too. We sat beside each other like nothing had happened, content to be in each other's company again after growing bored of arguing, unsure of how much of it actually had to do with splurging on a handful of spontaneous treats.

Hal walked with Austin. Kim walked beside me. She could tell I was struggling, and not just with the incline, not just with the rain. I could use something else to get over this hill.

"Have I told you about the woman I wrote a book with, the Russian pilot who fought on the Eastern Front?" she asked, referring to the memoir *Red Sky, Black Death*.

I shook my head. Water pelted my leaky, secondhand poncho. I could feel my mesh shoes filling up. Evergreens lined the path. The ground began to turn to liquid, so red it reminded me of tomato soup.

"Anna Yegorova was a fighter pilot, a total badass." Kim told me stories of Yegorova's resolute optimism, faith in her country, and unwavering determination to help the cause that led her to become a pilot despite sexism and serious resistance along the way. She flew into some of the bloodiest war zones in a wooden biplane. Yegorova's plane was shot down, then she survived five months in a Nazi concentration camp. But instead of a hero's return, the Soviet secret police treated her like a spy. She wasn't acknowledged as a patriot until 1965, the day she accepted Moscow's highest award: Hero of the Soviet Union.

I held onto Kim's every word until we reached the top of the incline. Then, for the descent, she had another story ready.

"Have I ever told you about the time I helped Hal catch a suspect while he was doing his PI work?"

I was more than happy to keep listening.

As we ladies trekked under the wide sky, I thought about Kim and Hal's relationship. I felt the urge to ask Kim what I'd been dying to ask: *How do you and Hal do it?* They'd shared bits of their origin story: Kim was Hal's flying teacher. Hal, recovering from a divorce, was charming and quick on his toes with the right pilot jokes, such as "Parasite drag. Great name for a band." One day, a tornado ripped through Nashville and destroyed Kim's small aircraft—a cherished, hard-earned, joint investment with her father. The loss wrecked her. Kim turned to Hal, who comforted her through that long night (they grinned and tapered off when they got to that part of the telling). They later married in the Belize jungle under a *palapa*, standing on a Maya mound.

I wanted to understand how they sustained their connection after fifteen years of marriage. They made it look deceptively easy: Kim's effusive enthusiasm for Hal's GoPro footage, Hal pausing mid-stride to ask Kim how her feet were feeling, Kim ensuring Hal tasted the most delicious tapas on the table, Hal's regular compliments on Kim's writing and on her sexy body, no matter how sweaty or unshowered or sleep-deprived. They jested and laughed with abandon. Respect. Support. Loyalty. I saw all of that in a glance, the way they looked at each other—that way the movies and books talked about. I'd never seen anything like it. Ever. And I wanted to know the secret. I wanted to believe there *was* a secret.

"I really admire your relationship with Hal," I said, careful not to sound too eager. I thought of their mutual acts of generosity, like Hal taking the initiative to organize a dinner so Kim could enjoy a slower morning in Burgos. But it was more, so much more, than chivalry. I admired how well Hal and Kim treated each other, how they talked *about* each other. They asked after each other's well-being and put their partner first, saying things like "How are you? Are you sure? Can I help?"

"I just really like him," Kim said. She didn't pretend to be an expert and probably felt strange being put in a position of authority to comment on something as vast as partnership, though she warned me about the dangers of eye-rolling, contempt, and complaining—things she'd seen sneak in and sour relationships she'd observed. "I give him the benefit of the doubt and try to remember that we're not mind readers. If one of us needs a hug, we need to be open and ask for it."

These were probably common enough things I could have read anywhere, but hearing them from Kim made them matter.

"Do you think marriage is too much work?" I asked, though perhaps this was more a question—the *real* question—for me than for her.

"No," Kim said. "Life is work. Love makes it easier."

Kim knew the power of a story. But she also knew what a story could not do.

"Do you think you should get some new shoes?" she'd suggested, as firmly as I'd known her to suggest. Lately, I could feel a pulse burning in my arches.

But in my stubbornness, and out of concern for money and perhaps a final hurrah to martyrdom, I'd passed. My Chacos, for all their obvious limitations on the Camino, had taken me all over the world for as long as I'd been traveling. They had become part of my own narrative, one I wasn't ready to change. Yet.

Frida played a Swedish version of "Hakuna Matata" on her phone as the three of us descended one final hill covered with stones the size of fists. At last, we strolled up to the Hornillo albergue. Ladies' day had been a success.

"Welcome," James called out, his enormous Sicilian body leaning against a stone wall. Austin sat on a bench outside the albergue. He looked up as we entered, placing his book facedown and wrapping me in a tight hug.

"Dinner is almost ready," he said.

I leaned into him and breathed in traces of cooking herbs. *I like you*, I thought. And I always had. We weren't the smooth brand of Hal and Kim's compatibility that I admired so much. We weren't anyone else but ourselves. Maybe that was okay. Yes, things sometimes felt hard. But there was also a sense of safety, contentment, and pleasure in being together. Maybe I wouldn't always wonder if I was feeling the "right" thing like an incessant itch and, instead, just *feel*. Perhaps we could still learn from others, continue to become the best version of us. But this, *us*, I was beginning to comprehend, was a long-term endeavor only we could do for ourselves, an act of creating and sustaining and believing in our own story as we went along. Maybe marriage was better experienced than understood.

Suzy was giving out oil massages to pilgrims with sore legs: friends and newer faces. Frida jumped into Suzy's queue. Kim looked around.

"Where's Hal?" she asked. Then he emerged from the communal kitchen, the steam of boiled potatoes following after him and his salt-and-pepper beard.

"How was your walk?" he asked Kim with an expression that betrayed his excitement for the mouth-watering chicken and pasta we'd soon enjoy. He'd even toasted bread to make croutons for the fresh salad. The sheer energy Hal put into the details of his creation after a laborious day of walking touched every part of the meal.

Kim didn't say a word. Instead, she beamed with a proud look that said it all. Or did it? It was a love that was theirs alone.

Kim had one more invaluable gift for me.

She cornered me after dinner before everyone slipped in their earplugs and pulled on their eye masks. "Can you say you're a writer without making a face or a self-deprecating comment?"

I grimaced. She understood, better than anyone, and she intimidated me with her sincerity. Kim was a *real* writer, I imagined. She professionally did this thing I'd done compulsively but minimized as a hobby for myself. I'd mentioned my amateur writing a few times in passing conversations. How was she able to read me, to know writing may be one way into the abstract hope for happiness I'd shared around the table in Ventosa?

"By Santiago, I want you to own it. Say it: 'I am a writer.'"

Who was I to claim I had a story worth telling, let alone the confidence to tell it? *A twenty-something, millennial, know-nothing, married, Utah Mormon girl.* But then I remembered the bitter, small place where that thinking came from. That story wasn't true. That story wasn't true for anyone. That story had *never* been true.

I was more than the histories I'd casually and actively consumed: more than my parents' divorces, more than my mother's decline, more than a tally of hardships I'd overcome, more than what was said about women at church or in the grocery-store-aisle magazines, more than any label glued to my forehead or any that I'd stuck there myself, more than my marital status. I could be the narrator, shaper, of my own life and not just a character. Is that not what I'd always wanted?

"I am a writer," I said to Kim, practicing, my stomach in knots.

I am a writer.

CHAPTER 23

Snapshots to Carry Home

NEVER LET ME FORGET THE NOISE of plastic bags rustling in the morning before anyone dared to flip on the lights.

The stench of still-warm shoes lining albergue entrances.

That sometimes the phrase *buen camino* can also mean "move it" or "f— you" when a cyclist whizzes past.

That in the ongoing debate between southern and northern Europeans on whether or not the window should be opened or closed in the dormitory at night, the correct answer is *opened.*

The middle-school teacher snoring on his back, mouth agape, boots still laced, poles in hand, and a pilgrim's shell centered on his chest as if in burial.

How a few of Austin's snot rockets splattered on my sandals.

What it felt like to pull on dirty, crusty underwear again after a lukewarm shower.

Those stretches along blazing-hot pavement, my skin drier than a raisin and lips scabbed, as tree cotton blew like snow.

The blustery man who insisted on ordering the *hecho recientemente*, pointing at those words atop the café poster featuring dozens of *bocadillo* options.

How locals left bakeries with newspaper parcels cradled under their arms. How my jaw ached from gnawing on hard baguettes, my mouth ripped up a bit from the rough texture.

The night I was awake to witness Hal throw his hands in the air when "Vlad the Inhaler" forgot a pap machine.

How quickly and reliably news of bed bugs spread by word of mouth.

The sun rash that erupted over the left side of my body, leaving white bubbles on my foot and hand. How Suzy walked beside me, pacing her steps so her shadow would shade my feet. How she complimented me on my "nice bronzing."

The heat in my throat as I read the signs counting down the kilometers to Santiago: 571 . . . 570 . . . 569. How I didn't know what to think when I saw "WHY ARE YOU WALKING?" spray-painted on the curb.

But also, the pleasure of stopping for two breakfasts per day.

The glow of fresh-squeezed Spanish orange juice.

How long my silhouette seemed in the early morning, a skinny swatch of dark framed in a hot-pink sunrise, beams of light casting a star on the road.

The ticking sound of Joanina's walking stick hitting the ground, as rhythmic and consistent as a heartbeat.

What it felt like to be enamored with an earthworm as long as my leg.

The circular patterns cut into the distant grain fields like lines left by a vacuum cleaner.

How no one knew the English name of the flower covering the landscape in billowy yellow blankets—only the name in Czech, German, Italian, and Hungarian.

The satisfaction of watching my own grime swirl away in the shower drain.

How pilgrims used their scallop shells to lap red wine from a fountain outside a monastery.

The elderly village women in long dresses who set aside brooms to lean across their individual balconies, gossiping in quick, hushed Spanish.

The grocer wearing a Basque nationalist T-shirt who gave me a banana to help with muscle pain.

The Cuban guesthouse owner who bragged about having made love to his wife on every table—including ours—then mocked my stiff classroom Spanish as he served us homemade lemon yogurt for dessert.

When Austin introduced Elise to Oreos. How, from then on, she insisted she "didn't have a problem with Oreos, she had a problem *without* Oreos."

The best-selling book Frida and I vowed to write on how to hunt flies using a hiking pole, then a sequel on how to fix the pole using duct tape.

The pack of Scots who slipped into kilts in the morning and kept tabs on every other Scot on the trail.

The sight of two young pilgrims—an Italian chef and a German lawyer—sunbathing seminude outside a stone church, their clothes strewn about the entrance.

The Vietnam vet who sang, "We'll meet again, / don't know where, don't know when" as he spun, his voice and spittle flying in all directions.

What it felt like to pull up a chair next to perfect strangers at dinner without feeling awkward.

When someone picked up a nylon-string guitar in the corner of an albergue and strummed John Lennon's "Imagine." How the room of twenty people, regardless of nationality or primary language, joined the chorus as if we finally understood the lyrics.

The night Austin and I pushed two bunks together, creating something like a full-size bed, then fell asleep immediately in each other's arms.

The four-foot nun wearing navy loafers who gave me a Madonna pendant on a blue thread I would wear for the rest of the pilgrimage. How I practiced a thank-you conversation in my head but never saw her again.

When Sheila handed Suzy a fistful of wildflowers for being "a beautiful woman."

The way Kim sprang from her chair to help with meals, pairing feasts with platters of stacked white cheese and quince paste.

The middle-aged Austrian who rested her feet on a patio chair, her orange pedicure peeking through her flip-flops. How her three grown children couldn't believe she was here. But I could.

That listening is a gift I know how to give.

That happiness can feel sacred.

The lightning pain of metal ladder rungs on aching feet, and the people who still had the goodness to ask, "Would you prefer the bottom bunk?"

The man in a wheelchair pushing his way up a mountain, sweat glistening off his brow, while his wife walked behind to support him through rocky patches.

When Hal squeezed my hand and asked, "How are you?" a gentle gesture—such a small, simple gesture—that made my eyes water.

The grueling thirty-one-k day when Sheila didn't arrive at our destination. Someone had seen her vomiting off the side of the road. But what followed is a memory I am not at risk of forgetting, a seared image I examine over and over for clues of how we moved from discomfort to moments of intense presence, from self-interest to some semblance of belonging: Martin's flash of concern, how he ran back without hesitation. He found Sheila four k's away and returned with her. I did the math. Martin had a thirty-nine-k day, and he had spent the last part moving hard and fast enough to kick up dust in his wake.

The times James dragged on a Marlboro cigarette and asserted his mantra, "The Way provides."

How I came around to believe him.

CHAPTER 24

The Meseta

EVERYONE WARNED US ABOUT THE MESETA, the dreaded 220-k stretch of the dry plateau along the Camino. Some recommended a bus or a train, citing the unchanging landscape, maddening in the way field after field pummeled the eyes with no sign of a village. People spoke of it less like a place and more like a ghost. The Meseta was a psychological test, the Pyrenees of the mind. Each of us felt up to the challenge.

But the Meseta came for us, too, forcing us into our anger, into our insecurities, poking at our fractures.

The Meseta divided our group. Like any family I've known, real or imagined, we scattered.

Suzy, our tall gazelle, our cheerleader and massage specialist, was the first to leave. I knew why before Joanina and Michael told us.

"I have a serious boyfriend back in Australia," Suzy had mentioned the day before, the last time I'd seen her. "He cares a great deal about me, and so do his children. He's a *really* good guy." Suzy seemed less talkative than usual, slower in her pace. She winced, mentioning shin splints, pausing to stretch. Her hope was to return to Australia to be with him upon completing her Camino. "At least, that's my current plan," Suzy had said. She shared that her instincts were against her. She'd spent the past few years wandering, going from tango studio to tango studio in South America, living passionately and loving men who morphed into mirages. Suzy and I had chatted more than once about what constituted partnership. Suzy wanted to walk this path to come to grips with what she *really* wanted, to prep herself for the return journey.

Suzy also mentioned that she'd met a mysterious artist at a gallery called Hospital del Alma in Castrojeriz, a fairytale village stitched along the top of a lush hill crowned with a crumbling castle. I recalled that Suzy's chair had remained empty at dinner that night. The group had felt her absence. Apparently, the artist had invited her to stay, not just for a meal but for much longer. Suzy had declined the second invitation, but she couldn't shake the artist.

"It's hard to know what to do," she said to me.

"I hear you," I said, Suzy and I abreast, walking in step under the pounding sun. I thought of similar wrestles I'd experienced. I remembered Amanda, the British nomad I'd met on my first trip to India. Many incredible women resisted the pressure to remain in one place, with one person. I admired those lives of freedom, though I recognized the costs. A part of me suspected I might always ponder those *what-ifs* for myself.

I didn't have any answers for Suzy. There were no right answers in these cases, only choices.

Now, after one day on the Meseta, Suzy had turned back. She needed to know what lay behind. Later, I heard that she moved on again after a few months, forming a relationship with a handsome roadside hermit, a reformed drug addict who had been living in a two-walled shelter beneath a makeshift roof for the past six years, no matter the season. He offered up a cart of hand-squeezed juices along with biscuits, toasts, jams, fresh fruits, and sometimes full meals to passing pilgrims. Even our guidebook had mentioned him and his generosity. For all I know, Suzy is still there, strumming a guitar, wishing everyone a buen camino, and offering up her legendary massages. A part of me hopes so. Another part of me hopes she is still roaming, living and loving wherever she wanders.

The next to go was Neil.

"It is time to walk my own Camino," he texted the group. No in-person goodbyes, all sarcasm extinguished. Perhaps I shouldn't have been surprised. He'd been popping over-the-counter Tramadol and squinting at bus signs in Spanish, taking taxis between towns when his motivation wore down.

Elise—young, strong Elise in her pink knitted socks—went with him. The train whisked them away beyond our reality, to the other side of the Meseta.

I understood, or at least I told myself I understood, but I missed everyone immediately, along with the impression of unity. Their perceived "giving up" threatened my own waning confidence. Goodbyes, especially abrupt goodbyes, triggered feelings of abandonment—the fear and the impulse. *Leave or get left.* Though I'd stuck it out plenty in my life—school, jobs no matter how difficult, my complicated commitment to religion, my relationship with Austin—I imagined none of these added enough evidence to redeem me from my original sin of leaving my mother, or the haunt of her leaving me. Then there's the thing where I couldn't stop traveling—running, running, running. I did not consider myself a person known for staying. I didn't feel like one who commits.

A feeling of betrayal, perhaps a kind of distress at being left behind in a wilderness, permeated the mood. Frida cursed. Kim pursed her lips. James stormed silently and confessed he'd had a dream where he'd told Hal to "call a lawyer." Sheila wept openly.

Sheila was the next to depart. We walked her to the bus station. She wore a red coat and wobbled as she supported herself on hiking sticks, her backpack a large shell against her tiny, nymph-like frame. No flowers graced her dark hair. A heavy determination shone in her eyes. Sheila had a goal, an urgency about getting to Cruz de Ferro by a specific date. There was something personal there she had to do, something to lay at the base of the iron cross in the mountain—we'd find out soon enough.

We gave her parting hugs.

"See you in Santiago," we said. That's what everyone always said.

On day seventeen of the pilgrimage, the third day in the Meseta, the sky threatened rain. I hadn't been sleeping well due to loud snoring in the albergues—but also dreams. Vivid, strange dreams that disappeared the moment I opened my eyes, leaving the distinct trace of disturbance without the logic to usher the feeling away. Even my ever-present Camino appetite was gone. Sporadic drizzle wet my face. Long yellow grass and wheat stretched along each side of the road, interrupted only by the occasional scab of brown. The wind moved the strands like sea swells, making me feel as though I were swimming, drowning, in a waterless ocean with no end in sight. Each bend looked like the last. Villages were spread out, meaning fewer breaks. Suddenly, everyone had tendonitis. With so many pilgrims taking the bus or train to avoid this section of the Camino, the path felt emptier. Irritation worked on me, rubbing into a mental blister. I raged at my feet, still achy after weeks of endurance. My eyes watered. I hugged my thin jacket around me, fighting the cold, an attempt to tap into my body's inner warmth. A day had never gone by so slowly.

How many k's have passed?

I needed markers, signs, a way to track my progress—to know how far I'd gone, how far I had left to go, how well I was doing.

My quiet took on an inner, inexplicable despair. The occasional conversations faded and blurred. Hal, who had slipped on some rocks and bruised his arms and hip, wasn't feeling up to his characteristic charm. Joanina and Michael held hands and kept to themselves. Though I'd spent most of the walk in comfortable silence with Austin—my consistent, reliable friend and companion—I walked twenty feet ahead when I vaguely made out his voice discussing Mormonism with Kim and a Lithuanian walking the whole Camino without a pack, keeping his only belongings wedged inside the large pockets of his khaki cargo pants. Austin had been using the first-person plural: "We believe this" and "We do that." I pressed on, without the energy to weigh in on the discussion, assert my fringe interpretations. I was unwilling, unable, to hear another word.

How much farther? I wanted to ask Austin, or anyone else nearby, for the millionth time. But I knew the answer would be the same: seventeen k's until the next café, then nine more k's until our destination. Without markers, no one knew where we were on the map.

What am I doing here?

More swaying grass. More straight path flecked with relics from an original Roman road, the stones green and blue like corroded pennies, the color of seeping dyes transferred to my hands on days when my jeans became damp from the mist.

More silence.

More sameness.

More wind. Always, *always* the wind. I could taste sand between my teeth.

What's the point? I screamed inside. *I need to be done for the day.*

NOW. NOW NOW NOWNOWNOW.

But the end was not in sight. All I had was now, and now was a scary thing indeed. *Now*, sitting with stillness and letting it just be? That process rarely left me satisfied or better off. The quiet scared me more than the distracting suffering. People did not skip the Meseta because it was boring. They skipped the Meseta because it made them feel insane—and not in the comical Don Quixote way.

I need to escape.

But where would I go?

I don't want to go home.

Familiar fear followed the rage, then the realization that I didn't want to be here, didn't want to be anywhere else, and yet I'd be boarding an airplane again in a few weeks. My heartbeat kicked up, ready to fight, ready to escape.

But fight what? Run where?

I gritted my teeth, pressing forward. Gusts chafed my reddened cheeks. The vast emptiness allowed my mind to fill it. The Meseta brought out the unsorted psychological, the voice we drowned out with laughter, food, drink, the romance of the journey. But here, my mind had space for its own long version of the story. I wondered if the Meseta, more than any other part of the Camino, resembled the Great Plains in the US.

How did my ancestors do this?

All my life, I'd been told the stories of the Mormon pioneers: their conviction, their sacrifice, their religious persecution as they left behind their roots and comforts and relationships, fleeing from city to city, state to state—escaping mobs and a government-sanctioned extermination order and the sight of their temple aflame in the night—until eventually, they pressed beyond the then-boundaries of the US in search of a place to call home, a place to build a Zion and practice their religion in safety. Sometimes the telling of their stories veered into idealization or mythology, the emphasis always on overcoming their untold suffering, deaths, the martyrdom of their prophet and leader, Joseph Smith. There is no denying these injustices, though fewer stories examine the early Mormons' instigating role in their oppression—they weren't great neighbors. Utah celebrates Pioneer Day on July 24, marking their arrival into the Salt Lake Valley in 1847 as a multinational community forged from a shared tragedy and a united hope in creating a beautiful, radical future—building Zion on Earth. Few understood why Brigham Young allegedly declared, "It is enough. This is the right place" when they rolled into that desert landscape. Why this one? They made the most of a near-impossible situation and put out a call to gather. Growing up in Utah, our Pioneer Day celebrations seemed bigger to me than those of the Fourth of July.

In Primary, the children's Sunday school program, I had sung songs revering the pioneers:

> When pioneers moved to the West,
> With courage strong they met the test.
> They pushed their handcarts all day long,
> And as they pushed they sang this song:
> For some must push and some must pull,
> As we go marching up the hill;
> So merrily on our way we go
> Until we reach the Valley-o.

And:

> Pioneer children sang as they walked and walked
> and walked.
> They washed in streams and worked and played.
> Sundays they camped and read and prayed.
> Week after week, they sang as they walked and
> walked and walked and walked and walked.

Bullshit, I thought now, gazing out at the cruel Meseta. Who would have had the energy to sing in conditions like this, but much worse? I preferred another children's hymn about the pioneers, a dour one sung in a minor key:

> Here comes the oxcart, oh, how slow!
> It's pulled by an ox, of course you know.
> The wooden wheels creak as they roll along.
> Creak, creak, creak, creak, creak is their song.

Every one of my second-, third-, or fourth-great-grandparents were pioneers, making me 100 percent "Mormon pioneer stock." A handful uprooted to Utah from the eastern states. Most took boats from Denmark, England, Germany, or Sweden. Many took wagon trains. Some unlucky ones pushed handcarts across the dry prairie, through snowy Rocky Mountain passes, clawing at the frozen ground to dig graves to bury their dead family members. The luckiest ones arrived a decade later on the new Union Pacific Railroad.

Sometimes I didn't know how to relate to this heritage or where I fit within it. I wasn't a saint. I lacked conviction. I wasn't persecuted. I fled threats of expectations, whereas where they fled actual threats. Was I ungrateful for their sacrifices in my willingness to reverse their path, to abandon Utah and everything they'd built? Few in my direct family line had moved permanently away from the Intermountain West since the pioneers' arrival. Would they find my unconventional Mormonism an insult to everything they stood for? Or would they find it humorous that I was on a Catholic pilgrimage, also walking westward, simply because I wanted to? Maybe they wouldn't have found my wandering strange at all.

With only three more k's to go, my mind overthrew my fumbling body. My feet burned like someone was holding a flame under my soles. I couldn't walk a second longer. I was, in Hal's words, "seeing only the poop and not the pony."

I stopped and dropped my backpack. Then I lay flat on the damp earth, all drama, though I didn't care if anyone saw. The ground greeted me like an old friend, my skull pressed against the hard honesty of dirt. *What would it look like, for just this once, to give up?* I stared at the slate sky, then covered my face with my floppy hat, pinning it in place so the wind couldn't tear it away. Two blisters throbbed on my left foot.

I'm done.

In time, I would draw a kind of strength from knowing the long version of my own family story, which I researched on Ancestry.com—a massive database owned and operated by The Church of Jesus Christ of Latter-day Saints. My pioneer people, I discovered, were more particular than I had been taught, more than a measure of their incredible resilience, more than a lump of saints. They were stranger, more restless, more adventurous, more flawed, more human, perhaps more like me than I had supposed.

For a long time, I thought my mother was the first woman in my family line to go to college. But I've uncovered a sepia photograph of Nora Mae Roper, my third-great-grandmother, at the age of fifty-three, smiling, standing in a black graduation gown, a cap atop her dark bob, a scroll gripped with both hands. She graduated from the Northeastern States Teacher's College in Oklahoma, then went back for a bachelor of science, then again, for a certificate to teach ceramics and weaving. She taught until her death. The picture does not betray the pain of her earlier life, on the journey west, when Nora fell sick and had to return east. At that time, her husband kidnapped their son, Earl, my second-great-grandfather. Earl and his father spent the next year living in a tent, even through the winter, running from town to town in Utah and Idaho. Earl was described by others as "such a sad little boy." The runaway husband became a mail carrier to intercept any letters related to Nora's relentless search for her son.

Earl nearly ran away himself when he was fifteen—the same age I was as I made my own departure from home—off to the bright horizon of California. He and his childhood friend made it as far as the rail station in Garland, Utah, eighteen miles away from their small town. They slept at the station. The next morning, after a vivid dream where Earl saw words etched onto a boxcar that promised "a great reward" for staying, he chickened out. His friend went on to California, never to be seen by his family again. Earl chose to stay. He grew up, married. Then, just before his first child, my great-grandmother, was born in 1914, Earl was reunited with his mother. Nora had followed a fortuneteller's prompting that her son lived in a small town in Utah. She wrote letters to every tiny town until eventually, a letter finally reached him. When he held the note in his hands, his wife said he "cried and cried he was so happy." They were soon reunited.

Another third-great-grandmother, Lily Susan Walpole, defied all expectations at the age of thirteen by joining the Mormon church in Norfolk, England. Her family, proper members of the Church of England, felt disgraced when they found out she'd been baptized into Mormonism. One day, she came home from a church meeting at 9:00 p.m. to find the door locked. She wrote, "I shook it hard but none came to let me in so I stood out that night." From then on, she was forced to lodge with a neighbor. Lily worked nine-hour days at a silk mill, attending night school to finish her education. After two years, at the age of fifteen (seems to be a pattern), Lily had saved enough for the passage across the Atlantic to Utah. Her folks, perhaps wanting to make amends, tried to prevent the sail. Lily heard of their plan and disguised herself as a boy, passing by the officials in Liverpool without detection. Once she reached New Orleans, her travel companions lent her "a fine riding horse" for the journey to Zion. Unlike other pioneer stories I'd been told, Lily described the trip as "the most enjoyable" she'd ever experienced. The "weather was delightful." When they reached the Salt Lake Valley, Lily said she wished "the trip had been two thousand miles longer." In the black-and-white picture I have of Lily, she sits outside in a rocking chair with a book in her lap in Murray, Utah. Her wrinkled face is shaded and enigmatic. She wears a long white dress as bright as her hair.

I could no longer ignore, after reading these stories and others, the evidence that I come from a long line of brave people, particularly women, making their own way in the world and defying the status quo. Yes, I admired their grit. I was used to admiring their resilience and faith—in fact, I was taught to do so. But in reviewing their lives, I also had a chance to sit with their griefs, without seeking to minimize or moralize their pain. They knew struggle beyond the physical exertion to get to Utah. Each experienced separation and abandonment, yet I did not judge them for it like I sometimes did myself.

One of my favorite stories I've uncovered is from another set of third-great-grandparents: Ole Peterson and Sophia Nielsen. They were childhood friends back in Denmark before each of their families set out for Utah at different times. After five years of living in Clarkston, Utah, Ole—broke, hungry, and with little to say for clothing—found out where Sophia lived in northern Utah. Though he hadn't seen her in a decade, he had to find her. Perhaps it was the poet in him. In the spring of 1887, Ole set out on foot, working for food along the way. This was not a typical pioneer story but rather a pilgrimage for love. I wish I could observe the moment when Ole reached her doorstep, 213 miles later, and see the look in his deep blue eyes, his matted black hair. It was said that Sophia "could see the fun in everything." They were married the following year in the Logan Utah Temple.

Their children, like their father, became poets. One wrote:

> Dearie, do you remember Ole Petersen courting
>   Sophia true,
> Over where the choke cherries grew?
> That was when the good old horse and buggy
> Made romance so sweet.

One of Ole and Sophia's daughters described their home, a boarding house at one time, as having a unique feeling: "I remember a man saying to father one evening: 'There is something fine about your home, Mr. Petersen. You all seem to get along so well together.' Father, never missing a chance to preach the Gospel answered, 'This is a Latter-day Saint home, we try to have the Spirit of the Gospel here.'"

The boarder didn't seem satisfied with that generic answer. "'I have been to other Latter-day Saint homes,' the man replied, shaking his head. 'You seem to feel something more toward each other.'"

"What are you doing?" Austin said.

I pulled away my hat. He stood over me, amused. He seemed so handsome to me then, his face scruffy and hair wild. I closed my eyes.

"What does it look like I'm doing?"

"Are you okay?"

I moaned and muttered. With him, I could be my worst. By now, I trusted he wouldn't leave me when things got hard. That knowledge both comforted and frightened me. All these years, all these months, all these days together, and still I wondered if I was capable of the long-term, doubtful of my ability to stay given my restless heart forged by the east winds of my youth. Though I had days—full days—where I appreciated and loved my windy disposition, the restlessness that had brought me so far, *here*, this was not one of those moments. I was no longer a sobbing child holding my pigtails and watching trees snap and shingles fly down the road. But I was still afraid of blowing away—as I had done many times since—afraid of my inability to control the force of my nature. I didn't want to hurt or disappoint any more people, least of all him.

"Only three k's left. We're practically there." Austin nudged my bag with his shoe. "Let's keep going."

Why did he always have to speak in the imperative?

I opened my eyes to half-mast. He held out his hand. After a long pause, I decided to take it.

"We're flying home in eighteen days," I said without feeling. I brushed dirt off my butt and picked up my backpack.

To that, Austin nodded. He didn't say anything. He could tell how I felt about it.

"Well, I know one subject that will make you feel better," he said as we began walking again.

"Hmph."

"How should we organize our books?"

Despite *knowing* this was a setup, I felt a whisper of joy. Though we had no apartment in Boston lined up yet, I had a vision for the bookshelves. The thought of combining our books was perhaps the single part of marriage I took absolutely no issue with. From the beginning, his collection—his beautiful, extensive, irresponsible purchases—had won me over. I had so much to gain by merging our libraries.

"We should color code them," I said. "Moving from gradient to gradient. Maybe arrange them from tallest to shortest. Or we could stagger them, more like a rainbow."

"How will I find any of them if they aren't grouped by topic?"

"You'll have me," I said. "I remember everything visually."

"Okay." Austin didn't sound convinced, but, satisfied with his small victory, he didn't challenge me. "We can try that for a while and see how it goes."

I smiled for the first time all day.

Then he asked, "What should we hang on the walls?"

At last, the rain came, hard and deliberate, pelting our group continuously on day nineteen, one of our final days through the Meseta. We had waited and waited for the downpour for so long that we'd forgotten our annoyance. The rain hit us like a game of tag, like a joke that goes on and on without a punch line. We sloshed along, stepping over the stone relics of the unflinching Roman road—not a single village to stop at for the 24.5-k day. We posed for awkward poncho pictures. My braid looked like a single, frizzy rope dangling by my face. We kicked murky puddles, as everyone's feet were drenched anyway. We dribbled rocks. We laughed. We had descended past rage, past pain, past fear, past boredom, into something almost delirious. But it no longer scared me. We had broken the boundary of despair, the narrative of suffering, and entered the realm of hilarity.

And what did we do when we reached this level? We sang.

"Does everyone know 'Row, Row, Row Your Boat'?"

Everyone did. We sang it all together, then in rounds:

> Row, row, row your boat.
>   Row, row, row your boat.

Then we did it again, with another international nursery rhyme:

> Are you sleeping? Are you sleeping?
>   Brother John, Brother John.

"Who the f— is John? His name is Jacob. Let's try it in Swedish," Frida said, teaching us how to shape our mouths to make the new sounds in the familiar tune. Only Austin nailed the accent to the words:

Broder Jakob, Broder Jakob, sover du? Sover du?
Hör du inte klockan? Hör du inte klockan?
Ding ding dong! Ding ding dong!

She then taught us the Swedish National Anthem and, fittingly, a children's song about the glory of the sun.

Next, we took on different parts of the Potter Puppet Pals YouTube video, imitating each character. Hal started us off with a convincing base:

Snape. Snape. *Severus* Snape . . .
DUMBLEDORE! Austin shouted.
Ron, Ron, Ron *WEASLEY!* I added.
HarryPotterHarryPotter! Frida blustered.

For a while, Bonnie Tyler's "Total Eclipse of the Heart" kept us company. We belted the lyrics shamelessly, as if alone in the shower. The rain kept falling.

"I've got another one," I said. I told them about the pioneer hymns from Primary and taught everyone the words to the dour oxcart song. Austin somehow hadn't heard of it, had never sung it, though he came from pioneers himself.

"That's it?" Hal said.

"Yup. That's it."

"How inspiring," said Kim.

We sang it in turn:

Here comes the oxcart,
oh how slow!
It's pulled by an ox,
of course you know.

Never had the song sounded better than when Hal, in his soothing deep voice, added his vibrato to the "creak, creak" part.

For a moment, I could almost imagine the oxcart song playing in a Nashville honky-tonk.

Hours passed like that. We sang every international-friendly song we could vomit from our subconsciouses. The rain didn't tire, but neither did we. I now understood that urge to sing and walk, the particular mental landscape that creates such a dizzying headspace, a strange but surreal place where I found comfort in the sound of my own utterance, an assertion of existence, a sound in harmony with the voices of those around me—everyone who chose to remain—existing too.

I'm sorry I ever doubted that my ancestors, mavericks and pilgrims in their peculiar way, sang as they trekked westward in search of an uncertain future. I believe a lot of things now that I never thought I'd believe.

CHAPTER 25

Cruz de Ferro

BEFORE DAWN, OUR DWINDLING CAMINO FAMILY shuffled out of the scratchy, dun-colored albergue blankets and left Foncebadón, a mountain village refuge. Today we would summit the highest elevation of the whole pilgrimage, including the Pyrenees, peaking at 1,500 meters. Our group had decided to skip breakfast and pocket stale bread for the road. We wanted to reach Cruz de Ferro, Spanish for "iron cross," before the crowds. For many, Cruz de Ferro was the climax of the pilgrimage, a place with an aura as strong as the city of Santiago de Compostela, which we wouldn't reach for eight more days. Most people in our group carried a rock from home. Austin and I had only the two stones we'd plucked from Saint-Jean on the day we began the Camino. As I'd packed my bag in Foncebadón, I'd found my generic gray rock and held it in my palm. It felt jagged and light, but still—it was weight.

"You snored a lot last night," Austin whispered as we set out into the predawn mist.

"Ugh. How loud?" Snoring was the greatest of common offenses.

"*Pretty* loud."

I believed him. I felt as though I'd barely slept. A cold had settled into my lungs. Germs spread quickly on the Camino.

But why were we whispering?

The icy mountain air chilled my feverish body. I wore socks on my hands out of desperation and shivered as we climbed. Each person in our group was silent, determined. I couldn't tell if the change was from an earlier-than-usual departure or something else. To avoid tripping on the dirt trail, I stared at my feet—numb, red, swollen sausage-toes poking through my Chacos. When the sun did emerge, cracking like an egg over the horizon, the world seemed to ignite, illuminating Foncebadón behind us, flushing the purple-flowering bushes with gold, drawing attention to the contrasting fog.

I was still staring at the ground when everyone came to a halt.

I looked up.

There it was: Cruz de Ferro. An iron cross atop a massive stake like a thin sword or steeple. Thousands of deposited rocks and notes stacked at the base in a sprawling gray mound.

Austin took my sock-covered hand. The group stood in reverent silence, a new volume for our vivacious crew. I looked to Hal, Kim, and James to lead the way. They had walked this route before.

But Martin, a faithful Catholic, went first without hesitation. He approached the cross as if this was something he needed to do. He knelt in the thin morning light, a silver moon above him as he prayed. I couldn't hear the words he said, so earnest, his head bowed and brow furrowed. After adding his rock, Martin returned in silence to our huddled group.

Hal and Kim went next. They'd brought multiple rocks from various Nashville friends who'd asked them to place their contributions at this sacred site.

They returned. "Sheila's been here," Kim said. "You'll see."

Austin and I approached the cross. I marveled at the thousands and *thousands* of rocks, the tiny notes and trinkets, like flags or handkerchiefs, that many critique as a growing trash heap. I soon spotted Sheila's offering: a bundle of lavender placed beside a picture of a dark-haired man with a youthful smile. My eyes watered. The man was her great love, Beat, who had died a year earlier on the same date Sheila had promised herself she would be here at Cruz de Ferro.

A sobering stillness gripped me. Not a religious feeling per se, but the overwhelming realization of how it felt to stand among these stones—on *top* of these stones—and all the pain and struggle, pleas and hopes, they represented for the individuals who'd carried them so far, so long. The pile had large and small rocks, rough and smooth, some painted, others featuring full names or scriptures written in Sharpie. I assumed each embodied something specific, named, perhaps a challenge more difficult than any I'd ever experienced. Collectively, they overwhelmed me.

Then Austin tossed his offering into the ocean of others with a clink. He never told me what his rock meant to him, perhaps something that came to his mind at the moment. He has since forgotten. Austin wasn't one to ruminate. He looked at me. My turn.

I sniffed, trying to breathe through my stuffy nose. My chest ached from coughing. When I turned over my gray-speckled rock, I saw burden. I saw weight, but perhaps one I still couldn't truly define or measure. I saw my relationship to suffering and struggle and almost-desperate need to prevail that had been both entertained and challenged along this whole journey. I recalled my humbling morning through the Pyrenees.

Perhaps this rock was my currency.

By my fuzzy logic, the currency of suffering—earned through acts of resilience—could inch me toward an elusive goal of success that manifested as accolades, productivity, prosperity, righteousness, belief, being happily married with a family for eternity—being *happy* in every aspect. The currency lived in a spending account that could buy me protection from total tragedy. This hard-won currency acted as an insurance plan against fate and provided a false sense of control. *To pay* is a verb that can also mean "to atone, to suffer."

But who collected the dues, which were beginning to feel more like alms? Who was this murky god of suffering, and what did that god grant me in exchange for my constant loyalty? Certainly not the end of pain. Certainly not relief from anxiety. Certainly not balm for my lack of imagination in a brighter future or, even more radical, a brighter today.

Perhaps that god's name was Failure. Nothing unique. Big, looming, intangible, a terrifying shadow cast over everything. Real all the same, especially for anyone, like me, who'd lived most of their life trying to please others, ignoring the pinched voice welling up inside.

Who would I be without fearing the wrath of Failure? If I wasn't afraid, who was I? If I wasn't sad, where was life's meaning? If I wasn't the accumulation of all the hard things I had faced and overcome, how would I measure the value of my life?

I feared that if I stopped suffering or if I reexamined my narrative of struggle, I'd be left with something worse: grief. Real grief. Grief without any meaning. The chance to sit with all that I had lost—my home, my youth, my mother, my understanding of God, my entire framework of certainty, my stories that bound me safely to my community and family, my trust in forever. I worried that accepting grief, even for a moment, would risk me never getting back up again, my limbs freezing until I stopped moving, trying, reaching.

Everything could turn. Like a twig snagged along a riverbank. After my exhausting protests, I'd grow weary and give into the current. All my resistance for naught, become swept up in the trapped, the miserable, the inevitable that could be delayed but never escaped. I'd abandon my ambitions. Austin would become a stranger at best, an enemy at worst. He would leave me for another woman, a younger woman, leaving me alone with four kids. Enter the suspicion. Enter the paranoia. Enter the court battles and fights with growing children and the paycheck to paycheck and food from charities and dramatic phone calls to anyone who will listen, until they stop answering, because the tales verge on fantasy, the plots too absurd, the lonely years dragging on and the ungrateful children moving away until the woman finally picks up a pen, only to scribble incoherent notes she shreds as she spirals deeper and deeper into her own mind.

But that woman was not me. That woman was my mother.

Surely the god of suffering had the power to sink me, dragging me closer to the precarious line of how I perceived her fate: losing her adventurous spirit to marriage, then her mind when the marriage ruptured and the children left. Despite the many holes in this theory, I'd fought hard to stay away from that plot for myself. I could picture her in that moment: hair entirely gray, isolated at home, jittery as she dressed for her minimum-wage job, final notices she refused to tell anyone about taped to the locked front door, her brain sifting through the real and envisioned persecutions that vexed her—a scene nothing like how she used to be, the bright life she'd envisioned for herself, nothing of what she'd been promised if she married a worthy man in the temple who'd served a mission and then fulfilled her divine role as mother.

Still, I held my rock. For a moment, I wanted to keep it. Or chuck it, *far*, into a bush or over a cliff instead.

What if I failed? Really failed?

Is that the worst thing that could happen?

My marriage could fail.

What if it did?

What if *I* failed in my marriage?

What I was beginning to taste in small spoonfuls—flavored with liberation—was a *guarantee* that I would fail. I would be petty some days. I would be too critical. I would be angry, furious, selfish. I would be wrong. I would be right when it wouldn't matter. I would be sad and lonely. I would be afraid. I would be flawed. And I could be sorry. I could try again. Marriage was a daily negotiation, a daily act of faith—a faith different from my tenuous relationship with God, where I'd wrongly internalized that doubt had no place. Questioning, I had been taught, signaled a failure of faith. Faith meant knowing something with certainty. But marriage demanded an always-evolving faith, precarious, with two different *people* evolving.

How many people would I disappoint if I failed? A lot. Though probably fewer than I supposed.

But who was I until I did fail? Until I accepted, bravely, whatever that might mean?

Maybe one day, the wrongness of being with Austin would manifest—our differences too challenging to continue reconciling—the moment ringing like a bell of gutting clarity. But that day was not today. That day might never come. And if I could trust myself enough, I could almost believe that I would know if and when that moment arrived. Trust that even then, I would be okay.

Also:

What if things *did* work out?

What if my life, my relationship, could be wonderful, more than I dared imagine?

Phlegm rose in my throat. The cold sun failed to warm me. I looked over my rock one last time. Perhaps my relationship to resilience and suffering was not so special after all. Maybe there was something beautiful and freeing in knowing this, in letting at least that weight go.

I placed my rock beside Austin's, alongside the rocks of others.

And with that gesture, I felt as though I'd inserted myself in a larger human story while remaining keenly aware that some burdens I might always carry.

CHAPTER 26

The Walk I Choose

Solitude is certainly a fine thing; but there is pleasure in having someone who can answer, from time to time, that it is a fine thing.

—Jean-Louis Guez de Balzac,
Dissertations chrétiennes et morales

"THIS LOOKS LIKE SOMETHING out of Tolkien's universe," Austin said to me one morning as we crested a hill in Galicia, the northwest region of Spain bordering Portugal.

"This could be the Shire," I agreed. The beauty of Galicia bowled me over. All the bridges and buildings made of gray and brown layered stones carpeted with moss. The vibrant greens, the cheerful dewy mornings, the rolling knolls with sheep and black-spotted cows lounging in pastures. At home in the West, I'd never seen a cow lying down, as they seemed to always be on the move for grass, for survival. Here, they plopped in stone-fenced fields like sleepy lap dogs. Galicia was Celtic, named after an ancient Celtic tribe living there during the last millennium CE, and, in many ways, it reminded me of Ireland. When the fog lifted in the mornings, I often paused with whoever happened to be walking beside me, just to take in the landscape.

With the change in culture, our food changed too. The ever-nearing sea brought *pulpo*, oiled discs of octopus arms peppered with paprika. We began seeing an almond cake, called a *tarta de Santiago*, dusted with powdered sugar except for the stenciled outline of the iconic sword of Saint James, the patron saint of the Camino. We savored a *caldo gallego* soup of pinto beans and collard greens, farm-fresh yogurts, a particular cheese so white and soft it smoothed onto bread like butter.

I, too, was changing. The left side of my body was darker than my right due to walking mornings in the same east-to-west direction for almost a month. Both arms sported a farmer's tan, and the freckles along the bridge of my nose became more pronounced. The insides of my Chacos had collapsed slightly, and the rubber sole had become sticky from blister tape. My toes had developed calluses, and the deep tan from my sandal straps would last for almost a year. My jeans felt tighter in the thighs from new muscle. I paused less when summiting slopes and didn't dread thirty-k days. My floppy hat had lost much of its shape. But by then, I had stopped caring about how I looked.

The path to Santiago was also growing more crowded as we neared the edge of what was considered a "qualifiable" Camino length, the one-hundred-k minimum to earn a Compostela completion certificate from the pilgrim's office. New people arrived every day. Their fresh boots lined the storage racks outside the albergues. Some wore bright yellow vests affiliated with the tour company they came with.

In search of a second credential stamp in a city called Sarria, I stood in a long line at a local church. A woman holding shopping bags and wearing a sun visor turned around with a wide grin.

"First day for you too?"

"Twenty-eighth."

When my mind was not clotted with the monotony of *feet, pain, food, sleep, feet, pain, food, sleep,* I had pangs of a dull, pending panic. Arriving in Galicia, gorgeous as it was, meant that the Camino was almost over. And not just the Camino, but the envisioned honeymoon I'd planned for Austin and myself.

"How do you pick up the ends of an old life?" Frodo Baggins asked upon his return to the Shire. At my insistence, Austin and I—while passing a Spanish pear between the two of us, taking bites as the sweet juices dripped down our wrists—had spent one morning volleying our personal goals for the future:

Me: "I want to keep redefining success and happiness and stop equating suffering with meaning."

Austin: "I want to remain materially minimalist."

Me: "I want to cook more and plan out meals, like the kinds we've been eating this year."

Austin: "I want to keep working on managing finances together."

Me: "I want to prioritize our marriage and make room for quality time."

Austin: "I want to keep walking regularly."

Me: I want to maintain a sense of wonder wherever I am."

Though appreciative that we could see a shared trajectory moving forward, I'd also put more energy into what this trip represented than in imagining what came next. Though I'd met people from all over the world and heard about what marriage meant to them,

I wasn't convinced I'd come to a satisfying understanding for myself. I wanted to ponder what I'd learned, whether it was enough, and who I might be upon returning home. Up close, I could point to moments of revelation and sharp feeling, a reckoning with failure, but no cosmic shifts in myself. And did I want to change anyway? Wasn't changing part of what I'd feared and resisted from the onset?

In those final days of walking, some of my old questions returned, sneaking up on me with their familiar urgency, questions about whether or not I should have done this journey solo as I'd originally intended. How different would it have been? How different would *I* have been at the end if I'd had more solitude? I worried I might not be a serious enough pilgrim, or that I'd lost something in surrounding myself with so many people, great as they were.

Folks who'd walked the Camino before talked up the merits of going to Fisterra, the unofficial end of the pilgrimage on the coast, a three-day walk after Santiago. "You have to go," they said. The image of the ocean stuck with me, though I doubted Austin and I had the time—we hadn't factored this stop into our tight itinerary.

On one particularly pastoral walking day, Austin and Frida got into a lively conversation. About what, I can't recall. I took the moment as an opportunity to reflect, then disappeared over a hill.

I'm going to walk alone today, I thought with a sense of pride. Though I'd had my fair share of tromping-off moments on this trip, stemming from anger or pain or frustration, this felt like a more mature iteration. And though I'd had a few stretches along the Camino for solo walking, this felt different, deliberate, like something I had to do.

So I did. For an hour or so, I trotted along the dirt path in solitude. Funny, how solitude seemed to me the more romantic, more rebellious option—too often equated with loneliness or the alleged woes of singlehood. If I could just be more alone, I imagined, I might be wiser, someone without so many anxieties or unspooling questions.

Rocks piled into thick walls to mark farm borders. My sunhat flapped in the gentle breeze.

See? I'm so alone. I can do this alone. Look how alone I am.

More rocks piled into walls. More dark green grass. A few sheep stared. A strange structure popped up on every property, raised a few feet above the ground. It looked like a Greek sarcophagus, but was it for grain? There was no one to consult or speculate with.

I kept checking the time. How long had I been walking alone? I needed to know. Another forty-five minutes had passed. I wanted to time my noble effort, though I couldn't put my finger on what made aloneness so noble, despite the allure.

I walked on.

Another rock wall. Another farm.

Another black cow. Another blonde cow.

Another urge to check the time, followed by an impulse to fight the urge.

Then, a few hours in, without warning or much surprise, a thought popped into my mind. I chuckled aloud at the obvious realization.

You don't want to walk alone.

Wanting, *knowing* what I wanted. What a notion. I'd searched the globe for other people's answers to questions I hadn't dared to ask myself with any kind of specificity, though I was the only one who could make decisions about my own situation. *What does a good marriage look like?* I wanted to feel free, never trapped. I wanted to be seen, appreciated, for who I was—wanderer and all—and not who I "should" be. I wanted to offer that kind of love without conditions in return. I wanted a true partnership, actual listening, genuine intimacy, honesty, room to grow, space for independence, mutual support for the other's aspirations—no matter how unconventional. I wanted a marriage that felt like a choice, not a fixed state to begrudge and endure. I felt weary of enduring for the sake of enduring.

All along, Austin had professed the maybe not-so-radical idea that life was meant to be enjoyed.

It took me years of writing to realize that this book was a love story. Love. Whatever that meant. I had to make it so complicated, had to be so sure and exacting. I had to *know*, the same way I thought that to be spiritual, I had to *know* that God existed.

But I didn't know. Life does not pass out guarantees, forevers. But I believed, or I wanted to believe. I have found that desire to be enough.

My fears about marriage were so loud, so consuming, that I had a hard time hearing the tiny hum of my heart, the heart that had led me here, that tiny drumbeat telling me to stay, to be *here*, right now, present, while making space for faith—faith in the blue-eyed man with the coy smile and tousled hair, the one with a book tucked under his arm and a question on the tip of his tongue; the man with strong hands scarred from building barbed-wire fences, who would never balk at hard work; faith in the one who is never too proud to say sorry first, who reads every placard in a museum, who can't cross a bridge without gazing down to spot a fish, who can tell a proper story, enchant children, and whistle better than a bird; faith in the one who thirsts to sail around the world, start a ranch in Wyoming, build a cottage in England, take a research trip in the Amazon, or anywhere, really, for life to him is not too small or too logical to rule out dreams; faith in the fellow adventurer, unabashedly smitten with me, committed to me, who never fails to offer me the window seat on an airplane.

And if all this wasn't love, I wasn't sure what was.

Though my questions and concerns were never about loving Austin, that love mattered. Despite the terror, the societal pressures, the religious standards, the stuffy institution, the dire divorce statistics, the projection of bad futures played out by my parents before me, and the mental paralysis that in marriage I would somehow lose my wonderfully restless soul—despite every reason in the world not to get married, I did. And though people often ask, "Then why *did* you get married?" and though I *still* fumble for a simple answer and maybe always will in response to such a large, seemingly simple question, I sense that I trusted some fundamental part of myself that guided me here and always had, a feeling as real and powerful as my fear had been, a quiet voice that said:

Go.

Be brave.

This is the way forward.

Not for them.

For you.

Go.

Just because I could walk alone didn't mean I had to. And what was I trying to prove? To whom? Here in the forest, among the tall eucalyptus trees standing as if for a procession on the way to Santiago, with no other witness but myself?

It's okay to accept that you want to walk with him. I promise. You can still be you.

If I had learned anything, perhaps it was that I could trust my own feet.

Taking off my backpack and dropping it on the ground, I waited for Austin to catch up.

CHAPTER 27

Fisterra

BAGPIPES BLASTED AS AUSTIN AND I WALKED through a stone archway to enter the plaza of the Santiago de Compostela Cathedral. The sound rang to my core, my eardrums pulsed. Light assaulted us. My eyes began to burn from the excitement and anticipation, and then we saw it. The cathedral. The pinpoint to which we'd been walking for thirty-two days. The cathedral was every bit as gaudy as we'd been warned: the victim of too many centuries of decorating and then redecorating according to the latest fads. Blue plastic tarps covered two of the massive gothic steeples for restoration. The hint of green and the elaborate curves reminded me of a lost, underwater mermaid castle. We didn't bother with a picture of the front.

Every muscle in my body relaxed, flooded with the relief of arrival. I looked at Austin: his navy-checkered collared shirt with a tear in the elbow, his eyes exhausted but smiling.

"We made it," I said. I'd never felt more proud.

"I never doubted we would." He pulled me in closer, his scruff tickling my lips.

We followed a string of others to get to the final pilgrim's office to present our credential in exchange for a Compostela completion certificate.

"Ming! Shin!" Austin said. Behind us, we spotted a pair from Taiwan. We hadn't seen them for weeks. We waited in line together. I showed them a selfie I'd taken while leaving Saint-Jean before the hike up the Pyrenees, a picture with the two of them standing in the background. There were so few strangers now.

The Pilgrim's Mass was wall-to-wall packed. Austin and I smelled the sour breath of the woman close behind, but I didn't mind much. I absorbed the cathedral in pieces: enormous stone pillars, shells carved into the wooden pews, a gold altarpiece guarded by sculpted angels. A priest wore a white robe with a gold stripe down the middle featuring the red cross of Saint James. He read how many pilgrims had arrived and from which countries. The incense dropped from the cupola and swung through the nave in the famous Botafumeiro, sending smoke throughout the cathedral. Some say this enormous thurible and pulley system was added to the ceremony to rid the place of the rancid scent of pilgrims. I didn't doubt it. The impetus for such a sizable thurible could also be a manifestation of Psalm 141:2: "Let my prayer be set forth before thee as incense; and the lifting up of my hands as the evening sacrifice."

I smiled, closing my eyes to listen to a baritone sing a song I had never heard in a language I didn't pretend to understand. Then I remembered the beatitude written on the postcard given to me by a kind nun on the third day of the Camino just outside of Pamplona: "Blessed are you, pilgrim, because you have discovered that the authentic Camino begins when it is completed."

I still had a long walk ahead.

And I could probably use a shower.

For most of my life, I'd struggled to fathom the idea of heaven. I didn't want to live in a world where the toast didn't burn. Now, I imagined it might feel something like Santiago, like a triumphal gathering where one could sit in a rooftop café and watch friend after friend waltz into view, a great reunion in the field of stars.

Our group—my incredible, irreplaceable Camino family—celebrated wildly in the cathedral plaza, hollering and dancing, springing for hugs. Only half of them had wanted their official completion certificate, content to know they had done it for their own reasons. We held each other and spun in circles. Michael kissed Joanina. Martin lifted his bag over his head in triumph like many other pilgrims around us, including a few spandex-clad cyclists who hoisted their bikes for pictures. Hal filmed all the euphoria and led a yoga session in the square with James and others, striking power poses with glee. Sheila with flowerless hair leaned on her poles and giggled. Frida sat down on the ground and drank an Estrella Galicia beer. Kim left her walking shoes behind in the square.

Our friends spent the day in jubilation. That night, we gathered at a traditional Spanish restaurant with stone walls, filling fourteen chairs around a massive table with white placemats. One final feast. We made toasts. Wine glasses clinked against my cup of water. Kim had encouraged each of us to prepare a mock last will and testament of the items we'd carried. We took turns reading our lists aloud in the moody light:

"I bequeath my dirty underwear to that Italian who snored all night back in Hornillo."

"My travel towel goes to Hal, so he can wear it like a superhero cape."

"For Kim, my roll of stolen albergue toilet paper, since pee is 'always coming.'"

"To Rachel, my hiking boots, so she can cross mountains without sandals."

"Sheila gets my hand sanitizer in case she ever throws up her pulpo again."

"To Frida, I bequeath *nothing*. Cuz bitch gotta earn."

"For James, my Tramadol, so he doesn't have to spend so much money on Scotch."

"Martin can have my Ziploc bags to organize and label them in three different languages."

"To Michael and Joanina, my silken sleep sack."

"My journals are for Austin," I said, "so he will understand my side of the story."

We dreaded the following days when the group would split up, picked off one by one to catch a flight home, to head on to Portugal, or to walk three more days to the coastline, to a mystical place called Fisterra, considered by some to be the true end of the pilgrimage. Austin and I had just enough time to make the journey by bus.

"We're too late," I said with despair as we flung our backpacks onto the hostel bunks in Fisterra. "We're going to miss the sunset."

Austin also felt the urgency. "We might catch the end if we run."

The sunset was the reason we'd traveled three hours by bus, leaving our friends behind for one night, one glimpse, of this sinking daylight before going home.

But in true Camino Angel spirit, the albergue owner's son overheard our plight and, understanding the stakes, rushed to grab his keys. "I'll drive you. Let's go."

Fisterra is part of the rocky Costa da Morte, Galician for "coast of death." The remote fishing town sits at one of the westernmost points on the Iberian Peninsula in Spain. The name Fisterra—also called Finisterre, Finistère, or Finisterra—comes from the Latin *finis terrae*, meaning "the end of Earth." It was named by the Romans. To them, this was the end of Earth, the edge of their known, charted world.

We thanked our benevolent driver and raced from the car to the top of a cliff. A lighthouse stood guard as well as a marker, similar to those we'd seen throughout the past eight hundred k's on the Camino. The sign read: "0.00 K.M." A warm, yellow light flooded every surface, illuminating our faces. Austin held my hand as we skirted the rocky edge to find a comfortable place to sit in a patch of clover grass and wild daisies.

We made it just in time.

How strange the Atlantic looked: flat, waveless, endless, yet full of restless energy, a kaleidoscope of shifting blue diamonds. The horizon seemed to bulge into an arc while thin clouds stacked above, suspended at indecisive angles. The sun sank lower, lower until it began to dip into the ocean. The orb shot blinding white rays. Fire oranges singed the line where water met sky. We fixed our eyes on the slow descent, speechless. A lone rock offshore, shaped like an altar, darkened too.

Christian pilgrims had been making their way to the coast for centuries. But before the Christians, people called Cape Finisterre "Ara Solis," a place where the ancient Celtics worshipped the sun. Ara Solis was a sacred-yet-dangerous space, where the Land of the Living brushed the Coast of Death. *Ara* was a Latin, feminine noun meaning "altar," a structure for sacrifice. But the word also meant—curiously—"refuge," "sanctuary," "shelter," and "home."

Ara Solis. Sun Altar.

I was married at an altar. In Latter-day Saint symbolism, the sun represents the celestial kingdom, the highest degree of heaven. The sealing ordinance, believed to bind spouses and families forever, was considered the gateway to eternal life with God. For our wedding, the two of us knelt, facing each other, as mirrors on opposite sides of the room reflected our young faces endlessly, somewhat terrifyingly in the high-ceilinged white room trimmed with gold. Family and friends witnessed Austin and me hold hands across that altar. As soft as the plush top cushion was, draped in beautiful lace, nothing could hide the fact that this was an altar. A symbol of sacrifice. A symbol of death.

I chose to be married, for conscious and unconscious reasons, before an altar. But I also know now that I didn't have to.

I didn't have to marry in the temple. I didn't have to marry Austin. I think I would have been just fine *not* marrying Austin, or anyone. I didn't know myself well enough to plan for forever. People change. Marriage couldn't be reduced to a long, arduous journey—the longer you go, the more you overcome, the greater the reward—tempting and comforting as metaphors can be. But I did know I wanted to be with Austin then, there on the cliffs in Fisterra. I wanted to be with him tomorrow, and probably the next day too, and so very likely the day after that. Step by step, choice by choice. And for now, that was all I needed to keep going.

Faster, faster the golden disk fell into the hazy horizon.

"Well, good sir," I joked. "It has been a pleasure traveling the ends of the world with you."

"The honor has been mine." Austin plucked two daises at our feet and gave them to me. I tucked the stems into my notebook. "This has been the best year of my life," he said.

The beam along the ocean surface seemed to widen, like a searchlight in the reflection back to shore. For a moment, the sun seemed to hesitate, to hold on and resist—a line of fire, then a smear, then a hairline, until at last, it disappeared.

The temperature seemed to drop. The wind teased my hair. Austin and I lingered a bit longer, talking, nuzzling before heading back to town.

I reached up to touch my floppy hat. "I don't want to burn it," I said, pulling it off to examine it. How wilted the shape had become. Hard-core pilgrims often burned an item on the beach, such as a hat, a shirt, socks—anything—as an act of closure.

"You don't have to," Austin said. "Also, you don't have a lighter or anything to burn it with."

Though I'd experienced a full pilgrim's training in ruthless minimalism, perhaps there was still value in sentimental preservation, a way to gently honor old selves.

We stared westward over the Atlantic together, toward home in Boston where our lives would begin again and again on the other side of the water—where we'd unpack our storage unit a year to the date after we'd packed it, organize our books by color, hang our laundry to dry, budget, change jobs, lose jobs, frequent marriage therapy, take turns cooking dinner, support each other's dreams, graduate from master's programs, build community, visit family, travel together and alone, begin saving for a house, and continue our long, philosophical conversation. This was not the final chapter of our story. Maybe there was, paradoxically, refuge found—created—out of a mutual sacrifice for something bigger, without having to sacrifice myself. Despite what the Romans believed, Fisterra was not the end of Earth, not the end of the world. And marriage certainly would not be the end of mine.

Darkness fell as Austin and I rose to find the road again.

Author's Note

As Toni Morrison once said, "If there's a book that you want to read, but it hasn't been written yet, then you must write it." This memoir was the missing book I needed to read and thus needed to write myself, a soul-dive of a project extending eight years while wading through many selves. To create this book, I consulted my memory, loved ones' memories, documented interviews, a hoard of my photographs, and a rigorous daily journal that I kept throughout my trip from 2014 to 2015. I am indebted to so many people who have helped me throughout this adventure. Some names and some identifying information have been changed to protect people's privacy. There are no composite characters.

It should go without saying, but this memoir is limited to my own experience.

This is not a book seeking to essentialize entire cultures or groups of people and their beliefs about marriage. I explore the topic through personal interviews with individuals, filtered through my own lens. To learn more about partnerships in other cultures, read the words of the individuals within them.

This is also not a spiritual memoir or a book about Mormonism, nor is it trying to be. Mormonism refers to a distinct culture that lives alongside the Church of Jesus Christ of Latter-day Saints. Speaking personally, I have rarely seen my complex Mormon experience represented in mainstream media—created and at times sensationalized by people who have, more often than not, never been Mormon. My story is just one Mormon's experience, but it *is* one Mormon's experience.

The million steps to Santiago were nothing compared to the steps to get this story from my heart into your hands. Thank you for reading, and buen camino.

Acknowledgments

This memoir took more than eight years to write, and the events span much of my life. I'm overwhelmed with gratitude and humbled by the number of people who contributed to the making of this book, directly and indirectly. I'm well aware that I wouldn't be here, and writing, without the help of others. It didn't take a village; it took a metropolis. This meager summary feels insufficient, but know that there are many individuals, named and unnamed here, to whom I am indebted.

First, my family. I'm grateful for everything my mom was able to give me, including her wanderlust, and for my dad's unwavering support. Thank you for everything, Pappy. My in-laws are also some of the best people on the planet and were sports about letting me include them in a chapter. Okasan, thank you for your belief in me and for seeing the merits of my restless nature, which sparked a bonfire of needed confidence to go off the beaten trail in so many ways. Thank you, Angela, for your meaningful conversations, about books and things that matter. I'm also thankful to my Grandma Rueckert, who left this world before she could read the final copy. She was perhaps my first writing fan. Though she sometimes disagreed with my unconventional takes, she managed to save the newspaper clippings of them anyway. Thank you for seeing me, Grandma. Though my siblings and their partners are not listed by name in this book due to the scope of the project and a desire to honor their privacy, they are a huge source of strength to me, friends alongside the trials we faced so early together.

A heartfelt thank you to the many friends I met on this trip, including many who are not represented in the book. A few people I am especially indebted to: Lili, Miguel, Lina, Ivan, Patrick, Nita, Anan, Lucky, Jay, Alok, Radha, Vic, Nas, Jasmi, Maithili, and Ashish. Your conversations and insights were transformative for me.

Chaitra, you are worth all the gold in the world. Thank you for your patience with my questions, your curiosity, and your welcoming heart. I love you and your family, and how we've continued our meaningful friendship through the years on various continents.

I'm also grateful to my Camino family. I'm not sure how I got so lucky. Frida, you wonderful Swede. I love you bigger than your biggest blisters. Thank you to Joanina, Michael, Neil, Sheila, Elise, Martin, Suzy, James, Bob, Soyoung, and big-hearted Hal for all the laughs and support. If you get a chance, check out "older Austin's" paintings, *Drawn Down the Way: A Journal along the Camino Francés in Sketches*. There are so many others who could be named here, such as Paula, Stine, and Jan, and I wish I could have included everyone in the book.

Kim Green, you get your own line. Thank you for being a fellow pilgrim, on the road to Santiago and also on the long writing Meseta. You are so full of soul and heart, and I'd be lost without you. Thank you for encouraging me, then and now, in every way.

I eventually found my place and my people at BYU–Provo, and I am grateful for that education. As I think about the early support

I had in college, I especially want to thank my friends and mentors during my anthropology training at BYU. Ashley Barker Tolman Shuler, Dave Shuler, Jay Bostwick, and Butter Johnson—thank you for the Field Study prep class and the lessons in inquiry-based research. I had amazing field group cohorts in Ghana and India. Gideon Burton and John Bennion, thank you for being thesis mentors, writing sages, as well as friends, both through my studies at BYU and beyond. Rachel Morse, Maggie Christensen, Chase Arnold, and rem—you have been pillars to me.

To Sue Booth-Forbes, thank you for awarding my *Exponent II* winning essay a week-long stay in the magical artist retreat at Anam Cara in Ireland. Thank you also to Kelly, who kindly rented the "yellow apartment" to me when I needed months of solitude to revise and read the book aloud so many times I lost my voice. Those months felt sacred to me.

I've also benefited from writing groups and mentors and classmates who have helped me through all stages of drafts. Thanks to Grubstreet and Michelle Seaton, as well as to the Vermont College of Fine Arts community, where I had the privilege of learning from the likes of Anthony Swofford, Patrick Madden, Barbara Hurd, Sue William Silverman, Ira Sukrungruang, and others. Tali—thank you for being a breathtaking writer and dear friend.

At Columbia University, where I completed an MFA with *East Winds* as my thesis, I have countless people to thank. My instructors, especially Phillip Lopate, Wendy S. Walters, Nicholas Christopher, Margo Jefferson, Leslie Jamison, Michael Greenberg, Lis Harris, Alice Quinn, Gary Shteyngart, Monica Ferrell, BK Fischer, Brenda Wineapple, Meghan Flaherty, and Corinna Barsan all had a big impact on me. Many of my classmates will be lifelong friends. There are too many to list in full, but I owe special gratitude to the folks who saw almost the entirety of this memoir when it was all said and done (sometimes more): Stephanie Philp, Kevin Wang,

Kim Viders, Marcelle Shehwaro, Vera Carothers, Elena Sheppard, Elliott Eglash, and Aaron Newman—thank you. Your feedback made all the difference. Sarah Rosenthal, you have my forever appreciation for being so instrumental in helping me develop my book proposal.

Kim Ence, there aren't words to express my gratitude for your insights and friendship. Thank you for reading the full manuscript, then some, always with excellent feedback.

A special shout-out to the brilliant Rachel Keränen, my "$100,000" writing friend, who has been there with me through it all since our first day on campus (and through many, many drafts of this book). Solidarity forever, friend.

To the "Crane Writers"—Brittney Jenson, Megan Nordquist, Mikaela Benson, and Ryan Palmer—you have my whole heart and gratitude, plus my debt for the dozens of synopses and summaries of this book you waded through. Thanks for helping me pick up the pen again when I needed it most.

Arielle Kaden, thank you for your cheerleading when I was losing hope, and Rachel A.G. Gilman, thank you for your perfectly-timed cards, always written in your healing-green ink. Allison Hong Merrill, you are the best accountability partner I could ask for.

Allison K Williams has been my guru from behind the scenes—offering feedback, introducing me to pitching, lending first-chapter revisions, offering marketing advice, and so much more. Shauna Summers has also been supportive and encouraging throughout my agent search and publishing journey. My thanks also to the Center for Latter-day Saint Arts, especially Glen Nelson, who provided support on my book proposal. Laurel Thatcher Ulrich has also been a mentor and friend through it all. A hearty shout-out to Exponent II.

The most impactful moment of the writing of this book came

from sharing it with the Cambridge RS Book Group. I lucked out with the most incredible community. Your feedback reminded me why I wrote this book while also giving me many ways to improve it immensely. Thank you to Tory Hartmann, Mariya Manzhos, Carol Ann Litster Young, Sam Layco, Eliza Wells, Andrea Porras, Brenda Heaton, Eunice McMurray, Gwen Volmar, Joanna Abaroa-Ellison, Kami Coppins, Linda Andrews, Sydney Pritchett, Haylee Ham, Hailey James, Elizabeth Homestead Jafek, Amelia Sorensen, Stefani Anderson, Megan Palmer, Heather Allen Lehnardt, Natalie Taylor, Debra Marie Reynoso, Cici Wendel Klein, and Leslie and Rich Nielsen. (Rich was also kind enough to fix my decomposing Chacos when they broke, years later. Thanks to him, I can still wear them.)

Toni, you know me better than just about anyone and had to listen to many conversations where I banged my head against structure, confidence, and other mental barriers. I'm grateful for the support you've given me as I've waded through many dark moments and tried to make sense of it all. This book would not be as layered without you. Lucinda, the same goes for you.

I also want to give a shout-out to BCC Press. They operate as a writing collective, and the work they do is a true labor of love. To Margaret Olsen Hemming, thank you for your warm introduction to the press. Michael Austin, you have been a delight ever since I was first introduced to you—a true partner in this work and now a daily pen pal. Thank you to D Christian Harrison for the beautiful cover, to Connor Hilton for shepherding the project along, to Cece Proffit for the generous marketing support on social media, to Andrew Heiss for the typeset, and—for my amazing editor—a special thanks to Lisa Van Orman Hadley. Lisa is truly unrivaled with her talent, thoughtfulness, and trained eye. The process of working with her was a writer's dream. I'm also grateful to my team at InkWell, Kimberly Witherspoon and Maria Whelan, who championed this book from the beginning. Kristina Marie Darling, thanks for helping me get the word out. Kenny Pappaconstantinou, thank you for sharing your audiobook expertise, and Tavia Gilbert, for your incredible coaching and directing as I learned new ways to channel my story and own my voice.

Austin, I hope this book shows even a fraction of how much you mean to me. Thank you for always being so supportive of this book and of my writing, following me wherever the wind blows. You have my eternal love. I'm so grateful for our long, philosophical conversation.

Discussion Questions for Book Groups

1. What do you think the wind represents in this story?
2. Rachel travels the world searching for answers about what makes a good marriage and why people participate in this universal practice. Do you think she finds the answer in the end? If so, what is it? If not, why do you think that is?
3. Which insight(s) about marriage surprised you the most?
4. Were there any stereotypes or assumptions that you paused to examine (or re-examine) while reading *East Winds?*
5. What was a quote or scene that stood out to you? Why?
6. How might society's messages about women and marriage change?

7. Similarly, how might conversations around the relationship between faith and doubt, or love and certainty, evolve?
8. What do you make of the definitions for Part 1: South America (*cleave*), Part 2: Asia (*decide*), and Part 3: Europe (*pay*)? What about the marriage advice in the "brief layover" sections?
9. Rachel says, "It took me years of writing to realize that this book was a love story." How is this a love letter, and who is it addressed to?
10. How did this book impact you? Are there lingering reactions, thoughts, or questions from *East Winds* that are still on your mind?

RACHEL RUECKERT is a writer, editor, teacher, and a seventh-generation Utahn. She holds an MFA from Columbia University, an M.Ed from Boston University, and serves as the editor in chief of *Exponent II*. She is also the cofounder of KLEIO, a family history writing company.

rachelrueckert.com ~ linktr.ee/rachelrueckert

CPSIA information can be obtained
at www.ICGtesting.com
Printed in the USA
JSHW082113121122
33089JS00001B/2

9 781948 218689